THE ARCHITECTURE OF PRODUCTIVE LEARNING NETWORKS

D1712998

The Architecture of Productive Learning Networks explores the characteristics of productive networked learning situations and, through a series of case studies, identifies some of the key qualities of successful designs. The case studies include networks from a variety of disciplinary and professional fields, including graphic design, chemistry, health care, library science and teacher education. These learning networks have been implemented in a variety of settings: undergraduate courses in higher education, continuing professional development and informal networks for creating and sharing knowledge on a particular topic. They are rich in reusable design ideas.

The book introduces a framework for analyzing learning networks to show how knowledge, human interaction and physical and digital resources combine in the operation of productive learning networks. The book also argues that learning through interaction in networks has a long history. It combines ideas from architecture, anthropology, archaeology, education, sociology and organizational theory to illustrate and understand networked forms of learning.

Lucila Carvalho is a Postdoctoral Research Associate in the CoCo Research Centre at the University of Sydney, Australia. Her PhD combined research in design, learning technology and the sociology of knowledge. She has studied and carried out research in Australia, New Zealand, the UK and Brazil. She has presented her work at various international conferences in the fields of education, sociology, systemic functional linguistics, design and software engineering.

Peter Goodyear is Professor of Education, Australian Laureate Fellow and Co-Director of the CoCo Research Centre at the University of Sydney, Australia. He has been carrying out research in the field of learning and technology since the early 1980s, working in the UK, Europe and Australia. He has published eight books and over 100 journal articles and book chapters.

We never educate directly, but indirectly by means of the environment. Whether we permit chance environments to do the work, or whether we design environments for the purpose makes a great difference.

(John Dewey 1916/2004, Democracy and education, *p. 17)*

It matters that we recognize the very large extent to which individual human thought and reason are not activities that occur solely in the brain or even solely within the organismic skin-bag. This matters because it drives home the degree to which environmental engineering is also self-engineering. In building our physical and social worlds, we build (or rather, we massively reconfigure) our minds and our capacities of thought and reason.

(Andy Clark 2011, Supersizing the mind: embodiment, action, and cognitive extension, *p. xxviii)*

We shape our tools and thereafter our tools shape us.

(attributed to Marshall McLuhan; Lewis Laphan 1994, Introduction to Understanding Media, *p. xxi)*

The coincidence of physical space with existential space, once the realm of architecture, must be translated into cyberspace, whose information content is delivered not as a solid permanent artifact but in the form of dynamic images and representations.

(Daniela Bertol 1997, Designing digital space, *p. xx)*

The failure of architects to create congenial environments mirrors our inability to find happiness in other areas of our lives. *Bad architecture is in the end as much a failure of psychology as of design.* It is an example expressed through materials of the same tendency which in other domains will lead us to marry the wrong people, choose inappropriate jobs and book unsuccessful holidays: the tendency not to understand who we are and what will satisfy us. . . . The places we call beautiful are, by contrast, the work of those rare architects with the humility to interrogate themselves adequately about their desires and the tenacity to translate their fleeting apprehensions of joy into logical plans – a combination that enables them to create environments that satisfy needs we never consciously knew we even had.

(Alain de Botton 2006, The architecture of happiness, *pp. 248–249, emphasis added)*

The incredible acceleration of speed during the last century has collapsed time into the flat screen of the present, upon which the simultaneity of the world is projected. As time loses its duration, and its echo in the primordial past, man loses his sense of self as a historical being, and is threated by the 'terror of time'. Architecture emancipates us from the embrace of the present and allows us to experience the slow, healing flow of time. Buildings and cities are instruments and museums of time. They enable us to see and understand the passing of history, and to participate in time cycles that surpass individual life.

(Juhani Pallasmaa 2012, The eyes of the skin: Architecture and the senses, *pp. 55–56)*

Instead of the lock-step of compulsory schooling in a fixed place, work in piecemeal ways to decentralize the process of learning and enrich it through contact with many places and people all over the city: workshops, teachers at home or walking through the city, professionals willing to take on the young as helpers, older children teaching younger children, museums, youth groups traveling, scholarly seminars, industrial workshops, old people, and so on. Conceive of all these situations as forming the backbone of the learning process; survey all these situations, describe them, and publish them as the city's 'curriculum'; then let students, children, their families and neighborhoods weave together for themselves the situations that comprise their 'school'.

(Christopher Alexander et al. *1977, from the Network of Learning pattern, in* A pattern language, *p. 102)*

You think philosophy is difficult . . . but I tell you, it is nothing compared to the difficulty of being a good architect.

(attributed to Ludwig Wittgenstein; Rush Rhees 1984, Recollections of Wittgenstein, *p. 126)*

THE ARCHITECTURE OF PRODUCTIVE LEARNING NETWORKS

Edited by Lucila Carvalho and Peter Goodyear

Routledge
Taylor & Francis Group

NEW YORK AND LONDON

First published 2014
by Routledge
711 Third Avenue, New York, NY 10017

and by Routledge
2 Park Square, Milton Park, Abingdon, Oxon OX14 4RN

Routledge is an imprint of the Taylor & Francis Group, an informa business

Library of Congress Cataloging in Publication Data
    Carvalho, Lucila.
    The architecture of productive learning networks / Lucila Carvalho,
    Peter Goodyear.
        pages cm
    Includes bibliographical references and index.
    1. Internet in education   2. Computer networks.   I. Goodyear, Peter, 1952–
    II. Title.
    LB1044.87.C364 2014
    371.33′44678—dc23

                                                                    2013034760

ISBN: 978-0-415-81655-7 (hbk)
ISBN: 978-0-415-81656-4 (pbk)
ISBN: 978-0-203-59109-3 (ebk)

Typeset in Bembo
by RefineCatch Limited, Bungay, Suffolk, UK

Printed and bound in the United States of America by Publishers Graphics, LLC on sustainably sourced paper.

Editors' Dedication

We dedicate this book, with love, to our partners and children:
Mark and Bruno; Sonia, Emily and Michael

CONTENTS

FIGURES

TABLES

PREFACE

Learning in a richly networked society involves complex, shifting configurations of tasks, tools and people, with new distributions of activity across time, space and media. We argue in this book that networked learning has deep roots – it is neither esoteric nor entirely modern. That said, the shape of the intellectual space in which we are working is experiencing dramatic shifts. When we submitted the proposal for this book, in May 2012, few people had heard of Massive Open Online Courses, yet six months later *The New York Times* was calling 2012 'The Year of the MOOC'. Design for networked learning requires analytic concepts and techniques that can cope with complexity and also with radical change; its methods must be both sharp and agile.

This book investigates some of the key attributes of learning networks, exploring what characterizes productive networked learning and how one can create an innovative design that is, at the same time, suited to a particular context, and builds on tested experiences of supporting effective learning. Our aim is to present a coherent framework that can capture the essentials of productive learning networks. Such essential elements often include the physical, digital and human; tools, texts and artifacts; explicit and implicit rules. It is not just the qualities of individual elements that matter – it is also how the elements combine to provide a coherent set of arrangements. This is why we speak of 'architectures' for productive networked learning. At a suitable level of abstraction, our framework explains how such structures may achieve the functions necessary for learning to occur, and how particular design solutions facilitate and shape learning activities and outcomes.

With a focus on the *architecture* of networked learning, Part II of the book brings together a series of case studies, illustrating how the analytical framework can be applied to unveil key relations between the entities involved in productive learning networks. The case studies include networks from a variety of disciplinary and professional fields, including graphic design, chemistry, health care and teacher education. These learning networks were implemented in a variety of settings and have contrasting purposes. For example, some networks are from undergraduate courses in higher education, others are for continuing professional development, others again are informal networks for creating and sharing knowledge on a particular topic, and there are also some networks where learning may seem incidental, but where we would claim that learning is a significant side-effect of the principal productive activities in which participants are collaborating.

Some of the greatest challenges and sources of satisfaction in design for networked learning arise from the autonomy exercised by networked learning participants. On the one hand, educational practitioners involved in developing and teaching through networked learning (such as teachers, facilitators, designers and others) need to help create well-crafted environments that will support effective learning through interactions with new and evolving technology. In order to develop such environments these practitioners require tools and methods to help them produce successful designs. On the other hand, the users of these environments – the learners within networked learning – typically exercise considerable autonomy in making choices about the tasks they will tackle, the people with whom they will collaborate, and the tools and resources they will use. Moreover, the activity in which people engage does not just draw upon tools, resources, etc. provided by the people organizing the network, and it does not only involve people who see themselves as part of the network. Rather, a person's 'networked learning activity' needs to be understood as something that involves other things and people, by virtue of the activity being enmeshed with other activities in which each person engages. (Looking at a learning network from the perspective of each of its participants is not the only way to look at the network, as we explain in Chapter 1, but when we do look at it in this ego-oriented or personal, participant-oriented way, we cannot help but see that networked learning activities are woven in with other strands of a person's life.)

Effective design for networked learning needs, therefore, to work with this autonomy; its methods need to help people co-configure their learning activity and the environment in which it takes place.

We have divided this book into three parts. Part I provides the conceptual foundations needed to understand the approach taken in our analysis. Part III synthesizes results and draws out implications for practice, theory and further research. Part II is the most substantial section of the book. Each chapter in Part II focuses on a specific case – usually a single learning network – and illustrates key structural elements and relations, explaining how these create the functions necessary for learning to occur within that particular context. The chapters present aspects of our analytical framework, using each case study to illustrate how different design solutions address learning, connecting both technological and pedagogical innovation.

Many of the case studies in Part II are freely available to inspect on the Internet. Since the time that our analysis was conducted, however, these networks are likely to have evolved or changed in some ways, but if you are interested in trying out our methods, or testing them against your own, please take a closer look at some of the examples. Let us know what you make of them, and what you think about the strengths and weaknesses of our approach. We like to think that we are always ready to learn from the experiences of others.

Lucila Carvalho and Peter Goodyear
Sydney, July 2013

ACKNOWLEDGMENTS

The editors are pleased to acknowledge the support, enthusiasm, ideas, intellectual energy and good humor of the other members of the Laureate project team. In reverse alphabetical order they are: Pippa Yeoman, Dewa Wardak, Kate Thompson, Beat Schwendimann, Ana Pinto, Paul Parker, Martin Parisio and David Ashe. Our core team has been extended, from time to time, by visitors from overseas and we want to pay special thanks to Yannis Dimitriadis, Peter Sloep and Begoña Gros for their thoughtful contributions.

The work of the project team takes place in the stimulating and supportive environment that is the Centre for Research on Computer Supported Learning and Cognition (CoCo). Many thanks to our fellow CoConuts.

The editors would also like to thank: Mark King for his work on the cover design; Agnieszka Bachfischer and Pippa Yeoman for assistance in the closing stages of book production; our co-authors, both in the Laureate project team mentioned above, and the external co-authors, whose contributions are at the heart of this book: Marlies Bitter-Rijpkema, Doug Clow, Maarten de Laat, Wim Didderen, Chris Jones, Jaime Metcher, Crighton Nichols, Tracy Richardson, Lynn Robinson, Thomas Ryberg, Rob Saunders, Bieke Schreurs, Rory Sie, Tim Shaw, Peter Sloep, Rangan Srikhanta, Matthew Todd, Steven Verjans and Hanne Westh Nicolajsen.

Our analytical work depended on gaining access to various networks and so we would like to express our sincere gratitude to the many people who made this possible and also to those within these networks who granted us permission to publish the images in this book. In particular, we thank Eric Whitacre and Claire Long for facilitating and granting access to material related to the Virtual Choir; Price Kerfoot, Lisa Clark, Paulette Greene and Robert Mallin for authorizing the use of the images related to Qstream.

Many people have influenced our thinking in this area, even if they may not entirely agree with our conclusions. We would especially like to thank Karl Maton, Andy Dong, Lina Markauskaite, Peter Reimann, Rob Ellis, Yael Kali, Diana Laurillard, Simos Retalis, Viv Hodgson, Chris Jones, David McConnell, Christine Smith, Phil Levy and Bob Lewis.

Our gratitude also goes to Alex Masulis and Madeleine Hamlin at Routledge, for their support and prompt advice in the completion of this book project.

Much of the research reported in this book was funded by the Australian Research Council through an Australian Laureate Fellowship grant to Peter Goodyear: *FL100100203 Learning, technology and design: architectures for productive networked learning* (2011–2015).

PART I
Foundations

1

INTRODUCTION

Networked Learning and Learning Networks

Peter Goodyear and Lucila Carvalho

Human beings are unusual animals. When we learn – whether acquiring new skills or making sense of the world – our experiences are colored by the words and actions of others. For much of our history, *what* we have been able to learn has been delimited by the qualities of the place we inhabit and by the experiences of our kith and kin. Archaeologists, evolutionary psychologists, and experts in the development and capacities of language are vigorously debating the origins of the modern human mind. They are trying to assess the relations between speech, symbolic activities, the making and use of tools, planning complex actions and the reproduction of cultural practices. On current evidence, it is reasonable to say that humans have been learning from and instructing each other for at least 70,000 years (Brown *et al.* 2012, Botha 2010, Henshilwood and Dubreil 2009, Wynn and Coolidge 2010, Pradhan *et al.* 2012, Schuppli *et al.* 2012, Gibson and Ingold 1995, Sterelny 2012). Indeed, recent scholarship suggests that linguistically mediated collaboration, learning and instruction may predate the emergence of modern humans 500,000 years ago (Dediu and Levinson, 2013).

Looking across the history of our species, one sees much more experience of learning from networks of family, friends and acquaintances than of learning in formally constituted educational institutions, such as schools and universities. Indeed, some would argue that schools, colleges and modern universities will turn out to be a short-lived aberration – that they are suspect inventions that seemed to serve the needs of rapidly urbanizing and industrializing populations, but that soon turned out to be expensive and ineffective ways of meeting human needs (Illich 1973, Illich and Verne 1976, Varbelow and Griffith 2012).

There is, of course, a substantial difference between learning from someone with whom one is in direct, face-to-face contact and learning from someone who is at a distance. In the 'distance' case, some text or other kind of representational artifact is needed to serve a communicative role. At the limit, any moveable artifact to which meaning can be attached and interpreted can serve this mediating function. Notches cut in tally sticks or other objects that represent quantities in stores or in trade might serve as examples. But the richness of learning from others at a distance only truly opens up with the development of *written texts* capable of carrying richer meanings. As we shall see, learning from distant others raises new versions of questions about dependability and trust. Human beings had tens of millennia to develop methods of testing and gaining trust in face-to-face situations. Some current-day preferences for the face-to-face can still best be understood by reference to this history (see e.g. Boden and Molotch 1994). Trust turns out to be a serious matter in networks whose members rarely meet face-to-face. But it is not unique to networks. It appears as an issue, in different guises, in the other two main kinds of ways that people organize themselves (or find themselves organized) – *hierarchies* and *markets* (Podolny and Page 1998, Borgatti and Foster 2003; and see Chapter 2).

The status of texts in *hierarchical* forms of organization is reasonably well-understood: one thinks of the functioning of bibles in the Roman Catholic church and secular books in early universities, for example. In each case, there is an association between the text, practices of sharing the text and authority – in particular, the reproduction of orthodox understandings of the world (whether spiritual or secular). The *market* for texts comes later – being dependent on reductions in the real costs of texts brought about, in part, by improvements in the printing process. With the growth of markets, the links between texts and authority change in nature: more diverse arrays of influence emerge. It is difficult to explain the need for, and functioning of, schools, universities and other formally established ways of organizing education without reflecting on the admixture of texts, practices, authority, trust and skepticism brought together by intersecting hierarchical and market forms.

But our interest is in *networks* – and especially in networks where learning is promoted through combinations of textual and other forms of communication. The history of (pre-digital) networked learning is a less well-documented area, though interest among economists and historians is growing steadily (see e.g. Duguid 2005a, 2005b, Hancock 2005, Haggerty and Haggerty 2010, Mokyr 2009). In many cases, *learning* in these networks might be seen as incidental – as a by-product of commercial exchange, for example. But as we shall show in Chapter 2, the goals of establishing and maintaining trust, and building shared understandings of products and processes, at a distance, turn out to be core to the functioning of commercial networks (Hancock 2005) and are less well-served by either hierarchies or markets (Powell 1990, Podolny and Page 1998).

The aim of this book is to share ideas about how people learn with and from each other, when much or all of their interaction is mediated by digital communications technology – notably, when they connect with each other via the Internet. In tackling this topic, it should be clear that part of our purpose is to show that *networked learning* is no longer an esoteric matter.

We do not, for a moment, want to ignore the fact that access to the Internet, and to digital tools more generally, is unevenly distributed. Lack of access to the Internet is both a source and a consequence of other forms of social, political and economic inequality. But the number of active users of the Internet is still rising exponentially. Internet connectivity delivers substantial reductions in the cost of access to information and people. Its intrinsic cost structures compare favorably with older technologies of print-on-paper and 'corporeal' travel (Urry 2002). In this sense, it is less intrinsically exclusive than the technologies it is displacing. So *on a longer view*, there is more to be said for networked learning than for some of the ways in which learning has been organized over the last century or two. It warrants closer inspection, because it connects with a pre-industrial past and a post-industrial future.

On the next few pages, we introduce each of our key constructs – learning, networks, networked learning, (productive) learning networks, architecture, analysis and design. The chapter concludes with a first sketch of our analytic framework. There is much more to say about some of these ideas, so Chapter 2 reviews R&D on learning networks and Chapter 3 explains why we take an architectural approach to analyzing learning networks, and how this can be done.

Learning: Towards a More Holistic Understanding of the Participant in Networked Learning

'Learning' is conventionally defined as a sustained change in behavior resulting from experience. This interpretation has some merit, in that the explicit reference to experience distinguishes learning from maturation. But the insistence on 'change in behavior' rules out much that is of value. For example, it is possible to arrive at a richer understanding of some phenomenon, or to experience a change in one's sense of self, without anyone else being able to detect a change in behavior. The difficulty of detecting evidence of learning in others should not be used to marginalize what many would feel are important aspects of learning. That said, we do think that the term 'learning' should be reserved for occasions where some persisting change has occurred. It should be distinguished from 'studying' – a situated activity normally intended to result in learning, but which does not always succeed in having this result. Learning, therefore, may be intended or incidental – it is often both. Some learning outcomes are the intended result of participation in a study activity; some are incidental by-products of study activities; some are by-products of activities other than deliberate study.

There have been many theoretical twists and turns in accounts of learning over the last 100 years or so – much to the exasperation of people who are charged with practical action and who do not have the time or patience to make personal practical sense of research on learning. A useful strategy for reducing cognitive dissonance (between the imperatives of educational action and one's understanding of the science of learning) is to characterize this sequence of theoretical shifts as no more than fashions and fads. But this is only a partial truth, and we firmly believe that a serious account of networked learning needs to be informed by the best insights that the learning sciences have to offer. Otherwise, we lose all hope of achieving a holistic understanding of the participant in networked learning. In brief, our argument runs as follows.

Each major shift (or 'turn') in learning theory has added some aspect of human experience to the research agenda, but has also shifted other aspects away from center stage. Over the last 100 years or so, one could point to a:

- behavioral turn
- cognitivist or information-processing turn
- socio-cultural or practice or 'situative' turn
- linguistic or semiotic turn
- brain-based/neuroscience turn
- socio-material turn

in framing 'the person' in research on learning and in educational and social research more generally.

Each of these turns, or paradigm shifts, has been a *reasonable* response by a set of researchers to the neglect of what they see as important phenomena in the prevailing research perspectives of their time. The *unreasonable* consequence has usually been that the new paradigm displaces rather than builds on the old. This has knock-on effects for pedagogy and educational practice. For example, the cognitivist turn in the 1950s and 1960s led to a relegation of some associationistic models of learning and of methods such as 'drill-and-practice', which have a demonstrably valuable place in relation to some kinds of intended learning outcome, such as in some areas of vocabulary learning or mental arithmetic (Mayes and de Freitas 2007, Lehtinen 2011). Similarly, the practice turn of the late 1970s and 1980s was accompanied by a marginalization of psychologically based accounts of human competence and understanding – to a virtual abandonment, within this camp, of interest in the mind and the brain.

Each of the major paradigms for studying human learning, understanding and capability has something to offer that is neglected or unexplained in other accounts – and they are *not* incommensurable (*pace* Koschmann 1996). An important starting point for this piece of the argument is that even the most mundane of human activities are susceptible to complex, multilayered analysis. Close empirical examination of human accomplishments reveals a breathtaking harmonization of capabilities that involve perception, memory, action, discourse; the automatic and the reflective; fast and slow thoughts, and so on. For example, recent developments in brain science are leading to a view of human cognition as *essentially embodied* – a perspective on thought, problem-solving and memory that couples these 'higher-level' accomplishments much more tightly with supposedly 'lower-level' processes of perception and action (see e.g. Kiefer and Trumpp 2012). Similarly, studies of the 'relational expertise' that allows professionals to work effectively with colleagues from other fields and disciplines (e.g. Edwards 2010) reveal the importance of being able to rapidly and accurately interpret the utterances of others who are co-present – abilities that depend at least as much on the lengthy processes through which conversational skills develop as they do on familiarity with the professional practices and workspaces in which collaborative interactions are unfolding. In short, a social practice account that ignores the nature and development of the complex skills involved in listening and speaking will not properly explain what is observed when capable professionals collaborate. Similarly, an account of the expertise of a scientist that ignores everything except their knowledge of scientific concepts and principles will be of little use in explaining how they do what they do, or in designing educational pathways for the next generation of scientists.

Our goal of painting a more holistic picture of the participant in networked learning also means that we need to address another matter of terminology. In many areas of educational writing it has become commonplace to refer to the person at the center of things as 'the learner' or 'the student'. This can often prove to be an efficient shorthand, but from time to time it is necessary to scrutinize our use of language and make sure that language choices are not restricting our ability to see and describe what is happening. Some of the case studies in Part II of this book are drawn from informal learning situations in which it is not appropriate to talk of the participants as 'students', and to label them 'learners' would also seem to misrepresent the essence of what they are doing. A good example of this is when what participants learn is a side-effect of their engagement in an activity in which the explicit purposes do not refer to learning – see for example The Synaptic Leap (Chapter 12) or the Virtual Choir (Chapter 13). So we often talk of 'participants' in networked learning, rather than of learners or students. However, this is not just a stylistic or superficial matter. As Sanne Akkerman and Michiel Van Eijck (2013) point out, automatically labeling someone as a 'learner' can (i) obscure those aspects of their activity that are not seen as directly supportive of learning, and (ii) render less visible the connections between their current activity and their activities and experiences outside the immediate 'learning context'. Such 'external' activities and experiences can have intrinsic importance for the person concerned and can also be of considerable relevance to how they engage with a learning activity, how they make sense of new experiences and ideas, and how they make use of such ideas and experiences later on in other contexts. Akkerman and Van Eijck encourage educational researchers to think 'horizontally' (about how current learning activities relate to other 'areas' of a person's life) rather than just 'vertically' (how current learning may or may not transfer to subsequent contexts of application).

Jean Lave has also commented recently on this conceptual and methodological blinkering. She mentions the work of Ole Dreier (e.g. Dreier 2011) and uses it to remind us of the value of

> examining what it means for persons to engage in the changing day-to-day trajectories of their lives . . . setting persons, in practice, in motion across and through their daily contexts ... tracing persons' movements across the various contexts of their everyday lives [to understand] how participation changes in changing practice.
>
> *(Lave 2012, p. 162)*

Lave (and Dreier) thereby warn of the dangers of conventional 'site-constrained' research practices.

The cases we examine in Part II of the book can each be seen as just one context in which the people involved conduct parts of their everyday life. At first glance, this may seem to run counter to Lave and Dreier's advice (to avoid 'site-constrained' analyses). Our decision to analyze on a network-by-network basis is a logical consequence of our interest in providing *design-oriented* insights. That is to say, our primary goal is to understand distinctive, potentially reusable designed attributes of each of the example learning networks. This is a different goal from understanding the lived experience of the people participating in the networks. However, one cannot understand how the network (and its designed attributes) functions without understanding something of participants' activities and experiences. The lesson we are taking from Lave and Dreier is that understanding how people act in/with networks is best done in a way that foregrounds the fact that their engagement in/with a network is just one part of their everyday life – and that connections with other things that they do must be part of the story of how their network activity makes sense to them.

Networks

From a sociological or organizational research perspective, a network is defined as a set of two or more actors connected by a set of ties (Borgatti and Foster 2003). A social actor, often represented as a node, point or vertex in a network graph, can be a person, a team, a firm or other kind of organization. The ties, otherwise known as links or edges in a graph, can represent a variety of types of connection or interaction, though it is unusual, and potentially confusing, for any one network representation to involve multiple kinds of links. (For example, one is unlikely to use a single network representation to depict both 'loves' and 'hates' links simultaneously.) Ties can be unidirectional: as when Firm A sources raw material from Firm B, or when Person T sets assignments for Person S, but not vice versa. Ties can be bidirectional: as when two students review each other's work. Ties may represent relationships in a binary way (present or absent; linked or not linked), or they may be tagged with some value (e.g. using a score of 1–10 to indicate the strength of a relationship, or thicker lines on a graph representing more frequent communication).

Social networks are not the only kind of network with which we are concerned in this book. In fact, the earliest occurrences of the term 'network' in everyday English refer to *physical* structures, and never to connections between people (Hancock 2005). The word 'network' was used to denote a meshing of materials – textile, wire or rope, for example – and later on, to describe natural systems that resembled such networks (e.g. human veins, rivers and their tributaries) and even to chains of ideas.

> As best as one can discern, the idea of a network as an interconnected group of people was foreign to first users of the word . . . the links in the network did not have *agency*. People wove networks; they did not form them and were not links in them.
>
> *(Hancock 2005, pp. 470–471, emphasis added)*

Later again, we find the term being used to describe large-scale artificial as well as natural phenomena, including networks of roads, canals, railways (and telegraph lines), and systems for supplying water, electricity and gas.

To understand 'network' in digitally mediated networked learning, one needs to think about both material and human connectivity. The notion of *material connectivity* is, at one level, more straightforward – it refers to the connections between computers, realized through radio waves, copper wires and optical fibers, linking them in local networks, networks of networks, and the Internet. Less evident, but no less important, is that such network connectivity depends on software as well as hardware and on internationally agreed standards and protocols, as well as on patterns of demand and supply, bandwidth limitations and connection speeds. (The material and the social are intertwined and affect action at a variety of scale levels.) Connectivity between computers can be a precarious achievement, depending on a heterogeneous mix of wires, tubes, photons, sensors, rules, funds, contracts and treaties. Headlines about cyber-terrorism, denial of service attacks and snooping by intelligence agencies occasionally remind us of this precariousness. But our everyday experience of networked life is such that connectivity is taken for granted, other than when the phone dies or we hit a wireless deadspot.

Of course, *people* networked long before they used that term to describe what they were doing (Knappett 2013). They have done this face-to-face, as well as remotely – with the aid of material objects (such as gifts), through texts (such as letters) and through networked devices such as the telegraph, telephone and computer. One can speculate about the earliest human activities that might merit the use of the term 'network', as distinct from 'community', 'clan' or 'family', for example. 'Network' implies a degree of openness and flux that 'community' may not capture. It implies interactions between people who then interact with others:

A interacts with B, B interacts with C, C does not necessarily know A. If everyone who interacts knows everyone else, then 'community' or 'group' is better than 'network' as a distinctive descriptor. Networking involves travel – of people, objects or messages; community need not.

Care needs to be exercised in understanding what is being done when something is *called* a network. Chris Jones (2004), building on the work of John Law, warns that 'when we analyze in terms of networks, we also help to perform networks into being' (p. 82). Jones speaks of the network as a metaphor, rather than as something to be understood more literally. To analyze something as a network is, of course, to impose structures and terms that may be alien to the people whose activities and relationships are thus represented. This is not a reason for backing away from network analysis *as long as one maintains a reflexive consciousness about what work one is actually doing.* The risks may be smaller here than is the case with analyses that insist on the 'community' metaphor. 'Network' denotes something distinguishable from 'community' (Wenger *et al.* 2011, McConnell 2006), and its educational connotations are somewhat more neutral. As Barton and Tusting (2005), Roth and Lee (2006) and Quinn (2010) have argued, some writers and educational practitioners enamored of the 'communities of practice' or 'learning communities' labels can be accused of undue romanticism. 'Network' has fewer of these cozy connotations, though one still needs to be wary.

Networked Learning

In our view, networked learning will eventually come to be best understood as something that predates the computer age, takes on a particular character and salience in the period from about 1980 to 2020, and becomes normal and invisible thereafter. That middle 40 years will stand out because of a temporary awkwardness in digitally mediated human interaction – in large part due to the tyranny of keyboards and text.

The phrase 'networked learning' has been in use for almost as long as people have been talking about computer networks. The broad set of practices to which it generally refers *is* as old as computer networks, though other terms have had greater currency from time to time. Earlier uses of the phrase did not necessarily distinguish between (a) learning by accessing texts (or multimedia resources) over a computer network and (b) learning with and from other people, by interacting with them over a computer network. Thus, until the late 1990s, 'networked learning' could be used as a synonym for 'online learning', in the sense of learning with the aid of (inanimate) resources accessed over a computer network (see e.g. Bacsich and Ash 2000).

What has since become the most widely cited definition within the networked learning research community was originally crafted by Goodyear, Hodgson and Steeples in 1998. It had a conscious political and pedagogical function, and in its first use, was intended to demarcate an area for R&D, within which *interactions between people*, mediated by computer/information technology, were to be given particular importance.

> We define 'networked learning' as learning in which C&IT is used to promote *connections*: between one learner and other learners, between learners and tutors; between a learning community and its learning resources. Some of the richest examples of networked learning involve interaction with on-line materials *and* with other people. But use of on-line materials is not a *sufficient* characteristic to define networked learning.
>
> *(Goodyear* et al. *1998, p. 2, original emphasis)*

This definition was written as part of a successful research proposal to the UK's Joint Information Systems Committee (JISC) – the organization that provides networking and other services to UK universities and colleges and that has funded a great deal of research and innovation in the educational use of networked computers. The acronym 'C&IT' was, at that time, JISC's preferred way of referring to computer and information technologies. The phrase 'networked learning' also had currency with JISC (see e.g. JISC 1998, Levy 1997), but in the usage of the time it did not *necessarily* imply learning with and from other people via the Internet. So networked learning was not invented in 1998, but a firmer set of links was made, at that time, between the phrase and some distinctive educational ideas and practices (Hodgson *et al.* 2011).

The resulting two-year JISC-funded project on university students' experiences of networked learning (1999–2000) played a substantial, practical role in shaping the networked learning field in the UK and Europe. It funded the development of what has become a biennial international conference on networked learning – building on the foundations of David McConnell's 1998 Sheffield conference on networked lifelong learning (Goodyear *et al.* 2001). It funded the development of the first major book on networked learning, edited by two members of the project team (Steeples and Jones 2002). In turn, it provided foundations for Vivien Hodgson's work in bringing together communities of networked learning researchers at both national (UK) and European levels (Dirckinck-Holmfeld *et al.* 2004; McConnell *et al.* 2011). The evolution of empirical research, innovative practice and theory development in the field that has come to be known as networked learning is described in more detail in Chapter 2.

Learning Networks

In this book, we speak of *learning networks* – as well as *networked learning* – because we have a particular interest in design. As we will argue below, networked learning cannot be designed – it can be designed *for*. Some of the *components* of learning networks can be designed. And learning networks can be analyzed, with a view to informing future designs.

For this reason, we want to promote 'learning networks' so that they become one of the central phenomena for inquiry in research on learning. While most other research fields have achieved a workable consensus on their objects of inquiry – geologists have rocks, medics have diseases, architects have buildings – researchers in networked learning do not have a shared corpus of things to be analyzed and explained. In this book, for the most part, we have chosen learning networks that are visible to the general public, via the Internet. Our analyses can be checked and complemented by the analyses of others who are active in this field. Too much of the literature on learning networks has been written by those responsible for managing them. While such accounts are very valuable, they should not dominate the field.

Linda Harasim and colleagues should be given credit for popularizing the term 'learning networks' (see especially Harasim *et al.* 1997). However, in our view, Harasim *et al.* have too restricted a view of what a learning network is. In their 1997 book, they approach the definition of a learning network twice, but do not quite succeed in pinning the concept down.

> Learning networks use computer networks for educational activity – in primary, secondary, university, and adult education. They depend on the hardware and software that form the communications network, but they consist of the communities of learners who work together in the online environment.
>
> *(Harasim* et al. *1997, p. xi)*

> In short, learning networks are groups of people who use CMC [computer-mediated communications] networks to learn together, at the time, place, and pace that best suits them and is appropriate to the task.
>
> *(ibid, p. 4)*

In both definitions, Harasim *et al.* take care to distinguish between what they see as the learning network (i.e. just the people) and the technology and other resources that the people are using. They also do not explain what is special about a network, such that it is worth using this term, rather than 'group' or 'community'.

At around the same time, the US Sloan Foundation embarked on a major program of investment in R&D on the use of asynchronous learning networks. Frank Mayadas of the Sloan Foundation described them as follows:

> Asynchronous Learning Networks (ALNs) combine self-study techniques with asynchronous interactivity to create environments in which learners can access remote learning resources asynchronously – using relatively inexpensive equipment – to learn at home, at the work place or at any place

of their choosing. Remote learning can enlist dynamic resources such as other students, outside experts or the instructor, or more static resources such as assignments, course notes or libraries. Additional digital resources can include databases, spreadsheets or even software-generated simulations. . . . In an ALN we can think of every person on the network as both a user and a resource. This concept is crucial to the power of an ALN, making it not just an electronic network but a network of people – an interactive learning community that is not limited by time, place or the constraints of a classroom.

(Mayadas 1997, p. 2)

This definition clearly embraces both the 'electronic network' and the people; but it does not help us find a core or a boundary to the network, or indeed to distinguish it from a group or community.

There are four significant problems in the attempts of Harasim *et al.* and Mayadas to pin down the key ideas pertaining to learning networks. First, they are not clear about why it is useful to try to find the boundary of a network, or how this might be done. This makes it hard to delimit an entity that can become the core object of research, or about which a 'field guide' might be written. Second, they use established practices of formal education to explain and distinguish learning networks. Third, they show a strong need to emphasize people and learning rather than technology. Fourth, they are more comfortable talking about the individual and their 'environment' than they are about the collective. Each of these four issues needs examining in more detail.

If we want to have a science of learning networks, then we need to be able to distinguish one learning network from another, to say something about centers and boundaries, topologies and the rich mix of heterogeneous objects, people, activities and ideas implicated in the network. Ed Hutchins has some useful thoughts that can be applied to this type of problem:

Everything is connected to everything else. Fortunately, not all connectivity is equally dense. The nonuniformity of connectivity makes science possible. Choosing the right boundaries for a unit of analysis is a central problem in every science and the basic approach to this problem has been in place for 2,000 years. Plato advised that one should 'carve nature at its joints' (Phaedrus 265d–266a). By this, Plato meant that we should place the boundaries of our units where connectivity is relatively low.

(Hutchins 2010, pp. 705–706)

We will explore the methodological issues involved in identifying and putting a boundary around learning networks in Chapter 3. For now, it is worth saying that the matter is usually resolvable if one identifies a configuration of *tasks, tools and people* – and that just one of these (e.g. the technology used) will rarely, if ever, allow one to find the limits of a network: the points where connectivity becomes noticeably sparse.

The problem with writing about learning networks in relation to prevailing formal educational practices is that one misses the continuity with other kinds of network activity. For example, Harasim *et al.* (1997) talk about one's 'learning network classroom' as 'anywhere that you have a personal computer, a modem, and a telephone line . . .' (p. 3).

Networks are one of the three major forms of social and economic organization, along with markets and hierarchies. It is hard to get a sense of proportion about the range and complexity of contemporary learning networks if one's main point of reference is the school and the classroom.

Emphasizing people rather than technology in one's definition of a learning network is understandable if one is writing for an educational audience for whom digital technology is unfamiliar and off-putting, as would have been the case for many educators in the late 1990s. We do not go as far as some network theorists who insist on giving equal status to people and non-human objects in socio-technical networks. However, we do want to promote the understanding of learning networks as assemblages of tools, artifacts, people, ideas and practices. This is made harder by the fact that, rather surprisingly, the nature of tools in educational technology is still an under-theorized topic (Oliver 2013). We return to give this more serious attention in Chapter 3.

It is not unusual to find a strong flavor of methodological individualism in educational technology – as if the individual, their fate and their view out into the world provide the natural unit for analysis and explanation. We do see merit in looking at networks from the point of view of the individual – one can speak of ego-centered networks and of personal learning networks, for example (McPherson 2009, Richardson and Mancabelli 2011). But it is also important to be able to take a network and its attributes as a unit of analysis. Not everything consequential about a network can be inferred from the experiences of the people who participate in it. Not all its qualities can be defined as aggregates of the actions or preferences of individuals. Speaking from the perspective of network analysis in archaeology, Søren Sindbœk puts it thus: Network-based analysis and reconstruction methods can offer

> insight into local and global properties of systems of interconnected objects, which can neither be discovered by studying the interacting agents individually or in pairs, nor by studying the average properties of the system as a whole . . . network models have the power to facilitate structural comparison across different scales and source materials and to formulate hypotheses and models for further exploration.
>
> *(Sindbœk 2013, p. 72)*

Productive Learning Networks

We apply the prefix 'productive' to draw attention to certain characteristics of some selected learning networks. It is not, in itself, an evaluative term. It is not meant as the opposite of unproductive, ineffective or failing. Rather, we choose to use this word because it foregrounds acts of creation rather than consumption and because of the connotations of self-realization and/or identity formation associated with productive activity – with 'work' in its general sense.

Knowledge-building networks, broadly defined, have been quite influential in our thinking, but we are also keen to push at the edges of what knowledge-building means, and to make sure that conceptions of knowledge-building in networked learning are not trapped by ideas, however fertile, that originate in science education (e.g. Scardamalia and Bereiter 2006). Once one opens up to conceptions of knowledge and ways of knowing that are not limited to the explicit, declarative and propositional, thereby also accepting knowledge as skill, as tacit, as embedded in practice, as embodied, etc. (Ingold 2000, Barsalou *et al.* 2007, Collins 2010) then many more kinds of valuable human interaction can be seen to fall under the umbrella term 'collaborative knowledge building'. When we speak of networked learning as productive, or as a shared enterprise of knowledge creation, we are including – for example – the kinds of knowledge that eventuate when people learn to sing together (Chapter 13), learn to share freely their discoveries (Chapters 4, 12 and 14) and learn to transform the organizations in which they work (Chapters 6, 9 and 15).

A number of our case studies and, we suspect, a number of the other learning networks with which our readers will want to engage are situated in formal education. In such cases, important elements of the knowledge involved, the ways of knowing and the roles of knowers, need particular analytic care. We have found some of the work of our colleague Karl Maton on Legitimation Code Theory (LCT) very useful here. LCT is a framework for studying socio-cultural practices within both formal and informal educational contexts (Maton 2013, Maton *et al.* 2014). In Chapter 16, we explain how we have used LCT to help analyze knowledge and knowing, as a part of what we refer to as 'epistemic analysis' and 'epistemic design'.

Architecture, Analysis and Design

There are countless numbers of learning networks. Each is different. Each embodies some ideas that can be useful to people who are shaping, managing or providing leadership for other learning networks. How can we capture such ideas to make them shareable? Describing unique features with careful attention to detail can actually be quite helpful. The human mind can be very good at working analogically, translating salient features of one case into specific ideas for a different case. So some of the descriptive material in Part II of the book aims to provide such details, and of course it is also possible to then go and visit the network concerned, to experience its design and functioning at first hand.

But we also want to be able to work at a more abstract level: to try to strip away some of the specifics, and identify deeper, more broadly applicable ideas. This has to be done with sensitivity. It is all too easy to create bland, formal representations that have no communicative power. Nor is it much help to distill emergent qualities of networks and try to turn them into design principles, without saying what design steps need to be taken to get similar results. ('Make sure your network embodies an open, lively, democratic spirit' is a fine slogan, but it is empty of design content: it does not give the designer any indication of what they might do to help bring such a state of affairs into being.)

The core of our intellectual work is therefore concerned with *analysis for design*. When we set out to analyze a learning network, our main purpose is to create knowledge that can be useful for design. This commitment to utility distinguishes what we do from approaches that are essentially *critical*, but this does not mean to say that we do our work blindly. Rather, our position reflects a commitment to supporting the work of others – educational designers – who themselves have professional commitments to help create things that support the learning of others.

This commitment to creating knowledge which is useful to designers means that we have to be realistic about the kinds of knowledge that designers can use. In turn, this means having a realistic idea of who actually *does* design work (with respect to learning networks), how they do it, what kinds of guidance they can act upon, and what other elements of the functioning of a learning network have to emerge after the designer has done his or her work. Relative to the numbers of people who teach, there are very few whose job title includes the word 'designer' – whether 'instructional designer', 'educational designer' or 'learning designer'. Our use of the word 'design' encompasses some of the activities undertaken by teachers when they are preparing for teaching – a part of educational work that we have previously labeled 'teaching-as-design' (Goodyear and Ellis 2007, Goodyear and Retalis 2010). This does not just embrace lesson planning or the preparation of lectures, but all aspects of design for learning, including those activities that result in the creation of learning places (physical, digital and hybrid), learning tools and resources, learning tasks and the social organization of learning arrangements, proposed divisions of labor, etc. (Goodyear 2000).

Design for networked learning can involve many, sometimes all, of these components, even though attention might primarily focus on the digital communication platform(s) to be used, the core tasks to be performed and the protocols for collaboration (Persico and Pozzi 2010). The outcomes of learning network analysis therefore need to be of a kind that can guide the design thinking and design decisions involved in shaping new, or improving existing, networks. To be useful, such guidance *can* take quite a general form – there are broad epistemic, pedagogical, social psychological and usability principles that should be part of the professional repertoire of any educational designer. But more concrete and action-oriented forms of knowledge are also valuable – including ways of representing successful design components such that they can be identified as appropriate, customized and re-used. To this end, we have experimented in some of our earlier work with design patterns and pattern languages for capturing reusable design knowledge for networked learning (e.g. Goodyear 2005, Goodyear and Retalis 2010). In this book, we work at a slightly more abstract level – identifying distinctive and particularly valued components from the designs in our selected cases. We also pay particular attention to the relations between components, trying to identify important elements of structure – that is, of architecture.

We say more about this 'architectural' orientation in Chapter 3, for it is quite a distinctive aspect of our approach. Our commitment to this architectural perspective arises from four sources. First, the practice of architecture is an *indirect* practice. It results in the creation of built forms that are meant to have effects on how people act and feel. Second, it is neither an arbitrary nor a deterministic practice.

> Architecture may well possess moral messages; it simply has no power to enforce them. It offers suggestions instead of making laws. It invites, rather than orders, us to emulate its spirit and cannot prevent its own abuse.
>
> *(de Botton 2006, p. 20)*

Third, it is a multidisciplinary practice that engages forms of epistemic fluency (combining diverse forms of knowledge and ways of knowing) that are rare or even shunned in many accounts of educational work.

> Architecture has sometimes found ways of getting on with the job when education freezes in the headlights of epistemological or moral uncertainty. Educationalists talk about the dangers of combining contradictory epistemological positions, while architects combine ideas from mechanics, optics, acoustics, economics, aesthetics, human biology, social psychology and history. They can combine mathematics and astrology without blushing. They build terrible buildings and some great ones. They sometimes ignore crucial human needs and wants, but the best of them *do* tend to show an understanding of human nature and its relationship to the material world that is subtle and profound.
>
> *(Goodyear 2011)*

Finally, architects move fluidly across scale levels in the design process, keeping an eye on the overall form and style of the building, while also knowing how to get the devil out of the details.

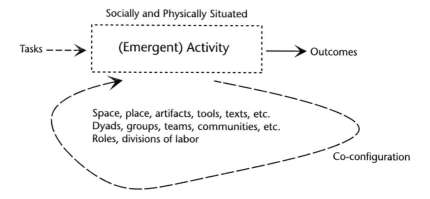

FIGURE 1.1 Activity-centered analytic framework

A First Sketch of the Analytic Framework: Activity, Tasks, the Setting, Social Organization and Co-configuration

In Chapter 3 we will provide a more detailed explanation of the main kinds of components that we look for when analyzing what a learning network consists of, how it functions, etc. To complete this first pass across our key concepts, and to help with some of the historical description presented in Chapter 2, we will very briefly introduce five key ideas here (see Figure 1.1).

First, our analysis is always *activity-centered*. That is, we take human activity to be key when one wants to understand learning. What people *do* – mentally, physically – is what matters. There is no experience without activity, nor any learning. Second, in formal educational situations, including in learning networks that have been created and are being run by an educational organization, one of the strongest influences on students' activity is the *tasks* set by teachers. We define tasks as 'suggestions of good things to do'. Students may be more or less compliant, more or less creative in their interpretation of a task. Thus, tasks are not identical with activities. Task prescriptions are resources on which students draw when they improvise their actual activities. In informal learning networks, it is not necessarily the case that anyone is formally giving out tasks. Nevertheless, there will normally be some shared practices, values and assumptions that stimulate activity in a similar way: suggestions of good things to do emerge in a variety of forms and ways. Third, activity is best understood as *situated* – it unfolds in ways that are shaped, subtly and powerfully, by the physical/digital tools and resources that come to hand, and by the social arrangements obtaining (divisions of labor, roles, etc.). Fourth, activity cannot be designed: it is *emergent*. Tasks, the physical/digital setting and divisions of labor *can* be designed. They are the three main kinds of *design component* for which we look. Finally, when we observe the physical/digital setting and social organization in a learning network, we need to recognize that what we see is partly designed and is partly created through the actions of the participants – that is, the network is partly designed in advance and partly *co-configured* in use.

The analyses presented in Part II focus on these four elements: the physical/ digital setting (or 'set', as in stage design), the social, the tasks (or epistemic) and co-configuration (Goodyear and Carvalho, 2013). In the next chapter, we provide some further background by sketching the evolution of learning networks and networked learning, while also drawing some connections with the development of ideas about network research in other areas of the social sciences. In Chapter 3, we describe and explain the elements of our architectural approach to analyzing learning networks.

References

Akkerman, S. and Van Eijck, M., 2013. Re-theorising the student dialogically across and between boundaries of multiple communities. *British Educational Research Journal*, 39(1), 60–72.

Bacsich, P. and Ash, C., 2000. Costing the lifecycle of networked learning: documenting the costs from conception to evaluation. *ALT-J: Journal of the Association for Learning Technology*, 8(1), 92–102.

Barsalou, L., Breazeal, C. and Smith, L., 2007. Cognition as coordinated non-cognition. *Cognitive Processes*, 8(2), 79–91.

Barton, D. and Tusting, K., eds., 2005. *Beyond communities of practice: language, power and social context*. Cambridge: Cambridge University Press.

Boden, D. and Molotch, H., 1994. The compulsion of proximity. In: R. Friedland and D. Boden, eds. *Nowhere: space, time and modernity*. Berkeley: University of California Press.

Botha, R., 2010. On the soundness of inferring modern language from symbolic behaviour. *Cambridge Archaeological Journal*, 20(3), 345–356.

Borgatti, S. and Foster, P., 2003. The network paradigm in organizational research: a review and typology. *Journal of Management*, 29(6), 991–1013.

Brown, K., Marean, C., Jacobs, Z., Schoville, B., Oestmo, S., Fisher, E., Bernatchez, J., Karkanas, P. and Matthews, T., 2012. An early and enduring advanced technology originating 71,000 years ago in South Africa. *Nature*, 491, 590–593.

Collins, H., 2010. *Tacit and explicit knowledge*. Chicago: The University of Chicago Press.

de Botton, A., 2006. *The architecture of happiness*. London: Hamish Hamilton.

Dediu, D. and Levinson, S. C., 2013. On the antiquity of language: the reinterpretation of neandertal linguistic capacities and its consequences. *Frontiers in Psychology*, DOI: 10.3389/fpsyg.2013.00397 [online]. Available from: www.frontiersin.org/Language_Sciences/10.3389/fpsyg.2013.00397/abstract [Accessed 2 August 2013].

Dirckinck-Holmfeld, L., Esnault, L., Gustafson, J., Hodgson, V., Lindström, B., Jones, C., Ponti, M., Ryberg, T. and Tickner, S., 2004. *EQUEL position paper: the theory and practice of computer supported collaborative learning*. Lancaster University.

Dreier, O., 2011. Personality and the conduct of everyday life. *Nordic Psychology*, 63(2), 4–23.

Duguid, P., 2005a. Introduction: the changing organization of industry. *Business History Review*, 79(3), 453–466.

Duguid, P., 2005b. Networks and knowledge: the beginning and end of the port commodity chain, 1703–1860. *Business History Review*, 21(2), 109–118.

Edwards, A., 2010. *Being an expert professional practitioner: the relational turn in expertise.* Dordrecht: Springer.

Gibson, K. and Ingold, T., eds., 1995. *Tools, language and cognition in human evolution.* Cambridge: Cambridge University Press.

Goodyear, P., 2000. Environments for lifelong learning: ergonomics, architecture and educational design. In: J. M. Spector and T. Anderson, eds. *Integrated and holistic perspectives on learning, instruction & technology: understanding complexity.* Dordrecht: Kluwer Academic Publishers.

Goodyear, P., 2005. Educational design and networked learning: patterns, pattern languages and design practice. *Australasian Journal of Educational Technology*, 21(1), 82–101.

Goodyear, P., 2011. CoPs, nets, knots and boundary work, Keynote lecture, *Annual Conference of the Australian Association for Research in Education.* Hobart, Tasmania.

Goodyear, P. and Carvalho, L., 2013. The analysis of complex learning environments. In: H. Beetham and R. Sharpe, eds. *Rethinking pedagogy for a digital age: designing and delivering e-learning.* 2nd ed. (pp. 49–63). New York: Routledge.

Goodyear, P. and Ellis, R., 2007. Students' interpretations of learning tasks: implications for educational design. *ICT: Providing choices for learners and learning – Proceedings of ascilite 2007.* Singapore.

Goodyear, P., Hodgson, V. and Steeples, C., 1998. *Student experiences of networked learning in higher education.* Lancaster: Lancaster University. Research proposal to the UK JISC, October 1998.

Goodyear, P., Jones, C., Asensio, M., Hodgson, V. and Steeples, C., 2001. *Students' experiences of networked learning in higher education, final project report* (2 vols). Bristol: Joint Information Systems Committee (JISC).

Goodyear, P. and Retalis, S., eds., 2010. *Technology-enhanced learning: design patterns and pattern languages.* Rotterdam: Sense Publishers.

Hancock, D., 2005. The trouble with networks: managing the Scots' early-modern Madeira trade. *Business History Review*, 79, 467–491.

Haggerty, J. and Haggerty, S., 2010. Visual analytics of an eighteenth-century business network. *Enterprise and Society*, 11(1), 1–25.

Harasim, L., Hiltz, S., Teles, L. and Turoff, M., 1997. *Learning networks: a field guide to learning and teaching online.* Cambridge, MA: MIT Press.

Henshilwood, C. and Dubreuil, B., 2009. Reading the artefacts: gleaning language skills from the Middle Stone Age in southern Africa. In: R. Botha and C. Knight, eds. *The cradle of language.* Oxford: Oxford University Press.

Hodgson, V., McConnell, D. and Dirckinck-Holmfeld, L., 2011. The theory, practice and pedagogy of networked learning. In: L. Dirckinck-Holmfeld, V. Hodgson and D. McConnell, eds. *Exploring the theory, pedagogy and practice of networked learning.* Dordrecht: Springer.

Hutchins, E., 2010. Cognitive ecology. *Topics in Cognitive Science*, 2(4), 705–715.

Illich, I., 1973. *Deschooling society.* Harmondsworth: Penguin.

Illich, I. and Verne, E., 1976. *Imprisoned in the global classroom.* London: Writers and Readers.

Ingold, T., 2000. *The perception of the environment: essays in livelihood, dwelling and skill.* Abingdon: Routledge.

JISC, 1998. *Circular 9/98: CALT Programme* [online]. Available from: www.jisc.ac.uk/fundingopportunities/funding_calls/1998/10/circular_9_98.aspx [Accessed 21 February 2013].

Jones, C., 2004. Networks and learning: communities, practices and the metaphor of networks. *ALT-J: Journal of the Association for Learning Technology*, 12(2), 81–93.

Kiefer, M. and Trumpp, N., 2012. Embodiment theory and education: the foundations of cognition in perception and action. *Trends in Neuroscience and Education*, 1(1), 15–20.

Knappett, C., ed., 2013. *Network analysis in archaeology: new approaches to regional interaction.* Oxford: Oxford University Press.

Koschmann, T., 1996. Paradigm shifts and instructional technology: an introduction. In: T. Koschmann, ed. *CSCL: theory and practice of an emerging paradigm.* Mahwah, NJ: Lawrence Erlbaum Associates.

Lave, J., 2012. Changing practice. *Mind, Culture, and Activity*, 19(2), 156–171.

Lehtinen, E., 2011. Learning of complex competences: on the need to coordinate multiple theoretical perspectives. In: A. Koskensalo, J. Smeds, A. Huguet and R. De Cillia, eds. *Language: competencies – contact – change.* Berlin: LIT Verlag.

Levy, P., 1997. Continuing professional development for networked learner support: progress review of research and curriculum design. *Information Research*, 3(1) [online]. Available from: http://informationr.net/ir/3-1/paper35.html [Accessed 2 August 2013].

Maton, K., 2013. *Knowledge and knowers: towards a realist sociology of education.* London: Routledge.

Maton, K., Hood, S. and Shay, S., eds., 2014. *Knowledge-building: educational studies in Legitimation Code Theory.* London: Routledge.

Mayadas, F., 1997. Asynchronous learning networks: a Sloan Foundation perspective. *Journal of Asynchronous Learning Networks*, 1(1), 1–16.

Mayes, T. and de Freitas, S., 2007. Learning and e-learning. In: H. Beetham and R. Sharpe, eds. Second ed. *Rethinking pedagogy for a digital age.* New York: Routledge.

McConnell, D., 2006. *E-learning groups and communities.* Maidenhead: Open University Press.

McConnell, D., Hodgson, V. and Dirckinck-Holmfeld, L., 2011. Networked learning: a brief history and new trends. In: L. Dirckinck-Holmfeld, V. Hodgson and D. McConnell, eds. *Exploring the theory, pedagogy and practice of networked learning.* New York: Springer.

McPherson, M., 2009 (May 8). A baseline dynamic model for ego networks. *American Behavioral Scientist.* DOI:10.1177/0002764209331530

Mokyr, J., 2009. *The enlightened economy: an economic history of Britain 1700–1850.* New Haven, CT: Yale University Press.

Oliver, M., 2013. Learning technology: theorising the tools we study. *British Journal of Educational Technology*, 44(1), 31–43.

Persico, D. and Pozzi, F., 2010. The three Ts of the structure of online collaborative activities. *Procedia Social and Behavioral Sciences*, 2(2), 2610–2615.

Podolny, J. and Page, K., 1998. Network forms of organization. *Annual Review of Sociology*, 24, 57–76.

Powell, W., 1990. Neither market nor hierarchy: network forms of organization. In: B. Staw and L. Cummings, eds. *Research in organizational behavior.* Greenwich, CT: JAI.

Pradhan, G., Tennie, C. and van Schaik, C., 2012. Social organization and the evolution of cumulative technology in apes and hominins. *Journal of Human Evolution*, 63(1), 180–190.

Quinn, J., 2010. *Learning communities and imagined social capital: learning to belong.* London: Continuum.

Richardson, W. and Mancabelli, R., 2011. *Personal learning networks: using the power of connections to transform education*. Bloomington, IN: Solution Tree Press.

Roth, W.-M. and Lee, Y.-J., 2006. Contradictions in theorising and implementing communities in education. *Educational Research Review*, 1(1), 27–40.

Scardamalia, M. and Bereiter, C., 2006. Knowledge building: theory, pedagogy and technology. In: K. Sawyer, ed. *Cambridge handbook of the learning sciences*. Cambridge: Cambridge University Press.

Schuppli, C., Isler, K. and van Schaik, C. P., 2012. How to explain the unusually late age at skill competence among humans. *Journal of Human Evolution*, 63(6), 843–850.

Sindbœk, S., 2013. Broken links and black boxes: material affiliations and contextual network synthesis in the Viking world. In: C. Knappett, ed. *Network analysis in archaeology: new approaches to regional interaction*. Oxford: Oxford University Press.

Steeples, C. and Jones, C., eds., 2002. *Networked learning: perspectives and issues*. London: Springer.

Sterelny, K., 2012. *The evolved apprentice: how evolution made humans unique*. Cambridge, MA: MIT Press.

Urry, J., 2002. Mobility and proximity. *Sociology*, 36(2), 255–274.

Varbelow, S. and Griffith, B., 2012. Deschooling society: re-examining Ivan Illich's contributions to critical pedagogy for 21st century curriculum theory. *ERIC Online Submission*. [online]. Available from: www.eric.ed.gov/ERICWebPortal/detail?accno= ED532618 [Accessed 30 June 2013].

Wenger, E., Trayner, B. and de Laat, M., 2011. *Promoting and assessing value creation in communities and networks: a conceptual framework*. Heerlen: Open Universiteit.

Wynn, T. and Coolidge, F., 2010. Beyond symbolism and language. *Current Anthropology*, 51, S5–S16.

2

PRODUCTIVE LEARNING NETWORKS

The Evolution of Research and Practice

Peter Goodyear

This chapter outlines some key aspects of the evolution and nature of learning networks and networked learning. The aim is to situate research into learning networks in a broader landscape of research in education, technology and the social sciences and to demonstrate that networked learning is an important, widespread way of going about learning, and that it has deeper roots than might at first be imagined. Networked learning is not an esoteric activity, and merits greater attention in educational research and in the social sciences more generally.

One of the reasons that networked learning may be seen as esoteric is that it is strongly associated with relatively new digital technologies. When the pioneering practical work and experimentation was being done in the 1980s and early 1990s, the digital technologies used were primitive, slow, unreliable and not widely available. There was little understanding of the nature and possibilities of digital communications technologies in the populace at large, nor even among the majority of teachers and academics. Educational technologists have seen their world stand on its head in the last two decades – the tools and infrastructure for which we were weird and lonely advocates have become pervasive and taken for granted in modern, industrial economies. Those of us who were active in the 1980s and early 1990s with what we now call 'networked learning' look back at our early writings as work from the margins. But we also see strong connections in that work, with ideas about learning that predate the digital revolution. In what follows, we try to sketch some of the continuities in networked learning, to help locate it more firmly.

Rapid, indeed accelerating, changes in the digital technologies that so many take so quickly for granted are (a) making it harder to distinguish clearly between what is digital and what is material, (b) thereby reweaving some of the threads that appear to have become separated in the recent history of networked learning.

Without exaggerating the role of technological aids to human perception and cognition – without redefining people as cyborgs – one can nevertheless see that technological change raises deep questions about learning, understanding, capability, agency and responsibility. It is easy to look back at our naive pioneering selves – including the pre-iPad, pre-Moodle, pre-Facebook, pre-Twitter, pre-blogging selves of 10 years ago – and smile wryly at how little we understood then of the dynamics of technological change. It is sobering to realize that more will change in the next 10 years than has changed in the last 10, and that as we move forward in times of accelerating technological change, we know less and less about the future.

An Introduction to Research on Networks

Research on networks in organizational science and in the business and management literature has regularly provoked comments that it is weak on theory and terminologically confused (Salancik 1995). Nohria, for example, described the network research field as a 'terminological jungle in which any newcomer may plant a tree' (1992, p. 3). Although not a complete explanation, it is likely that some of the terminological confusion has arisen because of the mixture of disciplines within which research on networks has been, and is being, undertaken. For example, there are some deep differences between how sociologists and economists regard networked forms of organization. In addition, some of the more influential work of a mathematical nature on network structures, topologies etc. uses different tools and has a very different epistemological base from those one finds in the mainstreams of social and educational research (Barabási 2002, Watts 2004).

For this reason, and to sketch some of the connections between network research inside and outside education, it is worth spending a little time reviewing key ideas from the broader literature on networks. Academic interest in networks as forms of social and/or business organization is largely a post-World War II phenomenon: one that received a triple boost in the 1980s and early 1990s with:

1. growing Western business interest in the organizational forms associated with the commercial success of Japanese industry (Gerlach 1992, Lincoln *et al.* 1996, Duguid 2005);
2. the development and expansion of digital communications technologies and especially the Internet (Castells 1996, 2001);
3. what Borgatti and Foster describe as a general shift away from 'individualist, essentialist and atomistic explanations toward more relational, contextual and systemic understandings' (2003, p. 991).

Paul Duguid (2005) eloquently makes the point that business interest in inter-firm networking, over the last 30 years or so, has created the impression that such networking is exclusively a modern phenomenon. This is far from being the case. As archaeologists and historians are beginning to show, networked arrangements have long played a significant role in the organization of trade and innovation and in the development of ideas (e.g. Hancock 2005, Sindbæk 2013, Mews and Crossley 2011).

According to Podolny and Page (1998), economists have tended to take a negative view that networks are a hybrid, inefficient form – an unsatisfactory combination of the two dominant forms of organization in economic life – markets and hierarchies. In contrast, sociologists have argued persuasively for the recognition of networks as a form in their own right – one with some inherent advantages not possessed by pure markets or pure hierarchies, while combining the flexibility of markets with the predictability of hierarchies (Powell 1990, Borgatti and Foster 2003).

> We define a network form of organization as any collection of actors (N≥2) that pursue repeated, enduring exchange relations with one another and, at the same time, lack a legitimate organizational authority to arbitrate and resolve disputes that may arise during the exchange. In a pure market, relations are not enduring, but episodic, formed only for the purpose of a well-specified transfer of goods and resources and ending after the transfer. In hierarchies, relations may endure for longer than a brief episode, but a clearly recognized, legitimate authority exists to resolve disputes that arise among actors.
>
> *(Podolny and Page 1998, p. 59)*

As the case studies in Part II will show, the idea of 'legitimate organizational authority' is actually quite complicated. Learning networks involve complex interweavings of authority and freedom: the exercise of influence and control is not always obvious, and yet it is often possible to identify a locus of power in the informal as well as the formal educational networks.

A distinguishing feature of networks as organizational forms in business is an orientation to reciprocity, building and maintaining trust, resolving differences through dialogue and consensus-building (rather than shifting to another supplier), and to constructing shared understandings of business needs and opportunities. On this view, networks are organizational forms 'characterized by repetitive exchanges among semi-autonomous organizations [or individuals] that rely on trust and embedded social relationships to protect transactions and reduce their costs' (Borgatti and Foster 2003, p. 995).

Trust can be infectious within networks. People are more likely to trust friends of friends than random individuals. Similarly, a new organization that becomes closely linked to a high-status organization tends to be attributed high status too. Trust and information sharing give networks the advantage of resilience in times of change.

By fostering more communication than the market does, network forms of organization facilitate greater coordination in the face of changes whose significance cannot be completely conveyed or understood through price signals. At the same time, because the boundaries of network forms of organization are generally easier to adjust than the boundaries of hierarchies, it is easier to modify the composition of network organizations to respond to those changes.

(Podolny and Page 1998, p. 66)

The topology of an actor's network can be interpreted as a way of measuring their social capital, though there are different views on how this might best be done. For example, in the early 1990s, Ronald Burt developed the idea that an actor's social capital is increased by the lack of direct ties between others in the actor's network. These 'structural holes' make the actor more valuable to those others, who would otherwise be less connected: 'Brokerage across the structural holes between groups provides a vision of operations otherwise unseen, which is the mechanism by which brokerage becomes social capital' (Burt 2004, p. 349).

Conversely, commentators like James Coleman and Robert Putnam argue that denser connections amongst other actors in one's network create possibilities for coordination and shared work that boost one's own value and benefits (Borgatti and Foster 2003).

Organizational science research on networks has also developed an interest in social cognition and transactive memory – the idea that knowledge is distributed in different minds, so that effective use of knowledge depends upon having easy, reciprocated access to the knowledge of others, as well as a good map of who knows what and 'who knows who knows what' (Borgatti and Foster 2003, p. 998). A complicating factor arises from the phenomenon of 'homophily' – the tendency to prefer to interact with others who are like oneself. While this can have positive functions, such as reducing conflict, simplifying coordination and facilitating the sharing of tacit knowledge (Cross *et al.* 2001), it also reduces access to different and novel ideas and can act as a barrier to those who are disadvantaged by difference and whose voices are not recognized (McPherson *et al.* 2001, di Maggio and Garip 2012).

Recognition of the special value of information passing between linked people (or organizations) in a network is a core characteristic of sociological research on networks. Indeed, understanding how information flow in networks enables individual and organizational learning and innovation has long been a central purpose of Social Network Analysis (SNA) (see for example Granovetter 1973, 1983). Granovetter (1973) developed the notion of 'weak ties' as being especially important in passing information across a network. 'Strong ties' are those binding people who have close, regular, repeated contact. They tend to be powerful in influencing the thoughts and actions of those involved. But we all also have 'weak ties' – such as connections to people who are acquaintances rather than friends or family, who may be located at a greater distance from us, and with whom we tend to interact less often. However, weak ties have an important role in distributing new knowledge. Within the tight-knit (socially) local sub-networks that are made by our strong ties, views of the world tend to be shared and stable; new insights come with information from (socially) distant parts of the network, via occasional interactions across weak ties. Learning stimulated and/or supported by encounters with new information, brought through weak ties, is therefore a valuable distinguishing characteristic of networks: 'Network forms of organization foster learning because they preserve greater diversity of search routines than hierarchies and they convey richer, more complex information than the market' (Podolny and Page, 1998, p. 62).

> the most useful form of information is rarely that which flows down the formal chain of command in an organization, or that which can be inferred from price signals. Rather, it is that which is obtained from someone you have dealt with in the past and found to be reliable.
>
> *(Powell 1990, p. 304)*

Podolny and Page (1998, pp. 62–64) describe two kinds of learning that occur in business networks. One involves the rapid transfer of self-contained pieces of information – network ties are thereby seen as conduits through which useful knowledge can pass. The second form of learning is more transformative, and occurs when new syntheses of information occur – creating something qualitatively different from the knowledge previously residing in any specific node.

Whether one is using nodes to represent individual people or organizations, network forms can be understood as promoting both additive knowledge accumulation and transformative change. They have been functioning in this way for a very long time.

Early Networks

Archaeologists, anthropologists and historians, using the distribution of related artifacts as evidence, have begun to use network analysis and network reconstruction techniques to model relationships between individuals and groups at various scale levels – from the house, through the village to the region – and across substantial slices of time. Gaps in the record, and the exercise of due diligence in interpreting the cultural role of any artifact, mean that such analyses are often suggestive rather than conclusive. Nevertheless, scholars are beginning to accumulate persuasive evidence about the social and spatial structuring of interaction, over substantial distances, at dates that are early enough to surprise those who think of networking as a phenomenon peculiar to the computer age.

For example, mappings of stone age artifacts in the Near East make it clear that, even 20,000 years ago, trade and travel were overcoming geography: material culture was not tightly localized and many artifacts overcame the friction of distance (Coward 2010). Similar studies have traced social interactions across time and distance, using evidence of trade and gift-giving from material culture – including in the Bronze Age Mediterranean (Knappett *et al.* 2008) and in South East Asia (e.g. Irwin 1978). Ideas and learning have also been followed as they spread. For example, using network analysis, Anna Collar (2013) has been able to trace the spread of religious innovations among the Mediterranean Jewish diaspora over the 400 years following the destruction of the Temple in AD 70. Research on intellectual networking among Muslim, Jewish and Christian translators in twelfth-century Spain is documented in several of the chapters in Mews and Crossley (2011).

Business historians have also become interested in network forms. David Hancock's research on the eighteenth-century Atlantic trade in Madeira wine shows how characteristic strengths of networks (a) made such trade sustainable, and (b) took significant care and skill to manage.

> The structures we can call networks – the open-work, netlike relational fabrics that Atlantic businessmen built in the eighteenth century – were solutions to problems, chiefly the challenges of doing business over oceanic distances, given the limits of transportation and communication technologies. At the same time, the solutions created their own management challenges. The inability to meet them could result in failure to build an adequate business network or to operationalize it fully or profitably.
>
> *(Hancock 2005, p. 473)*

One important key to understanding the significance of such networks – in contrast to markets – is that while the merchants' immediate goal was to sell Madeira wine, the long-term goal 'was to establish relationships with people who bought wine repeatedly and would recommend the distributor to others' (Hancock 2005, p. 477). That is to say, network relations enabled a growth in product knowledge and trust, as well as the development of a more nuanced understanding of the needs and capabilities of actors along the whole distribution chain. As Hancock points out, the maintenance of effective network relations demanded both skill and application. Not all merchants managed to achieve this, and their businesses suffered accordingly.

The exchange of knowledge through networking can also be seen as a central factor propelling the Industrial Revolution in eighteenth-century Britain – it is a key aspect of what Joel Mokyr has dubbed the 'Industrial Enlightenment' (Mokyr 2009). While sporadic and sometimes very significant innovation in agricultural and manufacturing processes had occurred in earlier times, the Industrial Revolution marks the beginning of *sustained* technological advances. One must be careful not to overestimate the short-term effects of science on industrial innovation during this period. Much progress actually derived from trial and error. However, as Kim Sterelny has pointed out, there is a big difference between 'blind' trial and error, and experimentation that takes place in an environment rich in tools, ideas and knowledgeable observers (Sterelny 2012, pp. 34–43).

The eighteenth century, particularly in Britain, marked a radical, ideological shift – to one in which there was widespread acceptance of the capacity of new knowledge to inform material progress. On Mokyr's analysis, this shift cannot be explained simply in terms of the growth of science. The reduction of the costs of access to useful knowledge was key.

What took place between the late seventeenth and early nineteenth centuries in Britain was the formation of networks linking those who were developing new knowledge to those who could exploit it, through both face-to-face meetings and the creation and circulation of affordable publications. The reduction of printing costs, and improved availability of published material through provincial libraries and coffee houses, gave affordable access to codified knowledge inscribed in journals, encyclopedias and manuals of various kinds. (Coffee houses had evolved to become important sites for intellectual life in the larger British cities by the end of the seventeenth century. As well as being places for discussion, many coffee houses had substantial libraries of their own – Mokyr 2009, p. 50, Peter and Farrell 2013.) Face-to-face networking between 'men of science' and the industrialists and merchants able to exploit their knowledge was important because of the difficulties of translating new propositional knowledge into forms that could be applied to practical problems and because of the complementary difficulty of making the tacit knowledge of industrial practice explicit and shareable. The creation of shared insights into practical issues – such as a manufacturing technique or engineering challenge – generally takes time, interactive discussion, joint problem-solving and trust. So in coffee houses, pubs and other shared spaces, informal meetings began to evolve into associations and into institutions such as the Royal Society and the British Association for the Advancement of Science (Mokyr op. cit., pp. 50–53). Both in London and in the provincial cities, these face-to-face meetings promoted an intermingling of scientists, businessmen and engineers and the forming of friendships and bonds of trust. They created opportunities to share tacit practical knowledge – a prerequisite for understanding the relevance of, and exploiting, the codified knowledge that was being generated by scientific advances, disseminated and discussed in lectures and demonstrations, and inscribed in the growing body of affordable periodicals and books. Crucially, these networks of learning and innovation reduced the real costs of access to useful knowledge.

> Rather than posing the question of whether it was theorists or practical people who brought about technological progress, we need to see the fundamental complementarity between them. It was precisely their presence

together and their ability to interact and produce something larger that has the power to explain Britain's technological successes.

(Mokyr op. cit., p. 61)

From this brief survey, it is clear that the sharing of information through networks is a well-established feature of human life. Its earliest forms depended upon human travelers – the traces of whose interactions can still be seen in the distributions of the artifacts they transported and left (Knappett 2013). With the development of writing, information could be passed within networks without either sender or receiver having to move – though a trader or messenger would have to carry the texts concerned. With the invention of the telegraph, telephones and radio, it became possible for complex information to travel independently – along wires, and then wirelessly, which brings us, by the 1960s, to communication using networked computers.

Early Experiments with Computer Conferencing in Education

The origins of networked computer conferencing are usually traced back to the EMISARI system, created in 1970–71 by Murray Turoff for the US Office of Emergency Preparedness. EMISARI – the Emergency Management Information System and Reference Index – evolved from pilot trials of using DELPHI techniques, linking geographically distributed experts (Turoff 2002). It included facilities for sharing text and other information items, tagging by topic and person, sending notifications triggered by updates, starting discussion threads attached to any information item, and keeping track of who has searched for what. It was also readily reconfigurable, to meet new emergency response needs (Turoff 2002).

Turoff and colleagues at the New Jersey Institute of Technology went on to develop the Electronic Information Exchange System during the late 1970s (see e.g. Turoff *et al.* 1977, Hiltz and Turoff 1978). From a user or functional perspective, EIES offered: (i) messages (private, one-to-one or one-to-many); (ii) conferencing (providing a transcript of a topic-oriented discussion, keywording and linking of entries, and a voting system); (iii) a notebook (personal online space for composing notes etc.); (iv) a bulletin (an online newsletter). EIES ran on a computer at NJIT and remote users typically connected to it via terminals, acoustic couplers and the telephone line. The standard connection speed for this dial-up service was 300 baud (30 characters per second). Those who recall using similar systems in the 1970s and 1980s will recognize the frustrating limitations of working with slow, unreliable connections, having to learn obscure sets of commands and managing the constraints of display technologies. That the EIES *User* Manual (not the technical manual) extends to 56 pages speaks to the complexities involved in carrying out tasks that these days are classed as 'intuitive'.

Evaluation studies run by Starr Roxanne Hiltz at the time estimated that users took 2–4 hours to learn how to use the EIES 'reasonably well'.

However, users do adjust fairly quickly. Within 20–30 minutes, they are able to learn the basic mechanics; within two to four hours, they report that they feel they have 'learned to use the system reasonably well'. From the approximately half-hour point until about *50 to 100 hours of practice*, they begin to master the social processes involved.

(Hiltz 1978, p. 160, emphasis added)

In writing about the planned field trials of EIES, Hiltz (1977) focuses primarily on its use to support distributed groups of *scientists* who are working on fast-moving topics. She mentions education, in passing, as a potential future application area (op. cit., p. 235) but the NJIT group's first actual use of EIES in teaching (which they dubbed the 'Virtual Classroom') was not until the fall of 1982 – with small numbers of additional courses offered in 1983 and 1984 (Hiltz 1986, pp. 7–8). Hiltz's assessments of the educational value and usability of EIES underscored the intrinsic difficulties of acquiring mastery of its more advanced features.

Learning advanced features is more problematic. In order to participate in an online course, students need to know only a few basic procedures and feel comfortable; however, instructors must be familiar with many advanced features in order to be able to control the delivery of long text items, construct tests or voting exercises, and moderate their conferences. About half of EIES users with less than 50 hours of time online never learned these features at all, and one-third of the high users with 50 to 99 hours online did not. Of course, they never may have felt the need to know how to use anything other than simple message and conference capabilities. . . . It may be concluded that only those experienced with the medium of computerized conferencing should undertake to offer a course using this medium. Further, 30 to 50 hours online will be necessary to gain this experience. Teachers with no knowledge of advanced features will need an experienced user to act as a technical facilitator.

(Hiltz 1986, p. 103)

The first live use of computer conferencing was also seen in 1982 at Western Behavioral Sciences Institute (WBSI) in California. The course WBSI offered in January 1982 is now widely recognized as the earliest example of an educational program being offered principally via computer conferencing (Feenberg 1986, Kaye 1992). Kaye (1992) describes the WBSI program of continuing professional development for business executives as being the paradigmatic example of what quite rapidly became a standard form for CMC – the *virtual seminar* 'in which a small group of articulate peers exchange ideas and information over a period of several months, in a text-based mode entirely free of any time or place constraints' (Kaye 1992, p. 6).

Robin Mason provides an exemplary analysis of virtual seminar transcripts from a WBSI course called *The Management of the Absurd* (Mason 1991). She identifies three important roles for the moderator of educational computer conferences: i) a *social* role – creating a friendly, social environment for learning; ii) an *organizational* role – setting the agenda, defining procedures, giving leadership; and iii) an *intellectual* role – that of educational facilitator.

Based on his WBSI experience, Andrew Feenberg shared some early reflections on design for educational computer conferences.

> Conference architecture consists of the distribution of tasks among the various conferences operated by a given group. It should be based on the answer to the question 'Who needs to communicate with whom about what?' Decisions about conference architecture might be compared with interior design decisions in the construction of a facility. Each conference on the network is a bit like a room in a building. Network design and interior design therefore ask the same question: How many conference rooms of what size are required for the tasks of the group? Good choices in this matter are essential; while it is not as difficult to change conference architecture once it is established as to redesign the interior of a building, it can be extremely confusing to a group to find the structure of its exchanges altered in mid-stream for reasons that may not be universally understood or accepted.
>
> *(Feenberg 1986, p. 5)*

Thus, out of the early 1980s experiences at NJIT and WBSI we begin to see elements of architecture – social and set – falling into place.

In passing, it is worth noting that Hiltz's (1994) account of her own first sketches of the Virtual Classroom (which she dates to 1977) also takes a distinctly architectural form. While enrolled in a postgraduate seminar in the sociology of architecture, Hiltz was given the assignment of designing 'an ideal classroom for the twenty-first century'. She started sketching classroom layouts but began to encounter some insurmountable design problems:

> How could you create a comfortable, upholstered discussion space for say, 30 people, without having to put in microphones so that participants could be heard across the huge circle without shouting? How could you possibly provide an adequate amount of computer and other resources, so that they would always be available to students for use in assignments, whenever they wanted them, without the endowment of a Princeton or Harvard? Suddenly it came to me. A teaching and learning environment did not have to be built of bricks and boards. It could be constructed in software. It could be Virtual!
>
> *(Hiltz 1994, pp. 5–6)*

The early 1980s also witnessed some experimental work with the use of digital communications technologies – email and/or computer conferencing – to substitute for in-class discussions in undergraduate teaching. Quinn *et al.* (1983) report on an experimental use of an email-based messaging system in one of Hugh Mehan's courses, in 1980, at the University of California San Diego (UCSD). Their analysis focuses on comparisons between the discourse in face-to-face classes and among equivalent students (studying the same course) who interacted via the messaging system. The interactions amongst the latter group were distinguished by a number of features associated with educationally richer situations:

- multiple threads of discourse – meaning that several strands of discussion were being developed over time, and that any one message from a student might refer to, and advance, more than one discussion thread;
- a higher proportion of students' responses to teachers' initiations – whereas the normal form of exchange in the face-to-face classroom was the familiar 'teacher initiates, student responds, teacher evaluates' sequence, in the messaging context, each teacher-initiated question or comment received multiple student responses;
- few teacher evaluations – compared with the face-to-face class, the teacher made few evaluations of students' comments; students made more peer evaluations (Quinn *et al.* 1983, p. 326).

UCSD was also home, in the early 1980s, to some pioneering developments in the use of email between schools – for connecting teachers and also students, both nationally and internationally. While there had been some use of electronic messaging in support of educational outreach projects by Dartmouth and Stanford universities as early as 1968–69, linking local schools to the universities' time-shared mainframe computers (Hunter 1992), the best-documented early experiments with educational use of email come from work by Jim Levin, Margaret Riel and colleagues (see e.g. Levin *et al.* 1987, 1990, Riel 1990, Riel and Levin 1990). These included some international collaborations between school children in the US, Mexico, Japan and Israel – working on problems specific to their own communities but that had points in common with problems being addressed in communities overseas (cf. Chapter 8, *Diseña el Cambio*). They also connected larger numbers of teachers and students, distributed across the US, Canada, the Netherlands, France, Germany and Australia, in 'Long Distance Learning Networks', to share curriculum ideas and experiences in learning circles.

In terms of the technological infrastructure, these experiments made use of personal computers, modems and email lists. They represent some of the earliest implementations of ideas about *community*-oriented work, as distinct from one-to-one communications. Also, while experiments with *locally-oriented* electronic community bulletin boards were well under way in the 1970s

(White 1977), Riel, Levin and colleagues were pioneers at *internationally distributed* educational interaction. They were among the first to speak of building internationally distributed electronic learning communities and the first to offer extensive analyses of success factors using the idea of 'network participant structures' (see especially Riel and Levin 1990).

> The most important factor leading to successful networks is *the presence of an important function* that the network serves for the participants. The nature of this function determines the particular form that the network should have. In these early days of the medium in which we are primarily concerned with building networks that work, a good design principle is to *have the form of the networks follow the functions* that the networks serve. As communication technology advances, 'user friendly' interfaces will become the norm and the technical barriers to networks will disappear. At that point, *the social design of networks will become the dominant issue*: what should be the nature of the interactions, how should leadership be provided, and how should activity be organized in this new communication medium?
>
> *(Riel and Levin 1990, p. 168, emphasis added)*

Thus, some of the key findings to emerge from their experimental work and analyses emphasize the importance of coherent pedagogical approaches. In our terms, they are prioritizing epistemic design and expecting set design to become less important than social design in the functioning of productive learning networks. (There are some interesting assumptions about system usability here. Riel and Levin are predicting that better user interfaces will reduce access barriers. It is worth adding that (a) usability is a *relational* concept – it is not solely a quality of the computer interface, but a relation between qualities of the interface and the knowledge, skills and expectations of the user; (b) some people bring more elaborate conceptions to the use of new tools and 'props', while other people may not have had the life experiences to interpret and use them so readily.)

A distinctive example of their ideas about epistemic and social design can be found in the notion of 'tele-apprenticeship' (Levin *et al.* 1987). This built explicitly on Jean Lave's contemporary writings about apprenticeship learning in traditional communities, which also turned out to be an important source of insight for the JITOL project, as we shall see shortly.

Professional Learning Networks

The decade or so following the ground breaking work described above witnessed an exponential growth in the educational use of Computer-Mediated Communication (CMC), including online discussion boards and email, with particularly well-documented programs of activity emerging at the Ontario Institute for

Studies in Education in Canada (see e.g. Harasim 1993), the NKI Electronic College in Norway (Rekkedal and Paulsen 1989), the UK Open University (Mason and Kaye 1989), the Jutland Open University in Denmark (Fjuk and Dirckinck-Holmfeld 1997) and at Lancaster University in the UK (Hodgson and McConnell 1992, Goodyear and Steeples 1993). Good overviews of these and related developments can be found in Kaye (1992), McConnell (1994, 2006), Harasim *et al.* (1997), Haughey and Anderson (1998), Steeples and Jones (2002). So in this section, we are going to focus on a linked series of European R&D projects exploring innovative designs for continuing professional development among geographically distributed networks of skilled workers. The ITOL, JITOL and SHARP series of R&D projects (1988–1999) is noteworthy for three connected reasons. First, the projects created a quite rare site for working out some of the meaning and consequences of ideas about open and collaborative learning, at a time when technology-enabled learning was dominated by strategies for optimizing individualized instruction. Second, the projects helped create a community of researchers, albeit mainly within Europe, who were interested in networked, vocationally-oriented collaborative learning for adults, when the vast majority of R&D work was aimed at education in schools. Third, the projects managed to interweave practical and theoretical goals, resulting in technical and pedagogical innovations and contributions to emerging theory.

ITOL

The ITOL project – *IT-based Open Learning* – started at Lancaster University in 1988 (Hodgson *et al.* 1989, Hodgson and McConnell 1992) and was the point of departure for several strands of research, writing and experimental teaching that collectively explored the ground for what we now call networked learning. ITOL was funded by a UK government agency whose remit covered adult vocational learning and skills. Through a separate grant, the same agency funded the creation of an experimental Masters course – Lancaster's MSc in Information Technology and Learning – which made extensive use of email and computer conferencing to support students' learning at a distance, interleaved with intensive one-week residential study sessions (Goodyear and Steeples 1993). The ITOL funding allowed Hodgson and McConnell to test the use of computer conferencing on the Masters program in Management Learning at Lancaster (see Hodgson and McConnell 1992, Hardy *et al.* 1994). Through these practical experiments, and guided by a strong commitment to open learning – encouraging autonomy, self-direction and negotiation of learning activities and assessments – the ITOL team developed a model to guide others who might wish to design and implement similar systems. This 'ITOL Model' was

> not intended to be prescriptive but rather to show how the component parts of an open-learning system of provision might inter-relate with each

other, and could benefit from the enhanced facilities for communication and information storage offered by new technology.

(Hodgson and McConnell 1992, p. 138)

From the perspective of our architectural analytic framework, the ITOL model foregrounded social design – focusing on roles for learner, tutor, counselor and manager of the resources – and placing the community of learners (rather than tutors or resources) at the center of things. Online and other information/learning resources were, of course, an element in the model. Given the high value placed on students' choice of learning goals and methods, the ITOL model was relatively silent about task design.

JITOL

The JITOL ('Just in Time Open Learning') project arose very directly from ideas sketched in ITOL and from the practical experiences of the Lancaster team. JITOL was a large project, with 70+ researchers, and was highly influential. It was funded in the early days of pan-European collaboration in educational technology R&D (the 'DELTA program'). It was conceived in 1991 and ran from 1992 to 1994, with some small extension activities continuing into 1995. The initial ideas guiding the project are summarized in Lewis, Goodyear and Boder (1992) and more extensive accounts can be found in Boder (1992), Goodyear and Steeples (1992) and Goodyear (1995).

Jean Lave and Etienne Wenger published their book on situated learning in 1991. In it, they coined the phrase 'communities of practice' and they argued persuasively for a fresh understanding of learning as a process of decreasingly peripheral participation in communities of practice. Lave and Wenger's most striking empirical examples described engagement in craft practices in traditional communities, within which learning and identity formation developed within local groups. In JITOL, we took this notion and applied it to *distributed* communities of practice, within which participation was largely or exclusively enacted through digital communications at a distance (Goodyear and Steeples 1992, Boder 1992). André Boder captured the essence of this nicely:

> The JITOL model includes two basic devices. One is a public debate, namely interactions between actors on the network. The other is a knowledge resource which serves as a reference for the interactions, but which in turn is constantly updated by the outcome of the interactions themselves. Therefore, reification is a recursive process through which the knowledge base progressively matches issues raised by the actors.
>
> *(Boder 1992, p. 178)*

So, core to the JITOL approach was the notion of members of a distributed community of practice collaborating in the construction of a shared, evolving knowledge base, partly or wholly through the traces left by their online interactions. In refining our design ideas about architectures for JITOL, we were also inspired by some related developments in North America – notably Mark Ackerman and Tom Malone's work at MIT on Answer Garden (Ackerman and Malone 1990) and, of course, Marlene Scardamalia and Carl Bereiter's work on CSILE (Scardamalia and Bereiter 1992) – later to become Knowledge Forum (Scardamalia and Bereiter 2006). Both Answer Garden and CSILE supported the iterative development of communal knowledge bases through inquiry activity. Answer Garden was essentially an organically growing help system. CSILE was explicitly designed to support intentional learning, especially in formal education. JITOL differed in so far as learning was seen as a valuable side-effect of the discussion of work-related issues (sharing new methods, problems etc.), and that learning was both an individual and a collective accomplishment, entailing the articulation and critique of knowledge embedded in existing working practices (Goodyear 1995, Bonamy and Haugluslaine-Charlier 1995, Manenti 1995, Lewis 1997).

SHARP

The SHARP project picked up some core ideas from JITOL and added multimedia capabilities to supplement what had previously been done through text. As Hodgson and McConnell (1992) and Goodyear and Steeples (1992) had pointed out, text is not ideal for professional communications. Capturing the knowledge embedded in working practices can be difficult and time-consuming when the primary medium is text. The SHARP project (Shareable Representations of Practice) worked on this problem. The main innovation in the 'set design' was a platform for what was called 'asynchronous multimedia conferencing'. This made it relatively straightforward for participants to upload digital video clips, embed them in a webpage, and then annotate both their own video clips and those of other members of the network (Sgouropoulou *et al.* 2000, Steeples and Goodyear 1999, Goodyear and Steeples 1998, 1999). Figure 2.1 illustrates what came to be known as the SHARP learning cycle.

The learning cycle involves a process of rendering the tacit knowledge embedded in local working practices into a shareable form, such as an annotated video clip. This is lodged in a shared online workspace, so that other participants in the learning network can get a better understanding of the knowledge, local context and practices. All the participants – professional and academic – can then discuss the issues at hand, make suggestions, critique, propose refinements, better ways of working, relevant practical and theoretical ideas, etc. (This is done through further annotations, using text, voice or video.) The final stage of the learning cycle involves closing the loop by (re)embedding the revised working knowledge into local work practices, e.g. through the creation of new procedures,

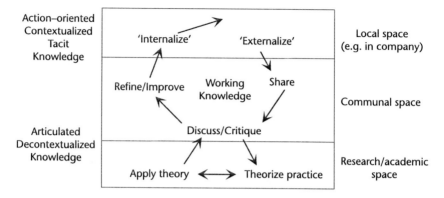

FIGURE 2.1 The SHARP learning cycle

techniques or job aids. And then the cycle begins again. As Figure 2.1 shows, the cycle involves translations between action–oriented, contextualized and often tacit knowledge (in the workplace) and more explicit, articulated and disembodied or decontextualized forms of knowledge (in the shared spaces of the SHARP platform). The sharing, critique, refinement and application of working knowledge can be viewed in terms of both individual learning and organizational learning. (In actuality, numerous individual and organizational learning cycles are active at any one time.) The academic participants in the SHARP learning cycle have a role that makes good use of their position on the interface between 'industry' and academia. They do not have to pretend to be practical experts, distilling advice for application in the workplace. Rather, they theorize the working knowledge and working practices that become visible in the discussion, make connections with ideas in the literature, and use these to help sharpen and orient the collective refinement of new working knowledge.

It is worth noting that SHARP preceded YouTube just as JITOL preceded the World Wide Web. Both projects can be seen as cases where strategies for professional networked learning ran ahead of the capabilities of the technology then available.

Mobile Devices, Web 2.0 and the Ubiquitous Nature of Networked Learning

Until the late 1990s, digitally mediated networked learning was largely a stationary affair. One needed a desktop computer and Ethernet connection to work efficiently. Sitting at a desk peering into the screen, the experience was a little like looking into cyberspace – one's immediate physical surroundings slipped away. With the growing availability of portable devices, and especially with the burgeoning availability of wireless network access and smart phones, this experience began to change dramatically. Network access is now at least as likely to happen 'on the move' as via a static desktop machine and many people possess several devices with which to stay connected. While use of a web browser, Facebook or Twitter on a mobile phone *may* distract the user from their immediate physical and social surroundings, at some risk to their safety and friendships, the overall shift has resulted in a complication of the sense of what is digital and what is not: the digital and non-digital become quite thoroughly entangled.

Two contrasting trends emerge from this mixing of the digital and the non-digital, both having some interesting implications for networked learning. One of these relates to the use of mobile, often personal, devices to extend and enhance (physically) place-based experiences. This genre can be thought of as 'mobile networked learning' and can include the use of location-aware functions on mobile devices. The other trend is to take aspects of the physical world into the digital, as with the creation of shared virtual worlds such as Second Life.

Learning in collaboration with others, using mobile devices, in situations where physical place is also significant, can take many forms. One example we have discussed in recent work (Goodyear and Carvalho, 2013) concerned the use of iPads and a complex assemblage of other artifacts in a training exercise for paramedics. This exercise took place in hill country and involved teams of experienced and inexperienced rescuers locating, treating and evacuating (simulated) casualties, over a two-day period. Successful participation in the exercise involved:

- learning to use each tool (e.g. a compass, flashlight, map, whistle, radio, stretcher, bandages, splints, iPad), at least with sufficient fluency to be able to act according to the established protocols, but ideally with a level of automaticity that binds tool and action in a smooth flow;
- integrating the use of the tools into a web of activity, involving smooth effective action, coordination with others, focus on the priority goals, etc.;
- turning the individual and aggregate experiences of the exercise into learning that lasts.

The point of the exercise, for each student, was not just to master the individual tools but to participate in the construction of a coordinated web of activity that could result in a successful rescue, minimizing danger to participants, and leaving traces (in some kinds of memory) that meant doing something like this again would not feel entirely new (Goodyear and Carvalho 2013, pp. 58–59).

While this example involved an *extensive* activity spread across a range of hills and bound together, rather loosely, with digital and analogue communication devices, other instances are more tightly place-focused. Here we are thinking of the integration of personal devices into the experience of visiting a museum or art gallery, for example. This is a rapidly evolving area of practice, with significant new technological capabilities appearing every few months. Among developments that we have begun to analyze are mobile devices such as The O – a mobile technology developed for the Museum of Old and New Art (MONA) in Hobart, Australia. On entering MONA, visitors are given a device with which they will interact during their visit. As visitors wander around the space, the device 'senses' the section of the museum in which the visitor is located, displaying pictures of the art pieces in that area. Visitors can then select which art pieces they want to learn more about, and they do that in interaction with The O – by reading a virtual label, hearing an interview with the artist or the insights of a curator about that work. There are no labels or any other written messages on the walls. This allows visitors to experience the space and the art in it in a very singular manner: both the architectural space and the positioning of the art pieces become more salient. Visitors are also invited to leave messages on The O for future users of that device, reporting their impressions of their visits. The adoption of mobile devices such as The O within museum spaces shows how new technologies are beginning to alter the traditional layouts of museum exhibitions, giving curators opportunities to repurpose the space in new directions. Such devices also allow the direct collection of evaluation data related to visitors' activities, likes and dislikes. And they can engage visitors in post-visit experiences, as visitors may choose to upload and download their visit through the web, or respond to questions or impressions left by the previous users of the device. Essentially, the devices reshape the museum spaces and the social experiences of those in that space.

While these examples can be understood as an incursion of the digital into the non-digital world, the reverse is true in shared virtual worlds such as Second Life. Although Second Life allows behaviors and constructed forms that are impossible in the physical world, it nevertheless gains much of its legibility from a loose emulation of the physical world. Indeed, some of the design problems and possibilities arising in shared virtual worlds stimulated some early thinking about relations with the architecture of learning places more generally (see e.g. Dillenbourg *et al.* 1999, Maher *et al.* 1999, Goodyear 1999). More recent analyses of learning collaboratively in shared virtual worlds can be found in Bayne (2008) and Peachey *et al.* (2010).

The other major line of development in the last decade has been the growth of so-called Web 2.0 capabilities, tools and practices (Dohn 2009, Mason and Rennie 2008). A core part of this development has been a shift from consumption to production, remixing and sharing. Web 2.0 developments have brought networked learning from a situation in which it depended on specialist technology for a platform to one in which learning networks can span multiple free platforms, assimilating new tools and ways of working almost without pause (Ravenscroft *et al.* 2012).

An additional corollary of the growth of Web 2.0 tools and practices has been, in our terms, to see a growth in the relative importance of the *set*. A good deal of the productive activity associated with Web 2.0 is concerned with the creation and furnishing of media-rich online places. As well as production of new material, the *curation* of content has become a salient activity, as people create and manage galleries of experience and know-how.

Massive Open Online Courses (MOOCs)

While it is relatively early to get a reliable perspective on the MOOC phenomenon, we can try to use some of the characteristics of MOOCs to locate them in relation to networked learning. The term MOOC was invented by Dave Cornier in 2008 to describe a course being run that year by George Siemens and Stephen Downes on 'Connectivism and Connected Knowledge'. The course had over 2,000 online students who participated without fee or credit. The course was both about connectivism and informed by connectivist pedagogy (Mackness *et al.* 2010).

MOOCs caught much wider educational and business attention in 2012, with the running of a number of courses by elite universities in the US and elsewhere, with much of the focus being on 100,000+ student courses run by staff associated with Stanford University (2011) and MIT (2012). The fact that these courses were not using connectivist pedagogies led Siemens (2012) to distinguish them from his 'cMOOCs' by labeling then 'xMOOCs'.

> Our MOOC model emphasizes creation, creativity, autonomy, and social networked learning. The Coursera [xMOOC] model emphasizes a more traditional learning approach through video presentations and short quizzes and testing. Put another way, cMOOCs focus on knowledge creation and generation whereas xMOOCs focus on knowledge duplication.
>
> *(Siemens 2012)*

Analyzing the design of MOOCs therefore needs to be done differently for xMOOCs and cMOOCs. The cMOOC's design places it somewhat more comfortably in the domain of networked learning than is the case with xMOOCs. cMOOCs entail more complex network structures than is typically the case with xMOOCs. A core feature of the xMOOC is a set of video recordings of short lectures (or segments of lectures) interspersed with online quizzes and supplemented with optional discussion forums. While some xMOOCs involve peer evaluation, the predominant design image is of a unidirectional *star network*, with the main connections radiating outwards from the lecturer to the students, very little opportunity for students to engage in discussions with the lecturer, and rather sparse connections between students. For example, MIT's own analysis of its first MOOC showed that only 3% of the 155,000 students who enrolled in the course participated in the discussion forums (Breslow *et al.* 2013, p. 22). There is some evidence to suggest that some students self-organize study and support groups using other platforms, such as Facebook – but this is not typically designed into the xMOOC. cMOOCs, in contrast, range over a broad array of platforms, with additional tools being used to offer some selective synthesis and to reflect a sense of community. Collaborative knowledge creation is at the heart of the epistemic design, and rich network structures emerge as participants engage with each other in fluid configurations, as tasks, time and interests suggest. While some researchers are questioning the coherence of connectivism as a theory of learning or a source for pedagogy (e.g. Clarà and Barberà 2013), cMOOCs nevertheless represent an influential paradigm for networked learning. Participants' experiences of the first cMOOC were understandably varied, with some reporting a gap between intentions and outcome. Autonomy and connectedness are not guaranteed, and have to be worked for. As Mackness *et al.* observe:

> The Connectivism and Connective Knowledge course was a courageous, ambitious and ground-breaking attempt to enable participants to experience the principles of connectivism – autonomy, diversity, openness and connectedness in practice. Our findings suggest that these might all be achievable in a complex learning network, but in a course (as opposed to a network), particularly a massive open online course, they can be compromised.
>
> *(Mackness* et al. *2010, p. 272)*

The design of, and response to, MOOCs in general and xMOOCs in particular raise a number of interesting questions about the future of networked learning. xMOOCs have gained some notoriety for their high rates of non-completion, though this is not a simple indicator of design quality or student experience (Breslow *et al.* 2013, pp. 21–22). It is rare for completion rates to exceed 10%. Given that the time cost of enrolling in an xMOOC is close to zero, it is reasonable to wonder whether the notion of completion is helpful, or indeed whether 'course' is a reasonable description of how most xMOOC users experience the resources made available to them. (In the MIT example reported by Breslow *et al.*, only one-sixth of the students tried even the first problem set.) Yet for some leading figures in the xMOOC movement, the attributes associated with being a course are what distinguish an xMOOC from a collection of open online educational resources. It is too early to say, with any confidence, but on current readings, the xMOOC design lacks logic unless it is a course, yet the vast majority of the users of an xMOOC do not treat it as a course. The inventors of the cMOOC want to move away from the idea of a linear course, yet the absence of some of the kinds of scaffolding provided in strong course designs turns out, in practice, to undermine the experiences of autonomy, diversity, openness and connection that are so close to the hearts of the cMOOC's creators (Mackness *et al.* 2010).

Concluding Points

This chapter has provided a selective overview of the evolution of ideas about networks and networked forms of human interaction, with particular attention to those that are supportive of information exchange, the generation of new insights, innovation and learning. Today's digitally mediated networked learning may seem a far cry from the stately pace of interactions involved in the Atlantic wine trade, or in the transport of rabbinical teachings in the Mediterranean. Nevertheless, there are theoretical concepts and analytic tools that can be applied to both historic and contemporary networks. There are some deep connections between Twitter streams and clay tablets, and the networks that they hold together.

References

Ackerman, M. S. and Malone, T. W., 1990. Answer Garden: a tool for growing organizational memory. *ACM Conference on Office Information Systems.* Cambridge, MA, ACM.

Barabási, A.-L., 2002. *Linked: the new science of networks.* Cambridge, MA: Perseus Publishing.

Bayne, S., 2008. Uncanny spaces for higher education: teaching and learning in virtual worlds. *Research in Learning Technology,* 16(3), 197–205.

Boder, A., 1992. The process of knowledge reification in human-human interaction. *Journal of Computer Assisted Learning,* 8(3), 177–185.

Bonamy, J. and Haugluslaine–Charlier, B., 1995. Supporting professional learning: beyond technological support. *Journal of Computer Assisted Learning,* 11(4), 196–202.

Borgatti, S. and Foster, P., 2003. The network paradigm in organizational research: a review and typology. *Journal of Management,* 29(6), 991–1013.

Breslow, L., Pritchard, D. E., DeBoer, J., Stump, G. S., Ho, A. D. and Seaton, D., 2013. Studying learning in the worldwide classroom: research into edX's first MOOC. *Research & Practice in Assessment,* 8, 13–25.

Burt, R. S., 2004. Structural holes and good ideas. *American Journal of Sociology,* 110, 349–399.

Castells, M., 1996. *The rise of the network society.* Oxford: Blackwell.

Castells, M., 2001. *The Internet galaxy: reflections on the internet, business, and society.* Oxford: Oxford University Press.

Clarà, M. and Barberà, E., 2013. Learning online: massive open online courses (MOOCs), connectivism, and cultural psychology. *Distance Education,* 34(1), 129–136.

Collar, A., 2013. Re-thinking Jewish ethnicity through social network analysis. In: C. Knappett, ed. *Network analysis in archaeology: new approaches to regional interaction.* Oxford: Oxford University Press.

Coward, F., 2010. Small worlds, material culture and ancient near eastern social networks. In: R. Dunbar, C. Gamble and J. Gowlett, eds. *Social brain, distributed mind.* Oxford: Oxford University Press.

Cross, R., Borgatti, S. P. and Parker, A., 2001. Beyond answers: dimensions of the advice network. *Social Networks,* 23(1), 215–235.

Dillenbourg, P., Mendelsohn, P. and Jermann, P., 1999. Why spatial metaphors are relevant to virtual campuses. *Learning and instruction in multiple contexts and settings. Bulletins of the Faculty of Education, University of Geneva* [online]. Available from: http://tecfa.unige.ch/tecfa/publicat/dil-papers-2/Dil.7.1.15.pdf [Accessed 30 July 2013].

di Maggio, P. and Garip, F., 2012. Network effects and social inequality. *Annual Review of Sociology*, 38(1), 93–118.

Dohn, N. B., 2009. Web 2.0: inherent tensions and evident challenges for education. *International Journal of Computer-Supported Collaborative Learning*, 4(3), 343–363.

Duguid, P., 2005. Introduction: the changing organization of industry. *Business History Review*, 79(3), 453–466.

Feenberg, A., 1986. Network design: an operating manual for computer conferencing. *IEEE Transactions on Professional Communications*, PC-29(1), 2–7.

Fjuk, A. and Dirckinck-Holmfeld, L., 1997. Articulation of actions in distributed collaborative learning. *Scandinavian Journal of Information Systems*, 9(2), 3–24.

Gerlach, M., 1992. *Alliance capitalism: the social organization of Japanese business.* Berkeley: University of California Press.

Goodyear, P., 1995. Situated action and distributed knowledge: a jitol perspective on electronic performance support systems. *Educational and Training Technology International*, 32(1), 45–55.

Goodyear, P., 1999. Educational technology, virtual learning environments and architectural practice. In: D. Ely, L. Odenthal and T. Plomp, eds. *Educational science and technology: perspectives for the future.* Enschede: Twente University Press.

Goodyear, P. and Carvalho, L., 2013. The analysis of complex learning environments. In: H. Beetham and R. Sharpe, eds. *Rethinking pedagogy for a digital age: designing and delivering e-learning.* 2nd ed. (pp. 49–63). New York: Routledge.

Goodyear, P. and Steeples, C., 1992. IT-based open learning: tasks and tools. *Journal of Computer Assisted Learning*, 8(3), 163–176.

Goodyear, P. and Steeples, C., 1993. Computer-mediated communication in the professional development of workers in the advanced learning technologies industry. In: J. Eccleston, B. Barta and R. Hambusch, eds. *The computer-mediated education of information technology professionals and advanced end-users.* Amsterdam: Elsevier.

Goodyear, P. and Steeples, C., 1998. Creating shareable representations of practice. *Association for Learning Technology Journal*, 6(3), 16–23.

Goodyear, P. and Steeples, C., 1999. Asynchronous multimedia conferencing in continuing professional development: issues in the representation of practice through user-created videoclips. *Distance Education*, 20(1), 31–48.

Granovetter, M., 1973. The strength of weak ties. *American Journal of Sociology*, 78(6), 1360–1380.

Granovetter, M., 1983. The strength of weak ties: a network theory revisited. *Sociological Theory*, 1, 201–233.

Hancock, D., 2005. The trouble with networks: managing the Scots' early-modern Madeira trade. *Business History Review*, 79, 467–491.

Harasim, L., 1993. Collaborating in cyberspace: using computer conferences as a group learning environment. *Interactive Learning Environments*, 3(2), 119–130.

Harasim, L., Hiltz, S., Teles, L. and Turoff, M., 1997. *Learning networks: a field guide to learning and teaching online.* Cambridge, MA: MIT Press.

Hardy, V., Hodgson, V. and McConnell, D., 1994. Computer conferencing: a new vehicle for investigating issues in gender and learning. *Higher Education*, 28(3), 403–418.

Haughey, M. and Anderson, T., eds., 1998. *Networked learning: the pedagogy of the internet.* Montreal: Chenelière/McGraw-Hill.

Hiltz, S. R., 1977. Computer conferencing: assessing the social impact of a new communications medium. *Technological Forecasting and Social Change*, 10(3), 225–238.

Hiltz, S. R., 1978. The computer conference. *Journal of Communication*, 28(3), 157–163.

Hiltz, S. R., 1986. The 'virtual classroom': using computer-mediated communication for university teaching. *Journal of Communication*, 36(2), 95–104.

Hiltz, S., 1994. *The virtual classroom: learning without limits via computer networks.* Norwood, NJ: Ablex.

Hiltz, S. R. and Turoff, M., 1978. *The network nation: human communication by computer.* Reading, MA: Addison Wesley.

Hodgson, V., Lewis, R. and McConnell, D., 1989. *Information technology-based open learning: a study report.* Lancaster: Lancaster University, ESRC InTER Programme.

Hodgson, V. and McConnell, D., 1992. IT-based open learning: a case study in management learning. *Journal of Computer Assisted Learning*, 8(3), 136–150.

Hunter, B., 1992. Linking for learning: computer-and-communications network support for nationwide innovation in education. *Journal of Science Education and Technology*, 1(1), 23–34.

Irwin, G., 1978. Pots and entrepots: a study of settlement, trade and the development of economic specialisation in Papuan prehistory. *World Archaeology*, 9(3), 299–319.

Kaye, A., ed., 1992. *Collaborative learning through computer conferencing: the Najaden papers.* Berlin: Springer.

Knappett, C., ed., 2013. *Network analysis in archaeology: new approaches to regional interaction.* Oxford: Oxford University Press.

Knappett, C., Evans, T. and Rivers, R., 2008. Modelling maritime interaction in the Aegean bronze age. *Antiquity*, 82, 1009–1024.

Lave, J. and Wenger, E., 1991. *Situated learning: legitimate peripheral participation.* Cambridge: Cambridge University Press.

Levin, J., Kim, H. and Riel, M., 1990. Analysing instructional interactions on electronic message networks. In: L. Harasim, ed. *Online education: perspectives on a new environment.* New York: Praeger.

Levin, J., Riel, M., Miyake, N. and Cohen, M., 1987. Education on the electronic frontier: teleapprentices in globally distributed educational contexts. *Contemporary Educational Psychology*, 12(3), 254–260.

Lewis, R., 1997. Sharing professional knowledge: organizational memory. *International Journal of Continuing Engineering Education and Life-Long Learning*, 7(2), 95–107.

Lewis, R., Goodyear, P. and Boder, A., 1992. *Just in time open learning.* Archamps, France: Neuropelab.

Lincoln, J., Gerlach, M. and Ahmadjian, C., 1996. *Keiretsu* networks and corporate performance in Japan. *American Sociological Review*, 61(1), 67–88.

Mackness, J., Mak, S. and Williams, R., 2010. The ideals and reality of participating in a MOOC. *Networked Learning Conference.* University of Lancaster.

Maher, M. L., Skow, B. and Cicognani, A., 1999. Designing the virtual campus. *Design Studies*, 20(4), 319–342.

Manenti, Y., 1995. Capitalising on knowledge: organisational issues and constraints. *Journal of Computer Assisted Learning*, 11(4), 225–230.

Mason, R., 1991. *Moderating educational computer conferencing. DEOSNEWS, 1* [online]. Available from: www.ed.psu.edu/acsde/deos/deosnews/deosnews1_19.asp [Accessed 22 April 2013].

Mason, R. and Kaye, A., eds., 1989. *Mindweave: communication, computers and distance education.* Oxford: Pergamon.

Mason, R. and Rennie, F., 2008. *E-learning and social networking handbook*. London: Routledge.

McConnell, D., 1994. *Implementing computer supported cooperative learning*. London: Kogan Page.

McConnell, D., 2006. *E-learning groups and communities*. Maidenhead: Open University Press.

McPherson, M., Smith-Lovin, L. and Cook, J. M., 2001. Birds of a feather: homophily in social networks. *Annual Review of Sociology*, 27, 415–444.

Mews, C. and Crossley, J., eds., 2011. *Communities of learning: networks and the shaping of intellectual identity in Europe, 1100–1500*. Turnhout, Belgium: Brepols Publishers.

Mokyr, J., 2009. *The enlightened economy: an economic history of Britain 1700–1850*. New Haven, CT: Yale University Press.

Nohria, N., 1992. Is a network perspective a useful way to study organisations? In: N. Nohria and R. Eccles, eds. *Networks and organisations: structure, form and action*. Boston, MA: Harvard Business Review Press.

Peachey, A., Gillen, J., Livingstone, D. and Smith-Robbins, S., eds., 2010. *Researching learning in virtual worlds*. London: Springer.

Peter, S. and Farrell, L., 2013. From learning in coffee houses to learning with open educational resources. *E-Learning and Digital Media*, 10(2), 174–189.

Podolny, J. and Page, K., 1998. Network forms of organization. *Annual Review of Sociology*, 24, 57–76.

Powell, W., 1990. Neither market nor hierarchy: network forms of organization. In: B. Staw and L. Cummings, eds. *Research in organizational behavior*. Greenwich, CT: JAI.

Quinn, C., Mehan, H., Levin, J. and Black, S., 1983. Real education in non-real time: the use of electronic messaging systems for instruction. *Instructional Science*, 11(4), 313–327.

Ravenscroft, A., Schmidt, A., Cook, J. and Bradley, C., 2012. Designing social media for informal learning and knowledge maturing in the digital workplace. *Journal of Computer Assisted Learning*, 28(3), 235–249.

Rekkedal, T. and Paulsen, M. F., 1989. Computer conferencing in distance education: status and trends. *European Journal of Education*, 24(1), 61–72.

Riel, M. M., 1990. Co-operative learning across classrooms in electronic learning circles. *Instructional Science*, 19(6), 445–466.

Riel, M. M. and Levin, J. A., 1990. Building electronic communities: success and failure in computer networking. *Instructional Science*, 19(2), 145–169.

Salancik, G., 1995. Wanted: a good network theory of organization. *Administrative Science Quarterly*, 40(2), 345–349.

Scardamalia, M. and Bereiter, C., 1992. An architecture for collaborative knowledge building. In: E. De Corte, M. Linn, H. Mandl and L. Verschaffel, eds. *Computer-based learning environments and problem solving*. Berlin: Springer.

Scardamalia, M. and Bereiter, C., 2006. Knowledge building: theory, pedagogy and technology. In: K. Sawyer, ed. *Cambridge handbook of the learning sciences*. Cambridge: Cambridge University Press.

Sgouropoulou, C., Koutoumanos, T., Goodyear, P. and Skordalakis, E., 2000. Acquiring working knowledge through asynchronous multimedia conferencing. *Educational Technology & Society*, 3. Available from: www.ifets.info/journals/3_3/a06.html [Accessed 1 July 2013].

Siemens, G., 2012. *MOOCs are really a platform* [online]. Available from: www.elearnspace. org/blog/2012/07/25/moocs-are-really-a-platform/ [Accessed 1 July 2013].

Sindbœk, S., 2013. Broken links and black boxes: material affiliations and contextual network synthesis in the Viking world. In: C. Knappett, ed. *Network analysis in archaeology: new approaches to regional interaction.* Oxford: Oxford University Press.

Steeples, C. and Goodyear, P., 1999. Enabling professional learning in distributed communities of practice: descriptors for multimedia objects. *Journal of Network and Computer Applications*, 22(2), 133–145.

Steeples, C. and Jones, C., eds., 2002. *Networked learning: perspectives and issues.* London: Springer.

Sterelny, K., 2012. *The evolved apprentice: how evolution made humans unique.* Cambridge, MA: MIT Press.

Turoff, M., 2002. Past and future emergency response information systems. *Communications of the ACM*, 45(2), 29–32.

Turoff, M., Johnson-Lenz, T. and Johnson-Lenz, P., 1977. *How to use EIES: electronic information exchange system.* Research Report 7. Newark: New Jersey Institute of Technology.

Watts, D. J., 2004. The 'new' science of networks. *Annual Review of Sociology*, 30, 243–270.

White, H. D., 1977. A directory of public services: utopian notes. *Information Processing & Management*, 13(3), 177–187.

3
FRAMING THE ANALYSIS OF LEARNING NETWORK ARCHITECTURES

Peter Goodyear and Lucila Carvalho

Introduction

The primary purpose of this chapter is to explain the framework that we have been developing to analyze learning networks and other complex examples of learning *in situ* (Goodyear and Carvalho 2013). We outline the evolution of the framework, and provide a rationale for its composition and use. Part of our argument is that more sophisticated methods of analysis are needed to represent the complexity of modern learning situations. We use some ideas from architecture, human–computer interaction, science and technology studies and a number of associated fields to analyze learning networks – including ideas about the relations between built forms (space, place, tools, artifacts, texts) and human activity.

As we mentioned in Chapter 1, a strong part of our motivation is to be able to analyze and depict learning activities in such a way that the resulting insights can be used for design. This commitment to generating *knowledge for design* has some consequences. Notably, it means that it must be possible to draw a credible connection between the results of analysis and the knowledge needed for real-world designers and design processes: there is a practical imperative at work here that helps pin down what counts as useful knowledge. The position we have adopted, with respect to design for learning, has been developed over the past two decades – studying the relations between design knowledge, design practices, the outcomes of design and the activities of learners (see e.g. Goodyear 1993, 1997, 2000, 2005, Goodyear and Retalis 2010, Kali *et al.* 2011, Goodyear and Markauskaite 2012, Goodyear and Carvalho, 2013). This work has been informed by ideas and practices from other fields of design, including product design, service design, architecture and urban planning. In particular, the work of Christopher Alexander on the generation of form, patterns and pattern languages, and the relations between built forms and human activity and experience has been a powerful inspiration (see especially Alexander 1964, 1979, 2006, Alexander *et al.* 1975, 1977, 1987). This body of work underlines the importance of recognizing (a) the subtlety of the links between what can be designed and what people then do and feel, as well as (b) the value of design and development methods that work by incremental improvement. So a key reason for our engagement in analysis is to help people who are involved in the ongoing improvement of existing learning networks, as well as those who are helping new ones come into being.

We start with a discussion of some of the more established methods that have been used for researching networked learning. We then draw some connections between the special challenges of researching learning networks and some of the ways of conceptualizing technology, and broader sociotechnical systems that have emerged in adjacent research fields. After that we present in more detail the main dimensions of the architectural framework, looking at the epistemic, the set, the social and their integration.

Approaches to Research in Networked Learning

In Chapter 2, we outlined some of the recent history of digitally mediated networked learning, identifying a number of core developments from the early 1970s onwards. While a wide variety of ways of researching networked learning have been tried out in the last 40 years or so, many studies combine one or more of the following: (a) user evaluation – testing the acceptability of the tools and educational methods being used, (b) interviews or focus groups eliciting participants' experiences of networked learning, (c) analysis of the transcripts of online discussions. Hodgson and Watland (2004) and Bliuc *et al.* (2007) provide useful summaries of the range of methods used and their application can be seen in a number of edited collections of networked learning research papers (e.g. Dirckinck-Holmfeld *et al.* 2009, 2011). To help locate our approach to analysis, we start with the tradition of analyzing transcripts of online discussions.

Online text-based discussions, of the kind that were central to much networked learning practice in the 1980s and 1990s, are self-documenting: the online texts that participants create lend themselves to analysis for signs of the processes and products of learning. Some empirical research and evaluation studies have limited themselves to producing quantitative summaries of online activity, counting the numbers of messages posted, by whom, and when. Such data can help paint a picture of the balance and rhythm of discussions, identifying people who may be left out of the discussion, or who may be dominating it, and looking at when discussion becomes more intense and when it flags. However, analysts can also dig deeper, looking for evidence of the development of ideas, for signs of metacognitive reflection and self-regulation, for collaborative knowledge-building, argumentation and so on. There are virtually endless possibilities, constrained only by the researcher's time and the ability of theory to support useful, reliable inferences.

TABLE 3.1 France Henri's analytic framework

Dimension	Definition
Participative	The numbers of messages (or statements) created by each person or group – a quantitative index of the scale of participation by each individual, or by subgroups of participants (e.g. students vs. teachers), or by the whole group
Social	Statements that are not related to the defined subject matter; statements aimed at strengthening relationships
Interactive	Chains of connected messages – indicating people building on and/ or arguing with other messages
Cognitive	Statements revealing knowledge and skills related to the defined subject matter
Metacognitive	Statements revealing awareness, self-control, self-regulation of learning

Source: adapted from Henri (1992, pp. 124–132)

Twenty years ago, France Henri produced a landmark methodological chapter that bridged between counting messages and analyzing content (Henri 1992). She took measures of participation in online discussion as a starting point and to them added four further dimensions of variation – the social, the interactive, the cognitive and the metacognitive. Table 3.1 summarizes her analytic framework. The first dimension is operationalized by a simple counting of messages. The other four dimensions require the use of content analysis.

Henri's contribution provided a foundation for subsequent researchers to develop and strengthen the research methods available. For example, Howell-Richardson and Mellar (1996) used speech act theory to provide a more theoretically defensible approach to segmenting online messages and to identifying connections between messages. Hara *et al.* (2000) used a more elaborate version of Henri's content analysis, coupled with graphical representations of whose messages built on whose, to show how the allocation of specific discussion roles to students could improve the quality of discussion. Schrire (2004, 2006), studying discussions for collaborative online knowledge-building, identified five main patterns for interaction:

> (a) *instructor-centered*, with responses initiated and triggered by an instructor message and responding mainly to the instructor message; (b) *synergistic*, including responses to the initiating message as well as follow-ups by conference participants from one message to another; (c) *developing synergism*, with mixed characteristics of instructor-centered and synergistic interaction; (d) *scattered*, involving small separate message clusters around loosely related sub-topics; (e) *student-centered*, with responses initiated by a student message.
>
> *(Schrire 2004, p. 486)*

Schrire's synergistic pattern, characterized by higher levels of student–student collaboration, proved to be associated with signs of high-order critical thinking.

This body of research, analyzing transcripts of online discussion – for content, discourse moves and interaction patterns – has now established a solid position in research on networked learning. Methodological reviews can be found in de Wever *et al.* (2006), Clarà and Mauri (2010) and Häkkinen (2013). There has also been some progress in automating or partially automating methods of analyzing online discussion transcripts (see e.g. Mu *et al.* 2012) and growing connections to other areas in the broader field of Learning Analytics (Suthers *et al.* 2013). A related development has been to triangulate multiple data sources, such that what is seen in the discussion transcripts can be understood from additional perspectives, such as through Social Network Analysis and debriefing interviews (e.g. de Laat *et al.* 2006, 2007a, 2007b).

Expanding the Framework for Research on Learning Networks

The research approaches sketched above took shape in a period where the dominant form of networked learning was through online text-based discussions – normally taking place as part of a formal educational program of some kind, stimulated, monitored and rewarded by a teacher, using a discussion forum provided as part of an educational organization's digital infrastructure.

A significant shift in research approaches can be seen from the late 1990s onwards, prompted in part by the growth in size and usage of the World Wide Web (WWW) and given extra momentum by a rapid expansion in the number and usage of tools for web-based content creation: so-called 'Web 2.0'. This opening out of networked learning was not *caused* by technological innovation alone – practices and expectations shift in a complicated interaction with technical advances. And within this mix, it begins to be seen that a much more expansive framework is needed to encompass conceptually the complex assemblage of tools, activities and social arrangements involved in a learning network.

How to develop such a conception? Educational technology is a field of research and practice in which theory plays an extraordinarily low-key and unbalanced role. It does make use of *theories of learning* – largely drawn from psychology, sociology and other disciplines in the human sciences. But it is virtually silent about the nature of technology (as distinct from describing the characteristics of particular devices) and it seems averse to actually *making* theory (Jones and Czerniewicz 2011, Oliver 2013). As a consequence, we need to spend some time trying to situate our approach to the analysis of learning networks in a broader framing – we cannot simply 'place' what we are doing in a familiar landscape, though readers familiar with some of our earlier work on ecological and architectural conceptions of learning environments will recognize parts of the argument (Ford *et al.* 1996, Goodyear 2000, 2005, Ellis and Goodyear 2010).

TABLE 3.2 Increasingly complex units of analysis

Unit of analysis	Description
Singular artifact	An artifact that is not easily reducible to constituent artifacts
Technical system	A system of artifacts: for example, understanding a bicycle as a system composed of wheels, seat, handlebars etc., or understanding a wheel as composed of rim, hub, spokes, tire etc.
Technological system	A combination of technical, social, organizational, political and economic elements
Sociotechnical ensemble	Understood as a technological system but without an *a priori* commitment to systems theory; also the term 'sociotechnical' gives parity to the social and the technical – it does not insist on one being prior to the other
Technological culture	Expands the unit of analysis to acknowledge that we live in a technological culture: 'technologies do not merely assist in everyday lives, they are also powerful forces acting to reshape human activities and their meanings'

Source: adapted from Bijker (2010, pp. 66–67)

We can trace the move to this more expansive vision of how to analyze learning networks by echoing some developments in science and technology studies (STS). Table 3.2 is informed by Wiebe Bijker's account of shifts in the unit of analysis in research on the social construction of technology (Bijker 2010).

Within the field of research on learning technologies, it can be argued that attention has most often been drawn to singular artifacts and technical systems, which are the simplest two of the units of analysis in Bijker's table. Some work in adjacent areas that has been very influential in shaping approaches to explanation in learning technology also has this (unconscious?) preoccupation with simpler units of analysis. A good example would be Don Norman's writings about the design of everyday objects and the associated concept of 'affordance' (Norman 1990, 1999, 2005). Norman (1990) sees affordances as referring to both the perceived and actual properties *of an object*; his use of the idea focuses on fundamental properties that regulate the ways an object can potentially be used. When we start to think about the range of things implicated in learning networks, it soon becomes clear that concepts and methods fit for analyzing singular artifacts and technical systems are not wholly adequate – so the idea of a learning network as a technological system or sociotechnical ensemble becomes more compelling (cf. Creanor and Walker 2012). As will become apparent at later points in the book, our language choices include 'systems', 'ensembles', 'assemblages' and 'networks'. We use 'ensembles' and 'assemblages' as synonyms, reflecting their use in the literature on which we are drawing. Like Bijker and others, we see 'systems' as having some distinctive theoretical connotations, evoking ideas about feedback and cybernetics from dynamic systems theory. Only when we specifically want to draw out such ideas do we deliberately talk about systems. The same applies with 'networks' – when we speak of networks, we want to foreground what is special about networks. So, some of the analysis in Part II of the book focuses on artifacts, some on sociotechnical assemblages, including those that lend themselves to being viewed as a network. (Bijker's 'technological culture' unit of analysis provides context for our analysis, but is not generally a focus of our work.)

In helping people position our approach, we find it useful to complement Bijker's description of units of analysis with Wanda Orlikowski's treatment of the ways in which technology is framed in the organizational and management studies literature. To make space for her own theoretical perspective on technology, Orlikowski (2010) sketches three pre-existing tendencies in the literature. The first she calls 'absent presence', referring to the way that technology is simultaneously recognized as being everywhere in life, yet nowhere in the (management) literature.

> A common explanation for this absence of materiality in the management literature is that technology is either invisible or irrelevant to researchers trained in social, political, economic, and institutional analyses of organizations. For these researchers, ontological priority is given to human actors and social structures, and as a result, technological artifacts (and materiality more generally) tend to disappear into the background and become taken for granted. With such a perspective, it is not surprising that scholars do not work on questions about artifacts, and research done on this view thus underestimates the role and significance of technological artifacts.
>
> *(Orlikowski 2010, p. 128)*

The same case could be made about educational research, within the mainstreams of which serious studies of the role of technology have been relatively rare.

The second position Orlikowski identifies in the literature is one that we can easily recognize in research on learning technologies. She sees it as a conception in which technology is treated as an *exogenous force* – as an autonomous driver of change. Researchers working within this framing tend to look for characteristics of specific technologies that can be held to cause change – shaping organizational processes, or, in the educational case, influencing the efficiency or effectiveness of technology-assisted learning.

> Most scholars adopting an exogenous force perspective ... [seek] to theorize the relationship between technology and organization sufficiently generally, so that predictions about technology effects may be made across types of organizations and technologies. ... While acknowledgement of various contingencies has served to check excessive claims of technological determinism, a strong commitment to the powerful effects of technology

> on people and organizations has continued to inform this research tradition
> ... scholars proceeded to conceptualize technology as a material deter-
> minant of organizational characteristics, while paying limited attention to
> either specific technological details or the role of human agency in shaping
> technology.
>
> *(ibid, p. 129)*

Looking across the decades of research in educational technology, one can see
an almost continuous stream of studies, each attempting to isolate characteristics
of a new device, resource or tool, in order to make claims about its educational
benefits.

Orlikowski labels the third perspective in the organizational literature
'emergent process'. In contrast to the technological determinism associated with
the 'exogenous force' perspective, this view gives primacy to human agency in
technological change.

> Central to an emergent process perspective is the notion that understand-
> ings of technology are neither fixed nor universal, but that they emerge
> from situated and reciprocal processes of interpreting and interacting with
> particular artifacts over time. Thus, an emergent process perspective focuses
> primarily on the embedded and dynamic meanings, interests, and activities
> that are seen to produce an ensemble of technological relations. [Studies
> focus] ... on the broader ecology of people, infrastructures, resources, policy
> decisions, and social relations that affected the development, adoption,
> appropriation, and adaptation of information technology.
>
> *(ibid, p. 131)*

Whether in organizational studies or educational technology, the 'exogenous
force' perspective ignores or downplays the role of history, social context and
human agency in shaping technology production, use and change. It situates
digital tools and artifacts as 'rationality-enhancing devices'. It favors research
approaches that seek generalizable laws to describe effects of technology on
people and their activities. In contrast, the 'emergent process' perspective
privileges situated human agency. It ignores or downplays the physical characteristics and capabilities of material/technological artifacts. It favors research on
micro-interactions and is poorly equipped to relate characteristics of particular
technologies to broader organizational or social effects.

Orlikowski's preferred approach – a fourth, and as yet rather lightly populated
approach – is to conceptualize the relations between technology and the human/
social as 'constitutively entangled'. Where the 'exogenous force' approach gives
ontological priority to the technological, and the 'emergent process' approach
gives ontological priority to the social, both approaches position technology
and the human/social as fundamentally separate and different. Drawing on Barad

(2003) and Suchman (2007), Orlikowski argues for a relational understanding of the technological and the human/social – neither being prior or privileged and each being entangled in the evolution of the other (Orlikowski 2010, pp. 134–136). There is some room for maneuver in interpreting this notion of the social and technical as being constitutively entangled. In thinking about the analysis of learning networks, we find it useful to adopt Faulkner and Runde's (2011) distinction between harder and softer versions of the idea. The hard version insists that the social and technical cannot be separated – there is only the sociotechnical. A softer version suggests that, for some analytic purposes, it is possible to speak of a social that is not material (e.g. laws or conceptual artifacts) and a material that is not social (e.g. a mineral deposit, fossil or tree).

From a design perspective, being able to tease apart the material and the social is very useful. We do not want to enter here into a deeper discussion about the agency of things (see e.g. Barad 2003, Bennett 2010, Fenwick *et al.* 2011, Ingold 2013). We *do* want to be able to say that when designers are imagining the consequences of their design choices, they need flexibility in thinking about the likely relations between the elements implicated in their designs. In thinking about how elements are likely to influence each other, within a sociotechnical ensemble, such as a learning network, it can be useful to be able to allow for:

- the exercise of intentionality and interpretive capabilities by the human elements (and not by the material elements);
- reasonably predictable mechanistic relationships between material elements.

That said, such attributions can only be rules of thumb for designers. For example, the increasingly complex inferential work being done in software makes it dangerous to be dogmatic about the limits of agency, as does the way in which human activity can be carried along in a flow of sounds and images and the actions of others. As Tim Ingold has suggested, it may turn out that trying to understand *the lives of complex things* will provide sharper insights than we get if we focus on agency (e.g. Ingold 2013, pp. 95–97).

We will return to the question of how material things or technological objects can be said to influence human thought, feeling and action later in the chapter. But to prepare for that section, and to complete our gathering of ideas from the literature on sociomateriality, we need to say a few more words about the material and the technological. We start with Philip Faulkner and Jochen Runde's theory of technological objects. Faulkner and Runde (2011) conceive of technological objects as things (such as artifacts) 'to which members of some community of human beings have assigned one or more uses in pursuit of their practical interests' (p. 3). A few such objects are simple – having no internal structure – but most are structured: 'composed of a number of distinct parts that are organized or arranged in some way' (ibid.). Technological objects, on this view, overlap with Bijker's 'singular artifacts' and 'technical systems' – see Table 3.2. Faulkner and Runde

(2011, p. 3) then introduce a distinction that is vital for our purposes yet neglected in much of the literature on materiality. This is the distinction between material and non-material technological objects.

> Material technological objects are things such as bicycles, bridges and bathtubs that have a physical mode of being, namely that they necessarily possess spatial attributes such as location, shape, volume, mass and so on. Non-material technological objects are ones that do not have a physical mode of being and therefore lack attributes of this sort.

Faulkner and Runde then offer some examples of non-material technological objects, giving – as the most ubiquitous of all – computer files. This distinction between material and non-material technological objects is important because (a) much of the writing about the importance of materiality actually fails to deal with the differences between materials, and the effects of these different qualities of materials on what humans do (Ingold 2007); (b) very little of that smaller body of writing about the consequential properties of specific materials (e.g. Boivin 2008) has anything to say about non-material technological objects. In short, although the literature theorizing materiality offers incisive ideas about the role of tools and artifacts in human activity, it is not geared up to help so well with the digital. This is a shame, since the literatures that deal more squarely with digital artifacts tend to focus on language and meaning, semantics and semiotics. Many non-material technological objects present themselves as texts, still images, video and audio. They often appear on screens in complex arrays. They are somewhat susceptible to analysis using linguistic and semiotic ideas (see e.g. Kress and van Leeuwen 2001, 2006). But this leaves a deeply under-theorized space in between – such that we still struggle to find a conceptual framing that can be applied consistently across the material and the digital, and across tools, artifacts, infrastructures, images, sounds and texts. Developments such as augmented reality, haptic interfaces, wearable computers and other innovations that mix the material and the non-material are making it clear that, in educational technology and in sociotechnical research more generally, the conceptual foundations are under severe strain.

Analysis Informed by the Goals and Limits of Design for Learning

At the start of the chapter, we said that our approach to analyzing learning networks is guided by a wish to improve design. Crucially, this needs an ability to discriminate between things that can be designed and things that cannot. Much that is important and valued in networked learning emerges within an environment that is itself only partially the result of design.

That said, we do have a very expansive conception of what 'design for learning' can and should cover. It is not restricted to the design of instructional sequences, or textbooks, or learning materials. At the limit, anything that can be designed with the goal of supporting somebody's learning comes within our remit. This is because we are, in part, interested in mapping, modeling and theorizing 'design for learning' in a comprehensive way. We do not want to adopt narrow, conventional boundaries, spend all our efforts making sense of what is inside the design boundary, and then find that new technological developments, innovative working practices or an oversight on our part render our efforts useless (Goodyear and Dimitriadis 2013).

We think it is important to distinguish carefully between what can be designed and what cannot. Despite the popularity of the titles, we do not think it is right to speak of 'experience design' or 'learning design'. An experience is a relationship between a person and a phenomenon. We *may* be able to design the thing that is experienced, but we cannot design the experience itself. We can design tasks or tools or other things that help someone learn, but we cannot do the learning for them. Of course, 'experience design' and 'learning design' are shorthand terms. But they conceal an important distinction – between what can be designed and what emerges subsequently. These shorthand terms also distract attention from the important and tricky task of establishing what it is that connects (a) the 'thing(s)' that have been designed to (b) the learning or experience that eventuates. The possible connections between (a) and (b) lie at the heart of research and evaluation in educational technology, yet there is surprisingly little agreement about how those connections are best described. We also try to resist talking about *designing a learning network*. In our view, a learning network is a complex entity that takes on a life of its own. The work that designers do can lead to the creation of things that are of use to the network, and that greatly improve the way that it operates. But that is different from designing the network itself. Knowing the limits of design is important.

Ego-centered and Holistic Perspectives on Learning Networks

There are at least two perspectives from which learning networks can be analyzed. In sociological research on networks, one of these is known as 'ego-centered' – capturing how the network looks from the perspective of one of its members. The other perspective is more holistic, and looks at the entire network, as if from above. The first perspective is very good at reflecting the experiences of individual network members. The second is very good for capturing aspects of the network of a more structural or aggregate kind – indeed, it may even refer to aspects of the network that are invisible to most of its participants. (Data on the most and least active parts of a network, or hits on pages, might be of this kind.) In our view, neither the ego-centered nor the whole network perspective is entirely adequate on its own. Most of the chapters in Part II capture some key features of the networks concerned both from ego-centered, user experiential and from whole-of-network perspectives.

An Architectural Perspective on Learning Networks: Activity-centered Analysis and Design

We take an activity-centered approach to design and to the analysis of learning situations (Goodyear 2000). We focus on *what it is that people are actually doing*, and the tools and resources and social interactions that become bound up in their activity. For those people who are particularly interested in learning outcomes, activity should be seen as key. It mediates the relationships between tasks (what learners are asked to do) and learning outcomes, between tools and resources and learning outcomes, and between interpersonal relationships and learning outcomes.

In the context of orthodox forms of study, we find that people are usually engaged in some combination of activities like reading, writing, listening, speaking, reasoning, reflecting, procrastinating and searching for inspiration. They may be manipulating apparatus in a lab, outlining an essay with a word processor, chatting with colleagues in a coffee bar, reading a journal article on an iPad on the bus, brainstorming with a project team, listening to a lecture or walking to a seminar. Depending on the learning outcome(s) that are in focus, the most significant aspects of their activity may be cognitive, perceptual, physical or emotional, and are very frequently a combination of these. With learning networks, the main activity is conventionally thought to be reading and writing online texts, with some reflection, planning and reasoning in between. As many of our cases will show, networked learning activity tends to be much more diverse than convention supposes.

So activity is centrally important and it cannot be designed. What, then, shapes activity? It *is* possible to see a person's activity as closely determined by external forces. In some situations, orders are given and acted upon, or physical forces cause movement. There are situations in which we act as if matters can be explained by reference to tightly coupled cause and effect links of this sort. But there are very many other situations in which it rapidly becomes clear that people's activity is not so simply determined. Activity is often influenced by tools and other artifacts and material resources that come to hand, but usually in quite subtle ways.

To get a clearer sense of how analysts and designers might engage with the links between what can be designed and what people do, it helps to recognize the following attributes of activity. First, there is normally an *ongoing* quality to activity. It has its starts and stops, interruptions, and so on. But its normal state is in motion – people are usually already doing something, rather than idling at rest. Second, activity is often, but not always, oriented to some goal. Its detail may occasionally look random, or even counter-productive, and the improvisatory path towards a goal may not be as direct as rational models would predict.

But nevertheless, the general direction in which an activity unfolds usually bears some relation to a person's purposes. Third, activity is also shaped by the physical setting in which it unfolds. People typically open and walk through a gate rather than jump over the fence; they follow existing paths rather than make their own; they use tools that come to hand; they click Google search links that come up on the first page, and so on. It is often rational to conserve energy – physical, mental and emotional. Fourth, what people do is often influenced by the actions of other people around them, including their instructions, advice, encouragement and warnings. Fifth, social norms, rules and habits tend to have an effect, even if other people are not around to remind one of them.

In short, our architectural framework suggests that we focus on understanding how structures affect and influence activities, acknowledging that human activity tends to be goal-oriented (though not tightly goal-driven) and physically and socially situated (see Figure 3.1). Design can have an effect on activity indirectly, through the ways in which it creates *tasks* and through its shaping of the *physical* and *social* context in which activity unfolds. 'We never educate directly, but indirectly by means of the environment. Whether we permit chance environments to do the work, or whether we design environments for the purpose makes a great difference' (Dewey 1916/2004, p. 17).

We use the term *task* to mean a suggestion about something worth doing. It may be communicated explicitly and in detail, or it may be a barely perceptible invitation. Tasks often involve sub-tasks. Sometimes, our analytic work involves inferring tasks and task structures from observable activity. When the activity is imbued with learning and knowledge creation, we look for epistemic tasks – we

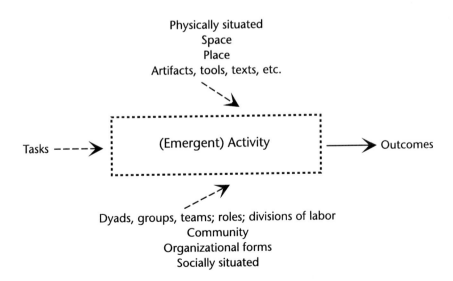

FIGURE 3.1 Tasks, tools and people

try to find characteristic ways of using knowledge and coming to know. It turns out that task structures often consist of nested explicit and tacit elements – not everything is, or needs to be, spelled out. We explore this in a little more depth in the section below: Task Structures and Epistemic Design.

The *physical setting* in which activity unfolds can also be heterogeneous and complex. For example, it may include a building, or a room in a building, or a room in a building on a campus. It may include physical artifacts within the room – including tools that come to hand, but also furniture (chairs, desks), hardware (computer, keyboard), books, notepads and pens. It may include non-material technological tools, texts and artifacts (a webpage, word processor, e-print, for example). We look at this below in: Structures of Place and Set Design.

The *social* situation is harder to pin down. From a design perspective, we can speak of things like roles, divisions of labor and organization forms – such as teams, working groups, learning communities etc. That is, it is possible for someone who is 'designing for learning' to suggest that students should tackle such-and-such a task in pairs, or that they should imagine themselves working as a member of a learning community. Design intention is reasonably easy to ascertain. What then eventuates is less clear-cut. As analysts, we can observe what people say, to whom they speak, with whom they work, what they say they feel about the others around them, and so on. But there are riskier inferences involved here than is the case when analyzing the effects of place and tools. We offer further thoughts on this in the section below: Organizational Forms and Designing for the Social.

Our approach to analysis therefore involves looking at unfolding activities and drawing connections with (epistemic) task design, with structures of place and social structures. An analogy that some people find helpful involves thinking about this in theatrical terms. Tasks are somewhat like the *script* of a play. The people who are going to act are given *roles*. Their activity during the play unfolds within a *set* – there is a backdrop, furniture, props and so on. Sets have to be designed and built, but they are not the play. They influence but do not determine the action. Similarly, neither script nor roles equate to the play: a play emerges as the actors draw upon the script, the props and each other, *acting* to create each performance.

The theatrical analogy can be pushed a little further to introduce a fourth construct: co-configuration. We use this term to capture the ways in which the participants in an activity reshape what is being done, and the context within which it is occurring, with many subtle factors influencing the 'live performance'. One way in which this happens is through improvisation. A script never fully specifies character or action. The actors and director have to work out the details and they may, indeed, override the playwright's intentions. Moreover, each actor's performance will vary from night to night and this affects how the other actors act, react and relate. Also, the action may move elements of the set – objects on the stage. This changing of the set through participants' activities turns out to be much more important in learning networks than is usually the case on the stage.

In a digitally mediated learning network, traces of participants' activity become part of the set – they are reified; they register as new texts, or other kinds of artifacts, visible on screen. Over the life-course of a learning network, the set evolves through the actions of network participants. The set shapes, and is shaped by, network participants' activities.

We now turn to a closer examination of the three major design components: the epistemic, the set and the social. After reviewing some features of each that are significant in our analyses, we conclude the chapter by looking at how they come together in networked 'ensembles'. It is important to remember that the distinctions between task, set and social are easier to make conceptually, and in framing design, than is usually the case when analyzing real cases. The epistemic inflects and is inflected by the social; tools have know-how embedded in them, and so on.

Task Structures and Epistemic Design

This section focuses on the structuring of knowledge-oriented activities, and on ways of understanding the potential influence of 'epistemic elements' in the unfolding activities of learners.

Knowledge-oriented activities are perhaps more evident in networks related to formal education where we can easily identify these activities in relation to learning tasks proposed. In less formal networks one may find tasks that appear less structured or less explicit. In any case, the epistemic elements of a network are those most closely associated with learning tasks, and those that seem to reflect a certain epistemic structuring, a certain way of communicating knowledge.

To design learning tasks, designers may engage in researching, thinking, planning, adjusting, conceptualizing the things that network participants may do or may engage with. Part of the work of designers involves choices about particular ways of expressing knowledge within a network. As these designers specify and refine the tasks participants will tackle, they make decisions about the sequencing, pacing and selection of what will be communicated, and so on. These decisions, in turn, do not happen in isolation. They often involve other stakeholders, interests, goals, pedagogical intentions and knowledge practices within a broader social context. For example, in Chapter 4, on Peep, the tasks the students are given only make sense because of the existence of certain kinds of work practices, and associated forms of knowledge, in the professional world of graphic design and in the world of higher education (with its need for assignments, grades etc.). Similarly, the work practices and characteristic ways of knowing of health professionals have a broader influence on task design in ISQua (Chapter 11). Other chapters in Part II reveal many variations in task design due to characteristic ways of knowing in professional work, chemistry, music, natural history, and so on.

In sum, when we speak about epistemic design, we are referring to the knowledge-oriented structures of a network; that is, we are often searching for and examining those elements that suggest things that participants will do. However, we are also searching for elements that are perhaps not explicitly associated with learning tasks, but which are likely to influence the way participants engage in tasks. Our analysis traces connections between knowledge-oriented elements (e.g. proposed tasks, resources and other elements that may be associated with these) and the learners' activities, with some alertness to the ways in which the unfolding of epistemic activity within the network echoes epistemic practices relevant to the network, but outside it.

This way of looking at epistemic elements of a network is underpinned by research in the sociology of knowledge which has found that knowledge may take a range of forms, and that these different forms are based on different organizing principles, underlying knowledge practices in educational or intellectual fields (Maton 2014, Maton *et al.* 2014, Maton and Moore, 2010). These diverse forms taken by knowledge are seen as potentially affecting policy and curriculum development as well as educational practices more broadly. For example, studies have investigated: ways that different subject areas evolve over time (Hood 2010, 2013); which types of pedagogy are best suited to helping a particular social group learn some specific subject matter (Chen 2010, Howard and Maton 2011, Maton 2014); and how principles from the sociology of knowledge can be incorporated into e-learning design (Carvalho 2010, Carvalho *et al.* 2014). In Chapter 16, we provide some synthetic analyses of epistemic design (of the networks in Part II) by drawing more deeply on this work in the sociology of knowledge – particularly on Legitimation Code Theory (Maton 2013, Maton *et al.* 2014) – and also by extending some of the ideas about knowledge-building found in the work of Carl Bereiter and Marlene Scardamalia (e.g. 2003).

Structures of Place and Set Design

This section introduces two groups of ideas: how to capture and organize the diversity of things that come together to constitute the physical context within which activity unfolds, and how to draw relationships between physical context and activity.

It is not necessarily the case that a large range of physical and digital things needs to be taken into account in every analysis of a learning activity or learning network. However, the conceptual framework for guiding analyses in general needs to have the scope to do so – it needs to be comprehensive, or at least easy to extend without conceptual disruption. Because of that, we need to understand 'place' as both nested and diverse. When we think about the physical situations in which participants' activity is unfolding, we need to be able to think of rooms within buildings, computers on desks, light and quiet, books and PDFs coming to hand, paper pads and electronic notepads, pens, mice, highlighters etc. Working on one's laptop on a train is different, in important ways, from working on someone else's PC in an Internet café. Highlighting a printed version of a journal article is different from highlighting an e-print. Having a chat with co-workers is different when it is face-to-face in an office or over Skype from one's home, or via text messaging while on the move. Forgetting you will need your copy of *The Oregon Experiment* (Alexander *et al.* 1975) has different implications if you are near your office, near a good library, or out in the mountains.

As a glance through some of the examples in Part II will show, understanding learning activity needs the analyst to be able to map it across what can be a complex mix of inter-dependent digital and material places, artifacts and tools. Sometimes a specific place, tool or artifact is key to the successful unfolding of the activity, or its absence blocks progress. In other circumstances, there may be workarounds. Increasingly, there are possibilities for swapping between the material and the digital; tangible interfaces, mobile and ambient computing and ubiquitous access to information amplify and complicate these possibilities. Relations between tools and places can be quite complicated. Sometimes, tools and other useful artifacts are only available in one (kind of) place – the place is important, in part, because of the tools and infrastructure that it makes available. In other circumstances, tools are what allow us to escape the constraints of a place. Access to the WWW and email or text messaging are cases in point.

The relations between place, tools and activity are key to both analysis and design. For the designer, a logic that can connect place or tool to activity is essential. Without some rationale that helps say 'this tool would be good for this activity' or 'this activity needs this kind of place', a designer's work is reduced to matters of taste and fashion. The complexity of the 'set' complicates the drawing of connections – which are typically 'many-to-many' rather than 'one-to-one'. Moreover, this is an area in which designers rarely have control over the full assemblage of tools and resources used by the learner – who may quite reasonably insist on bringing their own devices, for example. That said, there are some helpful constructs that can be used to sketch connections of different kinds. In particular, we would single out the notions of 'affordance', 'interpretation' and 'legibility'.

Affordance

We argued, earlier in this chapter, that technologically determinist causal connections are usually suspect. But the material qualities of artifacts are not irrelevant – meanings and uses are not infinitely variable. A term that has been used widely in educational technology to try to capture a non-deterministic influence of a tool or artifact on an activity is 'affordance'. Though widely used, the term is also widely criticized (see e.g. Oliver 2005, 2011, Goodyear and Carvalho 2013). Most criticisms fall into one of two categories – imprecise usage and underestimation of the human capacity to interpret, adapt and innovate. Among the problems of imprecision, it is possible to find uncertainties about whether an affordance is a property of an object, or is essentially a relation between an organism and an object; also, there are doubts about whether an affordance is directly perceived or socially constructed. Harry Collins observes:

> the terms 'afford' and 'affordance' are lazy terms ... these terms merely paper over deep cracks in our understanding ... of why, given the extraordinary interpretive capabilities of humans, anything affords any one interpretation better than any other ... something hidden and mysterious is going on whenever the terms 'afford' and 'affordance' make their appearance.
>
> *(Collins 2010, p. 36)*

Interpretation

In Goodyear and Carvalho (2013) we suggested that both 'affordance' and 'interpretation' are useful terms and that they can be understood by reference to what Daniel Kahneman (2011) calls 'fast' and 'slow' thinking. In brief, human cognitive activity – in Kahneman's view – has components that work automatically and reasonably well in familiar circumstances (the 'fast' system) and components that require much more cognitive effort, work more slowly and are best reserved for novel or otherwise problematic situations (the 'slow' system). We argue that the affordances of objects play to the fast system and the slow system is used when interpretation is necessary. Thus, both terms are useful in capturing different relations between things and places, on the one hand, and actions, thoughts and feelings, on the other.

The distinct roles of affordance and interpretation, and fast and slow thinking, are important for the designer. For example, in a learning task, there are often some aspects that require close attention – hard thinking – and others that do not. A well-designed task, and supporting resources, will act in ways that focus hard thinking on the parts of the work that are intended to leave a beneficial cognitive residue – in short, mental effort needs to be focused on what is core to the achievement of learning, on what is hard and important. Well-designed scaffolds, navigational cues and other kinds of procedural facilitation or performance support will mean that 'slow thinking' is not required for these enabling, but marginal, tasks. So, for example, good navigational cues can reduce cognitive load by ensuring that attention is paid to the core task, rather than to finding one's way around a website. Well-designed scaffolds mean that one can delegate to the 'fast' system some of the more reactive, peripheral aspects of task management, allowing the 'slow' system to deal with the core problem.

Some recent materially grounded accounts of skill, from anthropological rather than psychological sources, echo this distinction between the interpretive and the perceptual. Tim Ingold's account of 'walking the plank' is a case in point (Ingold 2011, Chapter 4 and see also Ingold 2000, 2013).

Notions of affordance and interpretation do not cover all of the ways in which activity can be linked to the physical world. A related, though distinct, idea from architecture and urban design is that of *legibility*. Legibility is the quality of a place that enables people to understand its layout. It helps with wayfinding in a building or in a town or city. By analogy, it can be used to characterize online spaces, websites and networks. A highly legible design helps people come to know what is there, what is available to them and how to find what they need.

There is not space here to provide an exhaustive set of constructs that connect places and things to activity. In earlier work we talked about re-use and updating of Vitruvius's architectural qualities of 'firmness, commodity and delight', which Mitch Kapor also used in analyzing software design (Kapor 1996, Cicognani 2003, Goodyear 2000). Additional constructs that relate the experience of built space to deeper human emotions can be found in the works of Juhani Pallasmaa (e.g. 2012a, 2012b), Christopher Alexander (e.g. 1979, 2006) and others. From very different perspectives, Don Norman and Danny Miller provide excellent accounts of how we feel about things and how things teach us how to use them (Norman 2005, Miller 2008, 2010).

> Objects don't shout at you like teachers, or throw chalk at you, as mine did, but they help you gently learn to act appropriately . . . before we can make things, we are ourselves grown up and matured in the light of things that come down to us from the previous generations.
>
> *(Miller 2010, p. 53)*

Organizational Forms and Designing for the Social

Designers can recommend a variety of ways in which people might work together – divisions of labor, modes of collaboration, roles etc. that participants in learning networks may find themselves adopting. This is one of the senses in which activity is socially situated – activity involves interactions with others. There is a second, deeper, sense in which activity is socially situated, by virtue of the fact that it is embedded in a broader culture. This second sense is not really amenable to design work; generally speaking, design for learning is informed by an understanding of culture, rather than being capable of effecting cultural change in any direct or immediate way. (We discussed some of these effects in the subsection on epistemic design, looking at relations between knowledge practices in a network and the sociology of knowers and knowing in the broader culture.)

As mentioned before, designers' recommendations are not necessarily followed, so while roles or divisions of labor may be suggested, they are not necessarily visible in practice. Moreover, people's capacity for self-organizing means that what we observe when analyzing learning networks may be emergent, rather than 'designed in'.

Suggestions about social organization for online work have quite a long history (Kaye 1992, pp. 14–15) and a wide range of structures have been tested. Early examples can be found in McConnell (1994) and Palloff and Pratt (1999).

They range in scale and complexity: from communities of inquiry, communities of practice and collectives down through teams and groups to dyads. Examples of a range of organizational forms, expressed in the language of design patterns, can be found in Goodyear (2005) and Goodyear and Retalis (2010).

Bringing the Epistemic, Set and Social Together

These three main dimensions for analysis and design – the epistemic, the set and the social – are useful reminders of what can be designed and how the outcomes of the designer's work may then influence what learners actually do. In practice, interesting things happen when multiple elements interact. For example, it is rarely the case that one wants to analyze the qualities of a tool, such as a hammer or word processor, without reference to the intended outcomes, users, their skills and experience, distributions of labor etc. In analyzing learning networks, such interactions can apply at multiple scale levels – a particular tool may be common across the whole network, or only used by a few strongly tied people; ways of knowing may be locally variable, or shared by everyone. The chapters in Part II illustrate the strengths, and some of the limitations, of taking this architectural approach to the analysis of learning networks.

References

Alexander, C., 1964. *Notes on the synthesis of form*. Cambridge, MA: Harvard University Press.

Alexander, C., 1979. *The timeless way of building*. New York: Oxford University Press.

Alexander, C., 2006. *The nature of order*. Berkeley, CA: Center for Environmental Structure (4 vols).

Alexander, C., Ishikawa, S., Silverstein, M., Jacobson, M., Fiksdahl-King, I. and Angel, S., 1977. *A pattern language: towns, buildings, construction*. New York: Oxford University Press.

Alexander, C., Neis, H., Anninou, A. and King, I., 1987. *A new theory of urban design*. Oxford: Oxford University Press.

Alexander, C., Silverstein, M., Angel, S., Ishikawa, S. and Abrams, D., 1975. *The Oregon experiment*. New York: Oxford University Press.

Barad, K., 2003. Posthumanist performativity: toward an understanding of how matter comes to matter. *Signs*, 28(3), 801–831.

Bennett, J., 2010. *Vibrant matter: a political ecology of things*. Durham, NC: Duke University Press.

Bereiter, C. and Scardamalia, M., 2003. Learning to work creatively with knowledge. In E. De Corte, L. Verschaffel, N. Entwistle, and J. van Merriënboer, eds. *Powerful learning environments: unraveling basic components and dimensions*. Advances in Learning and Instruction Series. Oxford, UK: Elsevier Science, 55–68.

Bijker, W., 2010. How is technology made?—that is the question! *Cambridge Journal of Economics*, 34(1), 63–76.

Bliuc, A.-M., Ellis, R. and Goodyear, P., 2007. Research focus and methodological choices in studies into students' experiences of blended learning in higher education. *The Internet and Higher Education*, 10(4), 231–244.

Boivin, N., 2008. *Material cultures, material minds: the impact of things on human thought, society and evolution.* Cambridge: Cambridge University Press.

Carvalho, L., 2010. *A sociology of informal learning in/about design.* Thesis (PhD). University of Sydney. Available from: www.legitimationcodetheory.com/pdf/2010Carvalho.pdf [Accessed 29 July 2013].

Carvalho, L., Maton, K. and Dong, A., 2014. LCT into praxis: creating an e-learning environment for informal learning. In: K. Maton, S. Hood and S. Shay, eds. *Knowledge-building: educational studies in Legitimation Code Theory.* London: Routledge.

Chen, R. T.-H., 2010. *Knowledge and knowers in online learning: investigating the effects of online flexible learning on students' sojourners.* Thesis (PhD). University of Wollongong. Available from: www.legitimationcodetheory.com/pdf/2010Rainbow.Chen.Thesis.pdf [Accessed 29 July 2013].

Cicognani, A., 2003. Architectural design for online environments. In: B. Kolko, ed. *Virtual publics: policy and community in an electronic age.* New York: Columbia University Press.

Clarà, M. and Mauri, T., 2010. Toward a dialectic relation between the results in cscl: three critical methodological aspects of content analysis schemes. *International Journal of Computer-Supported Collaborative Learning,* 5(1), 117–136.

Collins, H., 2010. *Tacit and explicit knowledge.* Chicago: The University of Chicago Press.

Creanor, L. and Walker, S., 2012. Learning technology in context: a case for the sociotechnical interaction framework as an analytical lens for networked learning research (pp. 173–190). In: L. Dirckinck-Holmfeld, V. Hodgson and D. McConnell, eds., *Exploring the theory, pedagogy and practice of networked learning.* Dordrecht: Springer.

de Laat, M., Lally, V., Lipponen, L. and Simons, R.-J., 2007a. Online teaching in networked learning communities: a multi-method approach to studying the role of the teacher. *Instructional Science,* 35(3), 257–286.

de Laat, M., Lally, V., Lipponen, L. and Simons, R.-J., 2007b. Investigating patterns of interaction in networked learning and computer-supported collaborative learning: a role for social network analysis. *International Journal of Computer-Supported Collaborative Learning,* 2(1), 87–103.

de Laat, M., Lipponen, L., Lally, V. and Simons, R.-J., 2006. Teaching and learning in networked learning communities: a multi-method approach to analysing students' experiences with e-learning. *International Journal of Web-Based Communities,* 2(4), 394–412.

de Wever, B., Schellens, T., Valcke, M. and Van Keer, H., 2006. Content analysis schemes to analyze transcripts of online asynchronous discussion groups: a review. *Computers & Education,* 46(1), 6–28.

Dewey, J., 1916/2004. *Democracy and education.* Whitefish, MT: Kessinger Publishing.

Dirckinck-Holmfeld, L., Hodgson, V. and McConnell, D., eds., 2011. *Exploring the theory, pedagogy and practice of networked learning.* Dordrecht: Springer.

Dirckinck-Holmfeld, L., Jones, C. and Lindström, B., eds., 2009. *Analysing networked learning practices in higher education and continuing professional development.* Rotterdam: Sense Publishers.

Ellis, R. and Goodyear, P., 2010. *Students' experiences of e-learning in higher education: the ecology of sustainable innovation.* New York: RoutledgeFalmer.

Faulkner, P. and Runde, J., 2011. The social, the material, and the ontology of non-material technological objects. *27th EGOS (European Group for Organizational Studies) Colloquium.* Gothenburg.

Fenwick, T., Edwards, R. and Sawchuk, P., 2011. *Emerging approaches to educational research: tracing the sociomaterial.* Abingdon: Routledge.

Ford, P., Goodyear, P., Heseltine, R., Lewis, R., Darby, J., Graves, J., Sartorius, P., Harwood, D. and King, T., 1996. *Managing change in higher education: a learning environment architecture.* Buckingham: SRHE/Open University Press.

Goodyear, P., 1993. Foundations for courseware engineering. In: R. Tennyson, ed. *Automating instructional design, development and delivery.* Berlin: Springer.

Goodyear, P., 1997. Instructional design environments: methods and tools for the design of complex instructional systems. In: S. Dijkstr, N. Seel, F. Schott and R. Tennyson, eds. *Instructional design: international perspectives.* Mahwah, NJ: Lawrence Erlbaum Associates.

Goodyear, P., 2000. Environments for lifelong learning: ergonomics, architecture and educational design. In: M. J. Spector and T. Anderson, eds. *Integrated and holistic perspectives on learning, instruction & technology: understanding complexity.* Dordrecht: Kluwer Academic Publishers.

Goodyear, P., 2005. Educational design and networked learning: patterns, pattern languages and design practice. *Australasian Journal of Educational Technology*, 21(1), 82–101.

Goodyear, P. and Carvalho, L., 2013. The analysis of complex learning environments. In: H. Beetham and R. Sharpe, eds. *Rethinking pedagogy for a digital age: designing and delivering e-learning.* New York: Routledge.

Goodyear, P. and Dimitriadis, Y., 2013. *In medias res*: reframing design for learning. *Research in Learning Technology*, 21: 19909 http://dx.doi.org/10.3402/rlt.v21i0.19909

Goodyear, P. and Markauskaite, L., 2012. Pedagogic designs, technology and practice-based education. In: J. Higgs, R. Barnett, S. Billett, M. Hutchings and F. Trede, eds. *Practice-based education: perspectives and strategies.* Rotterdam: Sense Publishers.

Goodyear, P. and Retalis, S., eds., 2010. *Technology-enhanced learning: design patterns and pattern languages.* Rotterdam: Sense Publishers.

Häkkinen, P., 2013. Multiphase method for analysing online discussions. *Journal of Computer Assisted Learning*, DOI: 10.1111/jcal.12015 [online]. Available from: http://onlinelibrary.wiley.com/journal/10.1111/%28ISSN%291365-2729/earlyview [Accessed 15 July 2013].

Hara, N., Bonk, C. J. and Angeli, C., 2000. Content analysis of online discussion in an applied educational psychology course. *Instructional Science*, 28(2), 115–152.

Henri, F., 1992. Computer conferencing and content analysis. In: A. Kaye, ed., *Collaborative learning through computer conferencing: the Najaden papers.* Berlin: Springer.

Hodgson, V. and Watland, P., 2004. Researching networked management learning. *Management Learning*, 35(2), 99–116.

Hood, S., 2010. *Appraising research: evaluation in academic writing.* London: Palgrave.

Hood, S., 2013. Ethnographies on the move, stories on the rise: an LCT perspective on method in the humanities. In: K. Maton, S. Hood and S. Shay, eds. *Knowledge-building: educational studies in Legitimation Code Theory.* London: Routledge.

Howard, S. and Maton, K., 2011. Theorising knowledge practices: a missing piece of the educational technology puzzle, *Research in Learning Technology*, 19(3), 191–206.

Howell-Richardson, C. and Mellar, H., 1996. A methodology for the analysis of patterns of participation within computer mediated communication courses. *Instructional Science*, 24(1), 47–69.

Ingold, T., 2000. *The perception of the environment: essays in livelihood, dwelling and skill.* Abingdon: Routledge.

Ingold, T., 2007. Materials against materiality. *Archaeological Dialogues*, 14(1), 1–16.

Ingold, T., 2011. *Being alive: essays on movement, knowledge and description*. Abingdon: Routledge.

Ingold, T., 2013. *Making: anthropology, archaeology, art and architecture*. Abingdon: Routledge.

Jones, C. and Czerniewicz, L., 2011. Theory in learning technology. *Research in Learning Technology*, 19(3), 173–177.

Kahneman, D., 2011. *Thinking, fast and slow*. New York: Farrar, Straus and Giroux.

Kali, Y., Goodyear, P. and Markauskaite, L., 2011. Researching design practices and design cognition: contexts, concretisation and pedagogical knowledge-in-pieces. *Learning, Media & Technology*, 36(2), 129–149.

Kapor, M., 1996. A software design manifesto. In: T. Winograd, ed. *Bringing design to software*. New York: Addison Wesley.

Kaye, A., ed., 1992. *Collaborative learning through computer conferencing: the Najaden papers*. Berlin: Springer.

Kress, G. and van Leeuwen, T., 2001. *Multimodal discourse: the modes and media of contemporary communication*. London: Arnold.

Kress, G. and van Leeuwen, T., 2006. *Reading images: the grammar of visual design*, London: Routledge.

Maton, K., 2014. *Knowledge and knowers: towards a realist sociology of education*. London: Routledge.

Maton, K., Hood, S. and Shay, S., eds., 2014. *Knowledge-building: educational studies in Legitimation Code Theory*. London: Routledge.

Maton, K. and Moore, R., eds., 2010. *Social realism, knowledge and the sociology of education: coalitions of the mind*. London: Continuum.

McConnell, D., 1994. *Implementing computer supported cooperative learning*. London: Kogan Page.

Miller, D., 2008. *The comfort of things*. Cambridge: Polity Press.

Miller, D., 2010. *Stuff*. Cambridge: Polity Press.

Mu, J., Stegmann, K., Mayfield, E., Rosé, C. and Fischer, F., 2012. The ACODEA framework: developing segmentation and classification schemes for fully automatic analysis of online discussions. *International Journal of Computer-Supported Collaborative Learning*, 7(2), 285–305.

Norman, D., 1990. *The design of everyday things*. Garden City, NJ: Doubleday.

Norman, D., 1999. Affordance, conventions and design. *Interactions*, 6(3), 38–43.

Norman, D., 2005. *Emotional design: why we love (or hate) everyday things*. New York: Basic Books.

Oliver, M., 2005. The problem with affordance. *E-Learning*, 2(4), 402–413.

Oliver, M., 2011. Technological determinism in educational technology research: some alternative ways of thinking about the relationship between learning and technology. *Journal of Computer Assisted Learning*, 27(5), 373–384.

Oliver, M., 2013. Learning technology: theorising the tools we study. *British Journal of Educational Technology*, 44(1), 31–43.

Orlikowski, W. J., 2010. The sociomateriality of organisational life: considering technology in management research. *Cambridge Journal of Economics*, 34(1), 125–141.

Pallasmaa, J., 2012a. Newness, tradition and identity: existential content and meaning in architecture. *Architectural Design*, 82(6), 14–21.

Pallasmaa, J., 2012b. *The eyes of the skin: architecture and the senses*. Chichester: John Wiley.

Palloff, R. and Pratt, K., 1999. *Building learning communities in cyberspace.* San Francisco, CA: Jossey-Bass.

Schrire, S., 2004. Interaction and cognition in asynchronous computer conferencing. *Instructional Science*, 32(6), 475–502.

Schrire, S., 2006. Knowledge building in asynchronous discussion groups: going beyond quantitative analysis. *Computers & Education*, 46(1), 49–70.

Suchman, L., 2007. *Human-machine reconfigurations: plans and situated actions.* Cambridge: Cambridge University Press.

Suthers, D., Verbert, K., Duval, E. and Ochoa, X., 2013. *Proceedings of the third international conference on learning analytics and knowledge.* Leuven, April.

PART II
Learning Networks

INTRODUCTION TO
THE CASE STUDIES

Part II illustrates the application of the architectural framework introduced in Part I, through a series of 12 case studies of learning networks. Each chapter offers an analysis by two or more researchers, discussing aspects of the network's design. They examine relationships between elements of set, epistemic and social design, exploring the influences of these elements on the activities that ensue, and the ways that participants reconfigure and reshape the design of these networks.

Chapter 4 introduces our first case study, which is situated in the context of higher education. The chapter presents the analysis of Peep, an online environment created to support a design programing course taught at the University of Sydney, Australia. Through interactions with Peep, but also with lecturers and peers, students are introduced to programing as a tool for designing and as a medium of expression in digital media. More broadly, Peep also introduces first-year design students to the social context of a profession, exposing students to ways of practicing design that are grounded on practices within the field, encouraging students to support and critique each other's work. Peep provides access to learning resources, guidance for completion of tutorials, a space where students ask for help and offer help, and where they can also showcase their work. The Peep chapter discusses how a special feature in its design – the code editor – helps to bring programing to the forefront of the environment, highlighting *code* as a 'first class object', like text or images. This first case study is co-authored by Lucila Carvalho, Peter Goodyear, Dewa Wardak and Rob Saunders.

In Chapter 5, Hanne Westh Nicolajsen and Thomas Ryberg apply the framework in the analysis of an experimental course run with undergraduate students at Aalborg University, in Denmark. The design of the experiment is underpinned by the authors' interest in helping students to become active and reflexive networked learners, by finding ways of stimulating their engagement in (or creation of) learning networks among themselves. The students are seen as able to draw on a wider array of resources and persons found outside the immediate surroundings of the 'classroom' or 'group room' in which they are situated. The case study discusses the use of specific tools and online environments to promote interaction and transparency between groups, as well as ways of encouraging students to interact with and learn from each other.

Lynn Robinson and Jaime Metcher introduce the next case study in Chapter 6, analyzing a network that brings together educational leaders in Australia. Leading Curriculum Change (LCC) is an online learning program created to support the reform of the Australian School Curriculum. It was commissioned by the Australian Institute for Teaching and School Leadership (AITSL). The program is delivered almost entirely online, and it runs across multiple Australian jurisdictions, sectors and educational contexts. The goal of the program is to support quality curriculum leadership and teaching and to provide professional development to lead teachers and curriculum leaders. LCC is open to all participants, offering them opportunities to engage flexibly in learning modules on topics related to curriculum innovation, leadership and teamwork, change management techniques. It also introduces participants to the vision and background behind the development of the Australian Curriculum. The modules were designed in consultation with various stakeholders and representatives from the participant group.

Martin Parisio, Kate Thompson, Tracy Richardson and Rangan Srikhanta apply the conceptual framework in the analysis of OLPC Yammer in Chapter 7: an online environment supporting the One Laptop Per Child (Australia) initiative. OLPC (Australia) is a charitable organization that provides XO laptops to children aged 4–15 years in Australian communities, with a focus on those in remote areas. OLPC Yammer uses the Yammer social network platform to create an environment for community engagement, where teachers and those involved in the initiative may ask for, access and offer support related to the initiative, its implementation and the ongoing use of the laptops within Australia. The majority of participants in this network are teachers and technical specialists, who come together to discuss aspects of the design and delivery of teaching activities, learning resources, technical support, development of educational software applications for children and other related matters. This case study analyzes a network that offers a shared space for teachers to connect and exchange experiences, independently of the type of school in which they work or the region of Australia in which they are located.

In Chapter 8 Crighton Nichols and David Ashe analyze the *Desiña el Cambio* platform, a Mexican online environment connected to a global movement initiated in India – Design for Change. Design for Change was created to offer children an opportunity to express their own ideas 'for a better world', encouraging them to put their ideas into action, thus becoming active agents of change. Design for Change has had an impact on 34 countries and over 300,000 schools, with hundreds of thousands of children, their teachers and parents, engaged in leading change. The purpose of the *Diseña el Cambio* platform was to create an online environment for Spanish speakers, where students and teachers could easily learn more about the program, such as how to register for the competition (Design for Change Challenge), the methodology for implementing the program in their school or organization and how to update their project profile as the project progressed. *Diseña el Cambio* was designed to be project-centric, but also encourages collaboration between schools, incorporating social networking elements and making it easy for users to exchange information by writing on walls, forming groups and so on. The platform was conceptualized for both online and offline use, and inherits design processes and lessons learned from previous projects, including through the use of design and pedagogy patterns.

In Chapter 9 Marlies Bitter-Rijpkema, Steven Verjans, Wim Didderen and Peter Sloep discuss the Biebkracht learning network (BLN): an inter-organizational network for library professionals in the Netherlands. The BLN case study discusses the work of a group of library professionals, researchers and learning technologists who came together to design, develop and implement a platform for innovation at a local and regional level. The chapter problematizes the profession of librarianship, and indeed the role of libraries, faced with social, technological, policy and funding changes. The case study applies the conceptual framework in an analysis of the creation and implementation of BLN, in this context of uncertainty and change. It discusses ways of addressing the specific needs of non-formal social learning among the individuals in the library workplace context, exploring how the network supports the whole organization, and ways of encouraging current and future learning.

David Ashe, Pippa Yeoman and Tim Shaw apply the conceptual framework in the analysis of the next case study in Chapter 10, a platform for the delivery of flexible learning programs for students or professionals working in fields of evidence-based practice. Qstream was initially conceptualized for learners and professionals in the health-care community, with a focus on the need for rapid recall of critical context dependent information. Qstream uses case scenarios and clinical questions distributed to participants via email at specific intervals, and these cases are then repeated under the control of an adaptive algorithm. Studies analyzing the use of these environments amongst the health-care community have shown that Qstream significantly improves students' retention of medical knowledge. Since then, the platform has been expanded to accommodate courses in different areas. This chapter analyzes Qstream as an environment that was created with a specific epistemic rationale – the spacing and testing effects – examining ways of combining the delivery of a flexible program and fostering both competitive and relationship-building social aspects.

Chapter 11 introduces another network for professionals in health care. Dewa Wardak, Paul Parker and Tim Shaw analyze ISQua Knowledge, an online environment created to foster and support the professional development of health care practitioners and managers. The online environment of ISQua Knowledge was first developed by the International Society for Quality in Health Care (ISQua), but the initiative included other partners and contributors, such as the Canadian Patient Safety Institute (CPSI), the Universities Research Corporation delivering the Health Care Improvement Project (HCI) for USAID and the World Health Organization (WHO). The environment was created so that members of the ISQua Knowledge network would have a space for sharing, developing and building on a collective knowledge base about quality and safety in health care. Free access to information and discussions related to health care were expected to be of significant help to professionals in the field, particularly those working remotely, in isolated areas and/or in low- and middle-income countries, who would generally have less access to discussions related to new knowledge and practices in the field. Thus, the design of the environment emphasizes making experts' knowledge accessible to all and fostering exchanges and collegiality amongst members.

In Chapter 12 Paul Parker, Beat Schwendimann, Kate Thompson and Matthew Todd introduce the case study of The Synaptic Leap (TSL). TSL is a web-based network where members use online collaboration to address research problems that are often neglected by the 'profit-driven' pharmaceutical industry. TSL embraces the concept of 'open science', where all data and ideas are freely shared. The network uses a decentralized approach in its deployment, taking advantage of various digital spaces and tools to promote collaboration. Members of this network include scientists and research students around the globe who come together to collaborate on research problems related to diseases found exclusively in tropical regions and diseases that have higher incidence among poor communities in developing countries, such as malaria, schistosomiasis, toxoplasma and tuberculosis. The network design allows people to join freely and to leave the project without affecting its continuity. Each member dedicates as much time and effort as they can. Conceptually, TSL applies a design-based model in the framing of research problems and so the projects follow a cycle for process improvement: initially, a research problem is posted and data is shared within the community, then members are asked to investigate, identify and reveal holes in the approach and to make suggestions about improving the current approach. Researchers in charge of the project then set to work on adjusting it, resulting in an improved approach, which is then posted online and the cycle begins again.

Our next two case studies involve networks that were neither specifically designed for formal education nor for bringing together a group of professionals in the same field. They represent a different type of network, where learning is neither central nor explicitly on the network's agenda. These networks nurture learning and foster collaboration in less direct and structured ways than the ones described in the earlier chapters. That said, these networks are not unusual: there are many others in which people choose to engage for leisure, relaxation, interest and/or a shared sense of achieving something worthwhile. In Chapter 13, Lucila Carvalho and Peter Goodyear apply the conceptual framework in the analysis of the Virtual Choir. The idea for the Virtual Choir originated with its conductor and composer, Eric Whitacre. Three choir projects have been completed so far. As part of each project, candidate choir participants individually record a video of themselves singing one of Whitacre's compositions. Participants receive instructions for the production of their individual videos, containing both musical and technical information, for example on how to record and upload their videos. Selected individual videos are then edited and cut together by a professional from Whitacre's team, to form the Virtual Choir. As with The Synaptic Leap, the Virtual Choir case study shows how the interaction between the participants and the facilitators of the project happens in a number of spaces (via email, Facebook, Blog, YouTube, the TED discussion forum etc.). Members interact within these environments in order to ask for support and information and share their stories, experiences and feelings in relation to participating in the project. Thus, this chapter also discusses the use of a distributed approach in the shaping of a network, where multiple spaces are used for collaboration. In this case study we analyze how design elements in the Virtual Choir engender experiences that some participants report as life-changing: including profound feelings of connection amongst people who have never met in person.

In Chapter 14, Ana Pinto, Kate Thompson, Chris Jones and Doug Clow present the case study of iSpot, a UK-based network developed by the Open University (OU). The main aim of iSpot is to help people identify species they have observed in nature: reptiles, birds, fish, fungi, mammals and plants. This network introduces people to practices within the natural sciences, by scaffolding ways of knowing within the sciences, offering a space to learn about wildlife and share interests with a like-minded community. iSpot can be accessed independently by anyone interested in learning, and sharing observations about, nature. It has also been used as part of a unit of study offered at the Learning Space (OU). Its members include people of all ages, both amateurs and experts. This chapter discusses some of the distinctive features in the design of iSpot, such as the ability to make topics and the levels of members' expertise visible, e.g. through the presence of icons adjacent to profile names.

While most of the case studies in Part II foreground online networks, our very last case portrays a different scenario. It describes the use of a web-based tool that enhances the visibility of existing relationships within a physically co-located learning network. In Chapter 15, Maarten de Laat, Bieke Schreurs and Rory Sie discuss the Network Awareness Tool (NAT), a web-based tool to help professionals gain awareness of existing learning networks within or between organizations. The main aim of NAT is to help professionals to deal with real, urgent, work-related problems that are part of their daily practice, for example, by revealing 'who' would have 'x' type of knowledge, which would be useful to solve 'y' type of problem. The NAT case study shows how the tool makes evident aspects of the architecture of an existing learning network, thus revealing relationships between elements in the social and epistemic dimensions. This case study explores issues associated with visualizations of an existing learning network in a secondary school in the Netherlands.

4

PEEP

Peer Support for Programing

*Lucila Carvalho, Peter Goodyear, Dewa Wardak
and Rob Saunders*

Overview

Peep[1] is an online environment that supports one of the courses (DECO1012) offered as part of the Bachelor of Design Computing at the Faculty of Architecture, Design and Planning in the University of Sydney (Australia). This degree program combines the creativity of design with a technical knowledge of computing; there is an emphasis on students exploring aesthetic possibilities in computer-expressed works. DECO1012 introduces first-year undergraduate design students to a computer programing language, with particular emphasis on its practical application. The course is designed to encourage students' experimentation with programing as a tool for designing and as a medium of expression in digital media and interaction design. The course comprises weekly one-hour lectures and two-hour lab tutorials, supported by Peep (Figure 4.1). DECO1012 is a compulsory core subject for the Bachelor of Design Computing and it is offered annually during the first semester for a period of 13 weeks.

Peep had supported DECO1012 in the three years preceding this case study; the current version incorporates feedback and adjustments from lessons learned through this earlier experience. Sixty-three students used the version reported in this case study, in two settings: at labs during tutorial activities (with tutors present in the room) and remotely from home or other locations.

Peep comprises seven main pages: front page, outline, tutorials, assignments, portfolio, forum and help. It is possible to access the environment as an observer, but students must 'log in' to participate in tutorials, complete exercises, work on sketches and assignments, and to add or modify information in their portfolios or profiles. The front page is the main point of entry to the environment and contains the latest information about activities within the online environment: any new

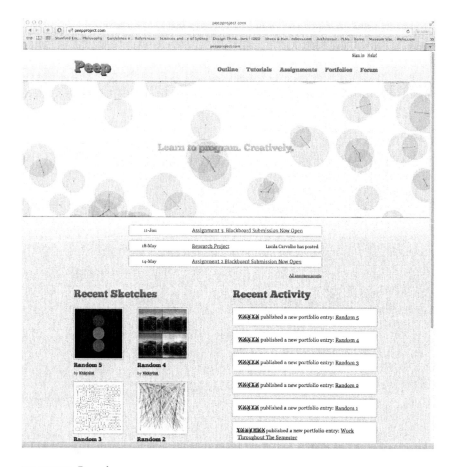

FIGURE 4.1 Peep: home page

announcements, recent activities, and recent sketches. The author's identification appears alongside each announcement, activity or sketch (Figure 4.1).

Within the online environment there are a total of 16 guided tutorials and three assignments. Students are asked to complete their assignments by developing portfolio entries that document their design concept, development process and final design implemented in code.

Students use the visually oriented programing language Processing.js. The programs that they develop are called sketches. Each student has a private 'sketchbook' where they can experiment with code. Students can publish their sketches in portfolio entries to share them with others. Peep provides access to learning resources, support for the completion of tutorials, a space where students can ask for help and offer support to each other, and a place for students to showcase their work.

A distinctive feature of Peep is that its design brings programing to the forefront of the environment, highlighting it as the core element. Code is considered as a 'first class object', and, therefore, within this environment code is as important as texts or images. One of the key elements of Peep's architecture is the embedding of code editors throughout, which allows for 'visibility' of something that is often 'invisible'. The code editors facilitate discussions about concepts through the use of different types of representations (text, code and image). As a result, first-year students are able to exchange ideas about these concepts and their experiences with them, to evaluate their programing skills immediately, and to help and support each other through the visualization of their object of study, while learning about programing.

This case study examines how designed elements in the online environment of Peep support DECO1012 students' learning of programing as a tool for design. We conducted interviews with the developer, the lecturer and one of the students enrolled in DECO1012. Moreover, we examined how key elements of the set design, in addition to the design of tasks and the forms of social organization, were conceptualized. We also observed students' activities and interactions with Peep and with others via the online environment. This chapter discusses some of the key elements of Peep's epistemic, set and social design, and how these elements influence learning activity within this context. The chapter also illustrates how these can be abstracted to inform the design of other learning networks and contexts.

Epistemic Design

Learning programing as part of DECO1012 requires that students acquire fluency with concepts that involve different types of representations. Students need to grasp the basic 'language' in order to practically experiment with it in their designs. That is, students need to be able to recognize the essential elements of the programing language and find ways of putting these elements together to realize a specific design intent. Guided tutorials introduce students to the basic elements of processing, and these are followed by other, more complex, tutorials, such as: using programing to draw with code, producing shapes and forms, adding color, drawing with randomness and with functions, and so on. Tutorials first introduce operational knowledge and gradually move towards conceptual knowledge. In each of these tutorials, students are exposed to and practice navigating between three types of representations: text, code and image. Once students have completed the tutorials, they are expected to apply the language in their own individual design projects. Here they need to show that they have acquired the programing 'vocabulary' and that they are able to structure this vocabulary into 'sentences', so they can communicate their own design intentions. There is, therefore, an emphasis on bringing the first-year students to a level of fluency as quickly as possible. Peep's epistemic design supports the lecturer and tutors in the delivery of teaching sessions at a high conceptual level, where meanings are highly condensed.

Task design involves the use of increasingly complex tutorials, introducing the specialist knowledge necessary for programing and building on the complexity of concepts. At first, programing language tutorials incorporate concrete examples based on everyday life; these help students to establish links within the new knowledge they are acquiring. For instance, Figure 4.2 shows how Tutorial 2 alternates the example of words and sentences in the English language with technical terms and expressions in programing. This tutorial moves from everyday experiences that students can easily relate to (the English language) to elaborated concepts in programing, and then again using everyday elements to explain

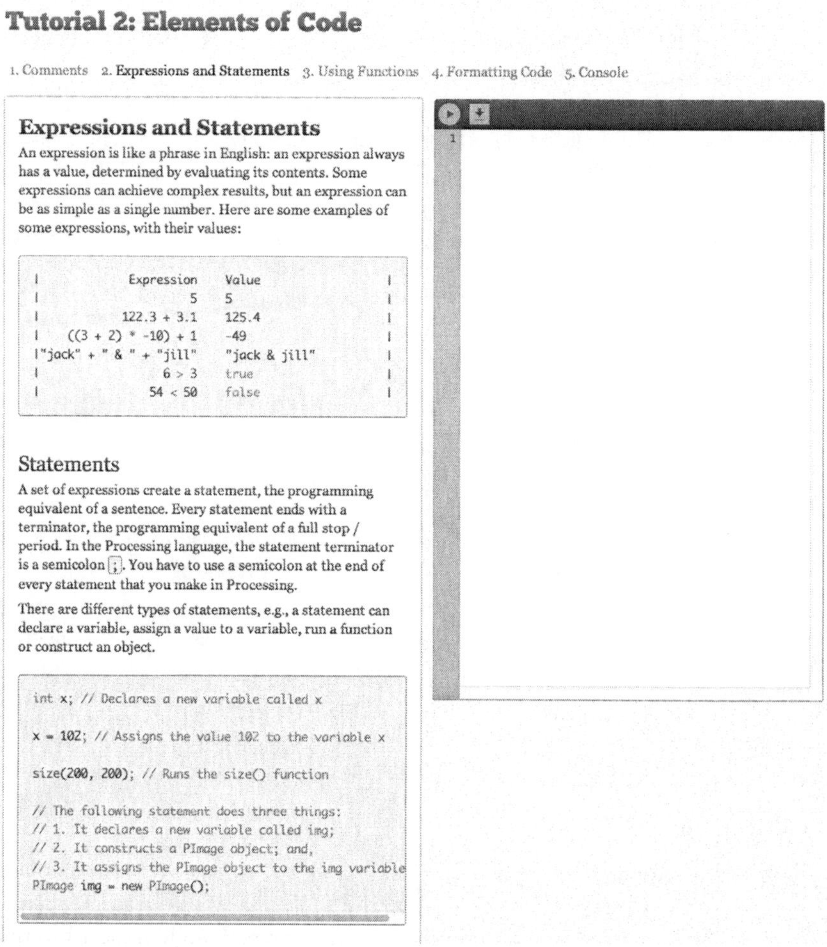

Tutorial 2: Elements of Code

1. Comments 2. **Expressions and Statements** 3. Using Functions 4. Formatting Code 5. Console

Expressions and Statements

An expression is like a phrase in English: an expression always has a value, determined by evaluating its contents. Some expressions can achieve complex results, but an expression can be as simple as a single number. Here are some examples of some expressions, with their values:

```
|            Expression    Value           |
|                    5     5               |
|            122.3 + 3.1   125.4           |
|    ((3 + 2) * -10) + 1   -49             |
|"jack" + " & " + "jill"   "jack & jill"   |
|                  6 > 3   true            |
|                 54 < 50  false           |
```

Statements

A set of expressions create a statement, the programming equivalent of a sentence. Every statement ends with a terminator, the programming equivalent of a full stop / period. In the Processing language, the statement terminator is a semicolon `;`. You have to use a semicolon at the end of every statement that you make in Processing.

There are different types of statements, e.g., a statement can declare a variable, assign a value to a variable, run a function or construct an object.

```
int x; // Declares a new variable called x

x = 102; // Assigns the value 102 to the variable x

size(200, 200); // Runs the size() function

// The following statement does three things:
// 1. It declares a new variable called img;
// 2. It constructs a PImage object; and,
// 3. It assigns the PImage object to the img variable
PImage img = new PImage();
```

FIGURE 4.2 Peep: a tutorial page

other conceptual ones. As tutorials progress and students move towards higher conceptual levels, fewer links to everyday life examples are used.

For the first eight weeks students are expected to complete guided exercises in Peep, primarily within the labs' physical space. As the course progresses and students become more proficient with both the use of the Peep environment and with programing, they are given increased opportunities to experiment practically with designing by applying the programing language to individual creative projects. During the final weeks of DECO1012, students have no formal tutorials to complete and instead use their lab sessions to work on their individual projects. Task design also incorporates operational knowledge ensuring students fully understand how to use the learning environment before they are asked to interact within it independently. For example, the very first tutorial is an introduction to Peep, and includes information about the functionality and behaviors of the code editor and 'how to get help' if necessary. Each tutorial is designed as a set of individual exercises; assistance may be provided via the 'help' link (which compiles a list of frequently encountered problems), via the discussion forum or in person via the lecturer, tutors and fellow students.

Once the essential elements have been introduced, task design shifts to using visual images as the basis for learning, as well as working with knowledge concepts related to programing and acquiring fluency in working to and fro between different types of representations. The code editors support a particular way of teaching programing – working with the visual image and what can be achieved by modifying a few elements of the code that produced it. Students are prompted to experiment in open-ended ways to explore what a particular piece of code is capable of producing; they are also challenged to 'reverse-engineer' images produced using code similar to that introduced in a tutorial, so that they start to think analytically about how to produce desired target images (Figure 4.3).

Set Design

Peep's set design consists of a digital space and at least two material spaces (the two labs in Figure 4.4) where students attend tutorials and interact with Peep. There is also a third potential material space: anywhere (home or other locations) with a web connection. The two labs consist of rooms with desks, desktop computers and larger screens on which the lecturer may project images or instructions. Desks are arranged in slightly different ways in each room: in one set up, students sit in rows, and in the second, students' desks face each other in groups of four (Figure 4.4). In the tutorials, students can choose which lab room they would like to be in, with seats allocated on a first-in, first-served basis. Within the lab spaces, students may interact with, and receive onsite support from, lecturer and tutors, and from other fellow students. The third material space – home or other location – is likely to involve other elements and people, mostly unknown to the designers and teachers and beyond their control. Students are left to make their

We can also combine tests on ⟨x⟩ and ⟨y⟩ to produce interesting, and unexpectedly complex effects:

Show Sketch

```
/** @peep sketchcode */
size(200, 200);
for (int y = 20; y <= height - 20; y += 10) {
  for (int x = 20; x <= width - 20; x += 10) {
    if ((x % 30) == 0 || (y % 50) == 0) {
      line(x-5, y+5, x+5, y-5);
    } else {
      line(x-5, y-5, x+5, y+5);
    }
  }
}
```

Experiment with the above code to produce different effects using conditional statements based on the values of ⟨x⟩ and ⟨y⟩. As a challenge, see if you can reproduce the following examples with simple tests on ⟨x⟩ and ⟨y⟩ to the ones used above:

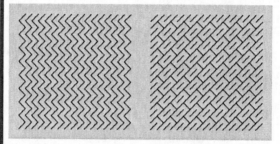

Experiment with combining the values of ⟨x⟩ and ⟨y⟩ together using math operations before taking the modulus. The following sketches differ only in the way they combine x and y together, see if you can produce similarly complex patterns:

FIGURE 4.3 Peep: using visual images as a learning resource

FIGURE 4.4 Physical spaces: set up of two labs

own decisions about whether and how to work in such spaces. In this case, these third spaces fall outside the scope of our analysis. (For a contrast, see Chapter 13 about the Virtual Choir.)

The digital space is represented by Peep's online space. The visual layout of Peep is simple and clear. It excludes inessential elements, with a focus on the content itself, allowing its core message on 'learning programing to design' to come to center stage. As described by one of the students in DECO1012, Peep has a 'simple and yet warm feel'. This description resonates with the idea that outward simplicity creates inner calm (see Christopher Alexander [2002] on simplicity and inner calm). Every element has a well-justified purpose (each earns its place) and therefore the environment's design avoids overload of textual or visual images or sound.

Every page in Peep follows a standardized layout. The use of a standardized global navigation system is a well-known principle in web design (Krug 2006, Nielsen 1999) but the application of this principle is particularly relevant in an environment such as Peep. Here it is essential that learners focus on specific content, which requires a design that excludes superfluous elements so that learners are not overloaded by unnecessary processes. Each individual page in Peep is divided into two horizontal spaces. The top part of each page contains a heading with the name of the online environment and five main navigational links on the left: outline, tutorials, assignments, portfolios and forum, in addition to two extra links ('help' and 'sign in') above. The bottom part of the page is where students find information about course content, and where they are able to work and interact with the environment and others.

Similarly, the setting for all 16 tutorials also replicates its layout: the left side of the screen is reserved for instructional text and the right side has the code editor where students work (see Figure 4.2). Replication of the same simple structure for each page (two horizontal spaces: one containing the title and navi-gational features, and a second displaying content and the workspace), coupled with consistency of operation for related actions across all the tutorials, enables students to quickly grasp how to act within the environment. These design principles (standardizing actions, layouts, displays) complement one of the environment's goals, namely, focusing on the key learning task – experimenting with programing as a means to design.

One of the essential elements in Peep's design takes into account the importance of making things visible (Norman 2002). This is particularly well expressed in Peep's use of the code editor. The code editor's design allows for both the visualization and running of the code, so that students can immediately see how their code looks and behaves (Figure 4.5). This design mechanism facilitates instant evaluation, and students know straightaway whether or not they have achieved the desired effect. The editor enables students to navigate between two modes of representation: code and image.

In addition, by embedding code editors in the tutorial pages, there is no need for a separate application program. Thus students can work on their code as they read information and learn about how to use the programing language, within the same page space. This design element prevents constant switching between screens, avoiding the need to navigate and manage two separate applications (Peep and a separate editor), which in turn contributes to situate programing activity at the core of the environment.

Peep also places importance on simplifying the structure of tasks (Norman 2002). For example, Peep's code editor automatically stores versions of code as students develop and test their work, and so the environment allows them to

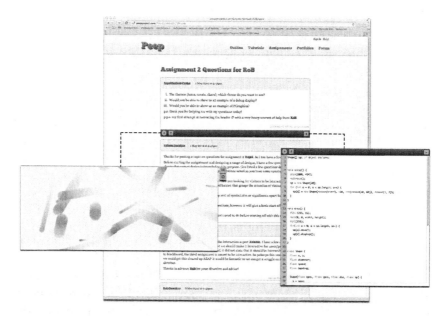

FIGURE 4.5 Peep: code editor showing image (left) and code (right)

concentrate on their learning and experimentation in programing, rather than having to worry about making mistakes or keeping back-up copies. Storing back-up copies and version control are important procedures in 'real-world' programing, and students will need to learn and develop such practices as they become professional designers. However, at this early stage of learning, Peep supports the students by automatically carrying out the version control, so they can concentrate on development and experimentation. A design decision was made to prioritize what were the key elements to be learned, and so, 'storing back-up' and 'version control' became automated procedures incorporated into set design, instead of being additional learning tasks in the epistemic design.

Social Design

Underlying the lecturer's conceptualization of this environment is the intention to facilitate a 'sense of community' and promote a 'friendly rivalry' amongst the students. The lecturer perceives these as desirable attributes that could potentially contribute to students' acculturation in design, as they enter the field of design. One of the objectives is to encourage first-year students (who are likely to be fairly new to both programing and design) to discuss their work openly, exchange ideas with peers, share their design thinking processes and help and support others. Peep's social design is therefore shaped by the belief that students are likely to benefit from being exposed to other students' work and from getting feedback from others about their own work. Such an exposure can create a learning context where students may build and elaborate on the design ideas of others. The design also allows for first-year students to practice interpreting critiques as a way to elaborate their designs, a practice that will be part of their future experiences in design education, where 'crits' are often used as a form of assessment (Horton 2007). The sharing of experiences and visualization of the group's creations contribute to form students' social identity as designers, as they start to recognize the nature of the designs the group seems to 'like' best. Thus, elements of the social design introduce students to practices and to what is considered meaningful and special within the field of design. Students share design ideas and come across the design creations of other fellow students within the particular context of Peep but also, more broadly, through examples and links to other professional designers' work as suggested by the lecturer. Students will use examples from the broader design field, and from their immediate social group within Peep, as the basis for establishing a richer understanding of the nature of the kinds of knowledge that are valued in design. Through this process students start to form their own identity as designers.

The nature of the social context of design is, nevertheless, introduced gradually. At the start of the course, for example, meanings are strictly bound to the social context of Peep's online learning environment, but as the tutorials progress they are gradually expanded to the social context of design more broadly. For example, while initial tutorials comprise straightforward exercises for learning specific technical concepts, later individual projects tend to provide a more 'real-life' mode, asking students to interpret design briefs and suggesting examples and links to the work of practicing designers. Although the environment mostly focuses on developing a set of skills related to programing (specialist knowledge), there is also considerable emphasis on the participant *as an author*, mirroring the way knowledge and practices are valorized within architecture (Carvalho *et al.* 2009).

The formal nature of undergraduate courses in higher education is often reflected in structured hierarchical roles. In the case study of Peep, these consist of the role of the lecturer, three tutors (usually senior design students) and the DECO1012 students. These roles are also reproduced within Peep, where students are aware of the symbolic authority figures represented by the lecturer and tutors. Tutors are third-year or honors-level students, and although they provide in-class support they do not tend to participate in the online forums within Peep. Nevertheless, such hierarchy is not explicitly visualized in Peep's design and so there are no icons or special features to denote the lecturer's or tutors' IDs.

The forms of organization conceptualized in Peep do not engage students in explicit collaborative work. The students are expected to complete their exercises individually and post their work for comments and feedback. However, the setting of the environment affords several spaces for students' social interaction, such as the discussion forum and comment bars in the announcements, portfolios and so on. In addition, students' interaction and participation in the environment are valued and encouraged through strategies adopted by the lecturer and tutors, as a way of responding to emergent activities. Tutorial classes supported by Peep, at least in the early weeks of the semester, implicitly reflect a hierarchical structure, and it is not surprising that students initially assume a more passive role and direct their questions to the lecturer and tutors. However, in order to nurture a sense of a working community, it is necessary that these initial relational boundaries become less rigid. The lecturer's challenge lies in how to encourage students to be progressively more autonomous, empowering them to help others, to exchange ideas, creating opportunities for students to shift from a narrower and more passive role to a broader and more active role. Students' active participation is a necessary step for creating a sense of belonging, and ultimately for developing Peep as a space that will nurture a design learning community.

Set, Epistemic and Social Co-creation and Co-configuration Activities

The diverse range of set ups – two classroom labs and the opportunity to access Peep remotely – implies that there are potentially a number of interactions and/or elements that are not necessarily visible within Peep's digital space, but that would nevertheless also influence students' activities and learning processes. Yet the students' ability to access the online environment from anywhere would require access to material resources, such as a computer, a web connection, electricity etc., necessary for them to be online remotely (home, university campus or other places). Connecting remotely, on the one hand, gives students the opportunity to work continuously on their projects irrespective of location and, importantly, allows them to be 'constantly connected' and engaged with the learning environment as they check for new announcements and new activities related to their peers' work production. Such an arrangement broadens the learning context, which is not restricted to the immediate surroundings of the two classrooms on the university campus. On the other hand, remote access also allows students to withdraw from personal interactions in the course, as they do not necessarily need to attend tutorials in the labs.

Within Peep's digital space, a core design feature is the embedding of the code editors, which directly influences students' activities. For example, this facilitates students sharing their code with others, bringing the object – a particular piece of code – to the forefront of their discussion, in a way that enables others to see what they are talking about. Students make use of these elements to share, talk about or ask for support with their code. Students exchange ideas about their knowledge production, asking questions if they are having a problem with their coding, or if they want to use one person's code as an inspiration for their own designs, or whenever they just want to praise a particular piece of work.

As students use the code editors, or as they produce sketches and publish their productions into their portfolios, they are also modifying Peep's set design. These elements and their productions are incorporated into Peep and from then on they become design elements available to be used by others interacting with the environment.

Activities related to epistemic design afford cumulative learning experiences, and throughout the environment there is an emphasis on students gradually building on specialist knowledge. Once students are introduced to programing concepts, they are expected to complete specific exercises where they will practice the skills they are acquiring. The tasks proposed envisage that students will work and experiment with modifying a given piece of code provided by the lecturer. They may use the code as the basis for their own creations, having the visual images of what can be achieved. In this way, students manipulate elements of the given code (building on the specialist knowledge) to achieve something unique in their designs. Similarly, the visualization of portfolios allows for students' work to be used as learning resources. That is, a student can build on a particular design they like, modifying or experimenting not only with the pieces of code in formal tutorials, but with codes and designs from their fellow students. The way the tutorials are structured allows students to work at their own pace, and to return to a topic as many times as they want to.

A few strategies have been created to address and nurture participation. One of these is seen in task design, where students are asked to input comments as part of formal activities in their tutorials. The idea here is to acquaint students with the act of posting; once students have experienced 'posting something', this practical experience of 'having performed the action' makes them more likely to do it in future. Another strategy used to promote participation involves redirecting questions that arrive via personal email or privately, for example by asking the student to publish a question in the Peep discussion forum. The act of posting a question in Peep allows the sharing of information: giving other students opportunities to acquire insight into a particular topic, but also empowering the author of the posting who has initiated a conversation within the learning environment. Again, in a cyclic effect, the likelihood of someone else commenting or exchanging ideas is increased once they have direct practical experience of it. Peep's design elements address this issue effectively, and this was demonstrated by the fact that, in the present version of Peep, students have independently answered each other's questions as early as the third week of the course.

The timing of replying to a post may also influence students' participation. The lecturer believes that it is important to avoid jumping in and replying as soon as a question is posted. This lesson was learned accidentally with a previous version of Peep – a student posted a question at a time when the lecturer was unable to provide feedback straightaway. As a result, other students had the opportunity to step in to fill the role, and so were able to offer their views on the particular question. While the optimal timing for replying to a post is unknowable, it is often helpful for the lecturer to choose to refrain from immediately answering a particular question so that other students have the opportunity to do so. Often, this lecturer will join a forum thread at a slightly later time to extend or expand upon the answers provided by students.

Students may choose to make their work public or not. It is only when students publish their sketches in their portfolios that these artifacts become part of Peep's shared setting. They become a potential source of inspiration for ideas and may be used as the basis for other students' own creations. As students examine these artifacts, they learn about how others have come to a particular solution to a design brief, how someone may have used a piece of code to achieve a specific effect, the different ways of interpreting a design brief, and so on. At the same time, as students publish their work in their individual portfolios to showcase their knowledge creations, they are also acting on the construction of their own design identities. The visualization of these portfolios, connecting authorship to artifacts, makes explicit the type of design this particular person produces. Peep enables a particular student to be identified as the author of a particular piece of work, and this mechanism may contribute to initiating conversation about a particular design (e.g. one may praise and recognize the work as interesting or special). In turn, it also contributes to the group design identity – as in identifying what types of design work Peep's participants like. It facilitates 'friendly rivalry' amongst students. For example, when students see something they value, or something that is recognized by others as really interesting, they become motivated by the feeling of potentially being recognized by the group as the author of a 'cool design'. This is clearly reflected in an interview with one of the students, who reported that it is very desirable to receive acknowledgment from their fellow students for a particular knowledge creation. As DECO1012 first-year students start to construct their identities as designers and build a sense of community through their interactions within Peep, peer recognition is perceived as fundamental and so are their wishes to help and support others. Students may be more likely to strive for learning and improve their designs when they feel acknowledged by their peers and mentors, but also when they can recognize and realize knowledge according to what is considered meaningful within that particular group. Within this process students start to create a sense of community and a feeling of belonging as they are gradually acculturated in design.

Abstracting and Synthesis

The case study of Peep illustrates potentially useful design elements for those online learning networks where learning and/or knowledge creation require dealing with concepts that involve different types of representations. The main problem this case study addresses is how to provide a space to navigate and experience different modes of representation as one explores specialist concepts, so that those involved in the learning network, particularly those who are new to the specialist knowledge, can have a common 'language' to share ideas and discuss these concepts.

This case study involves an online environment used to support a compulsory design programing course taught to first-year students in higher education. The course specifically focuses on learning programing to design. As part of the program, students are required to learn through experimenting with concepts that condense a lot of meanings, often relying on experimenting with visual images as the basis for learning. These learners are mostly new to programing (and its application within the design profession). As first-years, they are also new to teaching practices in tertiary education. Epistemic and social design, in this case, may potentially pose many challenges to them. First-year university students need, for example, to recognize previously unfamiliar social expectations in terms of what is required from them within the university's social context. These may include having to independently study outside classroom hours, to manage their own time, to complete different types of assignments, assessments and so on (Kantanis 2000). Such practices may differ from those the students have experienced within secondary education. In addition, these first-year students will need to cope with other implicit norms associated with learning within the specific disciplinary context in design. That means these students will not only be introduced to specialist knowledge, skills and design programing practices, but they will also be exposed to implicit values associated with the design knowledge and practices, which are expected to eventually form the basis for their professional work as designers (Carvalho *et al.* 2009). The material context includes two types of possible structural arrangements: one that includes using Peep in the lab settings, with the presence of tutors and peers, and one at home (or another setting) that would mainly rely on asynchronous communication with tutors and peers.

The code editors offer an interesting solution for those online learning networks that require instant visualization and manipulation of the object of discussion, making 'visible' what is usually 'invisible' and bringing the object of the discussion to the forefront. Figure 4.6 illustrates key structural elements in this case study. In the figure, tutorials introduce students to means to which they may navigate between three modes of representations: text, code and image. The navigation between these three modes of representing concepts is essential within the learning context of Peep, because it is through navigation that students may establish relationships between conceptual representations, learning to interpret concepts where meanings are highly condensed. That means navigation between 'code' and 'image' encourages them to notice that modifying a specific element of 'code a' will result in a certain effect in 'image b'. In addition, students also use

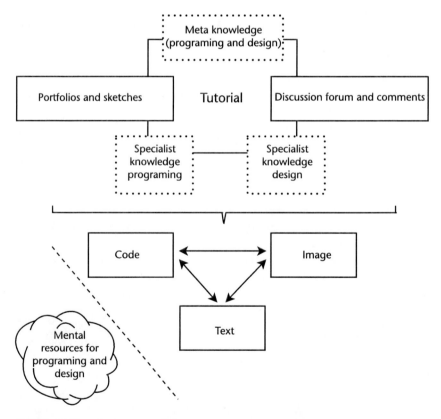

FIGURE 4.6 Peep: key structural elements

text – as they are requested to explain their design processes and development of their conceptual ideas, or as they engage in sharing ideas with their peers. As a result, the figure shows that students are also encouraged to practice fluent movement between the three modes as part of their design activities within Peep.

The code editors also support novices' practices by automatically performing essential procedures (such as version control) and by avoiding any need for these novices to use and manage more than one software application or different screens. It supports the novice, allowing them to focus on learning, bringing what is discussed to the center. The clean, consistent layout in the set design further supports learners who are new to the subject matter at hand. The set emphasizes what is to be the focus of attention in this particular environment by excluding inessential elements. The social design addresses the gradual introduction of the disciplinary social context of a profession. While meanings tend initially to be bound to the immediate online learning context, as tutorials progress they are gradually expanded to the broader social context of the discipline and profession.

Note

1 Accessed at www.peepproject.com. Please note that the network as described in this chapter may have evolved since the time of writing.

References

Alexander, C., 2002. *The nature of order: an essay on the art of building and the nature of the universe.* Berkeley, CA: The Center for Environmental Structure.

Carvalho, L., Dong, A. and Maton, K., 2009. Legitimating design: a sociology of knowledge account of the field. *Design Studies*, 30(5), 483–502.

Horton, I., 2007. The relationship between creativity and the group crit in art and design education. *Creativity or Conformity? Building Cultures of Creativity in Higher Education.* Cardiff, University of Wales Institute and the Higher Education Academy.

Kantanis, T., 2000. The role of social transition in students' adjustment to the first–year of university. *Journal of Institutional Research*, 9(1), 100–110.

Krug, S., 2006. *Don't make me think: a common sense approach to web usability.* 2nd ed. Berkeley, CA: New Riders Publishing.

Nielsen, J., 1999. *Designing web usability: the practice of simplicity.* Indianapolis, IN: New Riders Publishing.

Norman, D. A., 2002. *The design of everyday things.* New York: Basic Books.

5

CREATING A PEER-DRIVEN LEARNING NETWORK IN HIGHER EDUCATION

Using Web 2.0 Tools to Facilitate Online Dialogue and Collaboration

Hanne Westh Nicolajsen and Thomas Ryberg

Overview

In recent years there has been a growing interest in adopting social media to support students' learning within higher education. The promises of social media to support learning networks and engage students in more active learning arrangements seem to be an obvious opportunity for university teachers to tap into the rich digital learning ecologies students are already part of. However, while it is well established that students are heavy users of social media services, such as Facebook, it is equally becoming clear that they are not necessarily well versed in terms of creating productive learning networks or engaging in web-based activities particularly related to learning or academia (Clark *et al.* 2009, Luckin *et al.* 2009). We argue that learning networks based on social media and employed for academic purposes may challenge the traditional norms and practices for both teachers and students within institutionalized learning and therefore need re-negotiation and support.

In this chapter we present and discuss a design experiment, where one of the authors (Hanne Westh Nicolajsen) aimed to create a productive learning network among full-time, on-campus fourth semester students in an elective course within the program Humanistic Informatics (Aalborg University in Denmark). Aalborg University is characterized by being founded on a university-wide PBL pedagogy called the Aalborg Model of Problem and Project Based Learning. This approach emphasizes learning as knowledge construction and the main pedagogical principles revolve around problem orientation, project work, inter-disciplinarity, and participant controlled learning (Barge 2010, Dirckinck-Holmfeld 2002, Kolmos *et al.* 2004). The entire learning process is formed around the students' group-based inquiry into scientific and social problems. Therefore each semester is organized around approximately 50 percent course work and 50 percent project work in groups. The students work closely together for an extended period of time (four months), on formulating, identifying and 'solving' their problem, and writing up a final project report. Students at Aalborg University are therefore intensively engaged in collaborative problem-oriented learning and project writing, in tightly-knit groups. Here, however, we focus on an introductory course preceding, or running simultaneously with, the project work.

The design experiment was grounded in our interest in exploring and designing learning environments and architectures that are not restricted to servicing the needs of mutually dependent collaboration in tightly-knit groups. We wanted to explore tools and environments that seek to leverage the interaction and transparency between groups and help students interact and learn from each other. As such, we were interested in strengthening the students' capacities to become more active, reflexive networked learners, capable of engaging in, or creating, learning networks among themselves, and who are also able to draw on a wider array of resources and persons found outside the confines of the 'classroom' or 'group room'. This was one of the pedagogical aims of the design experiment that we discuss in this chapter.

The Design Experiment

The case was part of a course entitled: 'Interaction, learning and collaboration in virtual environments'. The course was planned to take 135 'student working hours' (five credits under the European Credit Transfer and Accumulation Scheme, ECTS). It is an elective course, and is passed through 'active participation', meaning the students need to attend the classes and fulfill the assignments given by the teacher. This included, amongst other things, the use of loosely connected blogs as a way to present and discuss self-chosen themes within a student cohort of 37 students. One of the goals was to establish a learning network, which would enable the students to learn together, by building up knowledge on a number of themes through short interrelated and reflexive posts, providing different perspectives and understandings. The discussions supplemented the more traditional and well-known teaching methods such as lectures and onsite group work. The main reason for designing for discussions was as a means to involve all students and encourage them to engage in a more active and reflective way. In the experiment, the students were asked to find and bring in relevant theoretical resources and real-life examples and discuss these by posting on their blogs and commenting on other students' postings.

The experiment was organized around a number of tasks (or assignments), which students would have to complete in order to pass the course. In the first task, the students (in groups of six) were asked to investigate a Web 2.0 tool of their own choice, which they then had to present and demonstrate in class to their fellow students. The second assignment (the experiment) was to engage in a number of online discussions. In this assignment all students were asked to make at least three contributions. Two contributions had to include theoretical reflections whereas one could provide case material, such as examples found in magazines or newspapers. One of the contributions could initiate a theme; the others should respond to entries by others. The students were encouraged to work together in groups, deciding on a theme to discuss. At the same time they were asked to contribute to other discussions. All initiated discussions had to be announced to everyone in class. In the beginning, Twitter was used for announcing new discussions, however this did not work well. On Twitter only the most recent entries (or 'tweets') are immediately visible, meaning the links to earlier discussions were lost (or out of sight and requiring an additional effort to retrieve), even though a particular hash tag (#insalæ) was used. As both the students and the teacher were more familiar with Facebook, a closed Facebook group was formed instead.

The discussion task was seen as an experiment providing an alternative way to unfold new themes or phenomena, in order to expand the learning design beyond the given course hours; and even more importantly, to involve the students as active learners. The students were encouraged to introduce different understandings and perspectives due to the request to draw on theoretical resources and practical examples. This way of working was intended to provide for multiple perspectives supporting critical thinking, as well as making the students more active and confident in finding, presenting and reading material on their own in a critical way, while also engaging in dialogues with other students.

In the third and final task in the course, the students were asked individually to reflect on the relevance of Web 2.0 technologies in support of learning. The two-page reflection had to be handed in to the teacher by email shortly before the final lecture.

The aim of the course was to introduce students to a wider understanding of networked learning by drawing on existing insights and theory, making them more active in taking on multiple roles and responsibilities, and experimenting with new forms of learning through the use of Web 2.0 tools.

Set Design

Setting up the Course

The course encompassed 12 teaching hours during which students and the teacher met at the university. The teacher decided to distribute these hours into weekly sessions of three hours spanning four weeks. Often these small courses are run within a week, but in this particular design, time in between the lectures was important, so as to ensure time for students to learn together and on their own.

The four class sessions ran between 9 am and 12 noon during February, which is a notoriously dark and cold month in Denmark.

A pleasant, flexible, well-lit lecturing room on the ground floor was booked for the weekly sessions. The traditional set up of the teaching room with rows of tables and chairs was changed into an arrangement for supporting groups. Seven tables were arranged, so students could sit together in groups of six. This arrangement was intended to support a flexible flow between lecturing and group work. Students needed to be able to see the whiteboards, since PowerPoints would be displayed and texts written on them, and they also needed to have eye contact with the teacher during lectures. However, students also needed to be able to engage with each other and see their peers as resources for interleaved discussions and group work. The grouping of tables was a way to create natural groups for the group work, rather than having to reorganize the room for student discussions and group work.

Students were asked to bring their laptops to class. The laptops were needed to access the different Web 2.0 tools to be used. For the group work, the students had to access and interact using Web 2.0 tools of their own choice (the choice of the group). During lectures, Twitter was introduced as a backchannel. In addition, students were expected to use Twitter to share links to their online discussions (Task 2). The Wi-Fi was thus an important element of the infrastructure. The teacher used a laptop and PowerPoint for the lecturing part. Students were also required to use their laptops and programs like Word and PowerPoint to make presentations to the class, and to write their individual or group posts in the assignments given.

As usual, the university-wide course management system Moodle was used to communicate about the course. Moodle primarily supported basic teacher-to-student communication, e.g. course schedule, content and materials, and announcements to the students. Email was used as a medium for handing in the final assignment.

Students were also expected to work in between the class sessions, engaging in different types of group work. Most students, if not all, have computers and network access at home, and most of the group work required only asynchronous interaction, which meant that students could work more or less whenever they preferred. Only when preparing the group presentations have students preferred to sit together to reflect on and discuss their experiences.

Epistemic Design

Collaborative Learning – Learning about, Trying Out and Doing E-learning

The design of the tasks envisaged that, throughout the course, activities would shift between the teacher lecturing about aspects of learning and networked

TABLE 5.1 Instructions for Task 1

Task 1. Web 2.0 Demo

- Form groups of max. six participants
- Create a walkthrough of a Web 2.0 platform. Play around with it first. You should be able to tell, what you can do with it, and how it works
- Create a 5–10-minute demo/presentation for the class
- Suggested technologies/platforms
  - Wikis
  - Blogs
  - Mahara

---

learning, and students experimenting, playing with and experiencing different Web 2.0 tools to support various learning activities.

Despite the expectation that most students were familiar with a broad range of Web 2.0 platforms, a gentle introduction was offered, before what was seen as the 'real' experiment. Three assignments to be done in between class sessions were given.

The first assignment was expected to make all students familiar with a broad range of Web 2.0 tools and to help them gain an understanding of how these might support learning (Table 5.1). The focus was thus on action-oriented learning, helping students learn by experimenting with the tool chosen (for example, students chose Mahara, Tumblr or Delicious). Likewise, students were expected to learn from the other groups' experiences, by getting introduced to a wider variety of Web 2.0 tools, and their potentials for learning; thus inspiring and encouraging their future choice of Web 2.0 tools to support learning (both within the course, but also for learning activities afterwards). They were asked to do this assignment in groups of approximately six.

In the second assignment, a mixture of individual, group work and networked interactions was designed for (Table 5.2). The set up required written contributions to be posted on a Web 2.0 platform of the students' own choice, and subsequently presented to the class. Everybody was expected to follow the discussions of their peers and contribute to any of the online discussions they preferred, so as to create a web of networked interactions between the individual or group-based contributions. Despite the formal requirement for three contributions per student, the students were allowed to create the contributions either alone, in pairs or in groups. The aim was to make students become peer-learners or co-teachers. First, as content providers, they had to find material – searching, reading, selecting and then condensing the material into a meaningful contribution. Second, students were also required to read and respond to others, thus providing a critical commentary on the contributions of their peers. Responding and following up on the content of others was a means to encourage reflection,

TABLE 5.2 Instructions for Task 2

Task 2. Web 2.0 Discussions

- Applying Web 2.0 technologies for common discussions
- Work with project themes or a problem related to this course
- Use a Web 2.0 technology to find and structure material, write and discuss together with the others in the course to create content on the theme
- You should respond to each other's (material) – no matter if you work in groups or individually
- Minimum effort
  - One initiating contribution
  - Two elaborative contributions
  - Input has to contain theoretical or empirical points
  - Short comments are allowed, but they cannot stand on their own ☺
  - Use material from class and in addition find at least three texts to support your contribution, of which two have to be theoretical
- Send a tweet/write on the Facebook group insalæ with a link to your Web 2.0 discussion
- Informal presentation (approx. 10 min.) – orally or podcast performance for presentation (Monday February 28)

constructive criticism and initiate relevant links/relations between the various contributions made.

In the final task the students were asked to write an individual reflection on 'Web 2.0 for education' (Table 5.3). It was expected that students would reflect on their own experiences from Task 2 and in this way bring their experiences and reflections to a higher level. Again students were asked to bring in theory to ensure a grounded reflection on their experiences and in the discussions. The students were encouraged to write up these reflections after participation in the online discussions to ensure some hands-on experiences to inform their reflections. We further used these reflections as a background to our final discussion. There is not space in this chapter to present a full analysis, or a detailed description of our methodology for analyzing the reflections. Further information on these matters can be found in Nicolajsen (2012).

TABLE 5.3 Instructions for Task 3

Task 3. Reflections on 'Web 2.0 for Education'

- Two pages
- Has to contain theoretical accounts (e.g. the learning triangle by Illeris, barriers to learning, social learning …)
- Hand in to westh@hum.aau.dk no later than Thursday February 24 at midnight! (you should have made your discussions before ☺)

Social Design

The design allowed for alternating roles and responsibilities between students and teacher during the course. During the class sessions there was initially a more traditional relation between teacher and student, where the teacher took on the role of an expert having the overview of, and particular insights into, the themes addressed. The first group presentations were a way to involve, engage and make students more active, as well as acknowledging that students may learn from other students. The choice of having students work in groups for the first assignment was to build a small learning network that would allow them to test a Web 2.0 tool in a small group, while also sharing these experiences with the wider learning network (the whole class). However, we often use group work for assignments that are presented in class to make students feel more comfortable, and less vulnerable to critique from other students and the teacher. Furthermore, it was expected that students would have different skills in mastering new technologies. Being in a group would allow for peer support, and if some students experienced problems using the tool, others might be able to help, or they could engage in a trial-and-error process together.

The second assignment, however, tried to move beyond distinctions and division of control over content and traditional roles between students and teachers. The idea was to position students as co-teachers and peer-learners, not only sharing their experiences and analysis, but also deciding on themes, theories and content to present to others (co-teacher), and deciding which questions to ask and how to engage (peer-learner). The ongoing transitions between individual/group contributions and engaging the broader network of the students in the cohort were seen as a way to improve the quality of the discussions. The aim was to encourage students to produce knowledge and understandings by changing between the roles of contributors and readers, as the interchanges were meant to mutually strengthen each other, particularly by encouraging the students to be critical of what they read and wrote. Likewise, the accumulated outputs were seen as resources that could provide the students with a better overview and insight into themes and theories, as these were communicated by other students on the same level and with approximately the same prior understandings. As previously discussed, it was expected that some students would feel insecure about the assignment and about writing 'in public'. The possibility of writing together (with an accompanying requirement of more or longer contributions) was seen as a way to overcome expected barriers of insecurity.

The final assignment (the individual reflection on the learning process) was handed in to the teacher. This re-established the familiar authority structure, placing the teacher back into a position of power, from which they decided whether students would pass the course – based on the quality of the individual reflections, as well as satisfactory participation in the required networked learning activities. In Table 5.4 we present an overview of the course, lectures and tasks.

TABLE 5.4 Overview of the course elements

	Class Sessions	*In-between*
		Individual study – self-regulated
Week 1	Lecture on learning theory	• Readings and group work • Task 1 given (group-based) – Choosing and experimenting with Web 2.0 platform – preparing presentation for class
Week 2	Lecture on e-learning Presentations of Task 1 – demonstration + reflection on pedagogical feasibility	• Readings • Task 2 given (network) – Engage in online discussions. Make one initiating contribution and respond to at least two (discussions to run until Week 4)
Week 3	Lecture on organizational e-learning	• Readings and discussions • Task 3 given (individual reflection)
Week 4	Summing up Presentations of online discussions Evaluating the outcome based on the presentations, the individual reflections and following discussion in class	• Tasks 2–3 presented

Set, Epistemic and Social Co-creation and Co-configuration Activities

Changes in the Set Design and Infrastructure

On the first day of the course the students came before the teacher and were already setting up tables and chairs to meet the requirements of the teacher (which had been communicated through the Moodle course forum). The students expressed interest in arranging the physical setting to support learning.

However, when it came to the use of Twitter during lectures, it turned out that only a few students had created an account, despite a teacher request asking everybody to set up a Twitter account and a Facebook account for the course. The prominent role we had imagined for Twitter as a backchannel during lectures, and as a way of linking to online activities, did not really take off. As a backchannel, a few funny comments emerged, but (maybe) due to the low number of students (37) and a nice relaxing physical setting and atmosphere, it was not perceived as necessary or useful to have a backchannel for questions and comments. When Twitter was to be used as a place to link to the online discussion it turned out that only the latest links would be seen, meaning it was not useful in providing an overview, or keeping track of the online discussions as intended. A third-party service or list at Twitter could potentially have solved the problem, but time and the teacher's insecurity about Twitter led to another solution. Another possibility was Moodle, but Moodle is not really favored by students, and the teacher preferred to use a more popular and immediate tool. Everybody seemed to be on Facebook and therefore a closed group on Facebook became the place to upload links for discussions.

The use of Facebook worked to some degree. On a closer inspection of their reflections and the online group activity, it was noticed that new forum posts and updates tended to push older contributions out of sight and attention. However, most students used the Facebook group to present a link to their online discussion when it started. In particular, one student used Facebook to advertise the latest developments on her blog and encouraged her peer students to visit. This turned out to have an effect, as her discussion got a lot of comments. Facebook was also used to ask questions about the assignments – deadline, formats etc. – rather than using Moodle, which is normally used for teacher–student communication.

Changes in or Challenges to the Epistemic Design and Social Design

The three tasks were received rather differently. The first and the third task appeared to be quite straightforward, whereas the second task – the online discussions – generated quite a lot of frustration among the students. There were minor issues in terms of how to use their blogs. It should be noted that, although students were free to choose any Web 2.0 tool to facilitate their discussions, they all chose to use blogs (e.g. WordPress, Tumblr and Blogspot). They appropriated the blogs in quite different ways, which also led to different patterns of discussions, as the students adopted different interactional strategies.

The main challenges or issues were not related to how to use the blogs (e.g. how to post, add or comment). Rather, it turned out that many of the students felt insecure and wanted more guidance as to what was expected in these 'online discussions'. We return to this point shortly. Nothing happened between the second and third sessions, even though the task had been presented. It seemed that everybody was waiting for someone else to start. Therefore, in the third class session, quite some time was used to talk about ways of getting started. The teacher provided the students with proposed topics/themes to discuss (e.g. quality assurance aspects, wisdom of the crowds), and the students were encouraged to decide on a topic in groups, writing together etc. While the intention was that students should find an interesting theme or topic on their own, this process needed more scaffolding and negotiation. In order to allow time for the discussions to flourish, the fourth session was therefore postponed for some days, and so was the deadline for contributing to the discussions and handing in the final reflection.

Shortly after, and on the same day as the third session, the first blog 'Organizational user involvement through Web 2.0' appeared with the contribution 'User involvement why?' This blog, however, was set up in a way that did not allow comments. Only the three blog owners could make posts, and therefore, the blog was seen as a 'closed', yet public, discussion. The next day, a student who was part of another group put a trial post on their blog 'Quality assurance on Web 2.0'. The first comment from another student in the group revealed that they were unsure about how they could use the blog, as they realized they all had to be 'authors' in the BlogSpot blog. The five blog owners then collaborated and agreed upon a common strategy, taking turns in providing one contribution a day, all relating to the theme of the blog. They also decided to end all posts with an invitation for contributions from other students. Despite their pedagogical efforts, most posts still were not attracting comments, except for one of the posts, which took advantage of social media and was 'advertised' on Facebook. This post received seven comments, resulting in an interesting discussion about the 'Wisdom of the Crowds'. Other blogs featured only one initial contribution, followed by a number of comments from other students, whereas one blog had an initial post and then a continuing dialogue and interaction between various commentators and the blog owner, who acted as a moderator/facilitator of the discussion. Even though the technological infrastructure used by the students was *relatively* similar (they all used blogs, albeit different platforms), the way students adopted them was different. They also adopted different communication norms and interaction strategies, thus also interpreting differently what contributions and dialogue might mean. Overall, 32 discussions were initiated, resulting in a total of 110 posts and comments on 12 different blogs. All the blogs took off rather slowly, and there was a peak number of contributions (32) at the time when the students had to hand in their reflections, including links to their contributions in the online discussions. This can be seen from Table 5.5, which illustrates the temporal distribution of contributions to the online discussions. The top row represents the dates and the bottom row the number of contributions. It should be noted that the task was set to start a week before contributions actually began, and end before handing in the reflections on February 27.

We are in the process of analyzing more closely the relations between the number of initial contributions, and the number of comments the different blog

TABLE 5.5 Distribution of the online contributions during and after course

	February										March		
Dates	18.	19.	20.	21.	22.	23.	24.	25.	26.	27.	28.	1.	2.	3.
No. of contributions	1	2	2	9	4	13	24	14	7	32	0	0	0	2

postings generated. For example one blog alone generated 33 comments, five blogs each generated eight to ten comments, while the remaining six blogs generated fewer or none. We are particularly interested in understanding how the relations between topic, interaction strategy, and 'advertising' might have affected the interaction and dialogue – but also how existing friendships and the reputation of the student(s) might have had an impact. This, however, extends beyond the boundaries of this chapter, although we do have some indications about the relations, which we will address in the coming section.

Analysis

The set design and infrastructure surrounding the course was 'hybrid' or mixed in a number of ways. Engagements shifted between online and offline (while these clearly were also intertwined and interacted), between different ways of working (individual, group, network), and featured a mix of different platforms. What is worth noting around the technical platforms was the students' preference for using Facebook, although this certainly also posed some difficulties and challenges. We do not consider this to make a point about students' nativeness with social media, as it was clear they had difficulties with blogs and were largely unfamiliar with Twitter. Rather, we would argue that Facebook has now become such a familiar technology that this preference could equally be interpreted as a 'conservative' choice or 'safe haven', contrary to exploring other platforms and technologies.

While many students argued in their reflections that the use of Facebook to communicate about the online discussions was encouraging, some also argued that it became difficult to refrain from following the flow of contributions even in their spare time. The use of Facebook thus seemed to result in blurring the borders between study time and free time, which created problems for some students. They adopted different strategies to cope with this, e.g. one student decided only to follow a few blogs whereas another decided to look whenever an interesting theme or a 'good' student or friend wrote something. The latter in particular suggests that there might also be a social element affecting the interaction in or between the blogs, but also some students became aware of unknown qualities of their peer students, and that some students were less ambitious than expected. In addition, the flow of forums/updates intermingled with many other activities on Facebook might also have clouded or pushed aside some of the contributions, and suggests that students did not really have a full overview of the blogs and conversations initiated. An alternative approach could have been to set in place e.g. aggregated RSS feeds from all the blogs/ comments, which students could subscribe to, and which could feed into Moodle, Facebook or a reader of the students' own choice. However, it remains to be seen if students are actually familiar with such technologies, as the experiment – more broadly – supports other observations that students might not be as familiar with advanced use of Web 2.0 technologies as is often assumed (see for example Bennett *et al.* 2008, Jones and Shao 2011).

In relation to the epistemic design, and the use of online discussions through blogs, a number of issues surface. It was clear from the initial lack of activity that students were insecure or doubtful about what was actually expected from them. While the first and third tasks were 'routine' student assignments, the adoption of blogs for dialogue and interaction was not. This adoption of blogs affected students' usual roles, situating them as co-teachers (selecting a topic, finding material, reflecting and presenting and initiating a dialogue). Some students found it easy and encouraging, whereas others found it to be somewhat scary, difficult and entailing a heavy workload. Most of the students recognized that the online discussions required them to become critical about the material to present, their own communication and the communication of their peer students. This, together with their option of choosing which discussions to contribute to, and the freedom to choose material and topics, were seen as encouraging by some. Others found the task too cumbersome, as it was perceived as difficult to find good material. In relation to this, an interesting issue was that although many students acknowledged the importance of becoming more critical, active and self-directed, one of the most requested elements was quality assurance by the teacher in relation to the postings. This demonstrates the enduring difficulties in reversing or altering roles between students and teachers, and that these do not disappear when adopting media and tools that are supposedly more participative, student-centered or even assumed to be ahierarchical. Obviously, the students were still enveloped in a formal learning context, and were also to be assessed for their contributions.

Another issue of interest was their different interactional strategies and ways of engaging in dialogues. The differently patterned performances also suggest that asking students to 'engage in online discussions or dialogues' may not be a straightforward enterprise, and it may not be a practice that students are immediately familiar with. For example, how to create a 'dialogical' post and a continuing conversation of knowledge-building might need more scaffolding and instruction.

Abstracting and Synthesis

The aim of the course was to introduce and engage students in a wider understanding of networked learning by drawing on existing insights and theory. Another, and more important, aim was to make the students more active in taking on multiple roles and responsibilities, through experimenting with new forms of learning via the use of Web 2.0 tools, and engaging in different types of collaboration and interactions (from small group to wider network) – thereby forming a more informal or peer-driven learning network. It seems that the experiment was in many ways successful in realizing these goals, but also faced some challenges. It is clear that more attention can be invested in the set design, the epistemic design and the social design.

The set design and infrastructure was in many ways a hybrid or heterogeneous mix of the material and digital, and of specially provided, institutionally provided, and student-provided elements. However, this mix also challenged the students in carrying out and keeping up with discussions. They purposefully or unknowingly limited commenting and had difficulties sorting out access and authorship. While these issues were resolved, it reminds us that adopting a mix of student-provided technologies can be challenging for teachers in case they are called upon to assist with a variety of platforms or services they might not be familiar with (and for which no institutional support exists). The specially provided spaces (the Facebook group) slowly displaced or replaced the institutionally provided Moodle space, and also 'mails' (messages) to the teacher. Even though the students had a preference for these spaces, they also proved troublesome, e.g. as the ephemeral and fast-paced nature of updates on Facebook and Twitter can be difficult to cope with (as they also enter a mix of friends' and families' updates). Equally, it seems they can make it difficult to store, archive or keep a record of the most important links (the advertised posts) that can escape students' attention. An aggregated RSS feed or maybe a social bookmarking service with groups (e.g. Diigo.com) could address these difficulties, but this would also add an extra layer of complexity (and would be an additional space to monitor and maintain).

Web 2.0 technologies are often assumed to be 'native tools' of the students and to be more participatory, collaborative, dialogical and ahierarchical in nature, opening up opportunities for more learner-centered pedagogies. This study, however, provides a more complex picture of these relations. While the epistemic design consciously aimed at positioning students as peer-learners and co-teachers – open to the formation of a peer-driven learning network – these roles were not comfortably assumed by all students. Most students were uncertain of how to engage in peer-driven dialogues as co-teachers and were expecting more teacher intervention in terms of quality assurance. They also adopted different dialogical strategies, thus interpreting differently the task of engaging in 'online dialogues', although the technologies chosen were relatively similar. This reminds us, as teachers and designers, that the adoption of Web 2.0 technologies does not, in itself, alter roles between students and teachers. Nor can we precisely predict the types of interactions that will occur. Nor do they entail a clear idea of what kind of performances or genres of writing are expected. In other words, the set design does not determine changes in the social or the epistemic. The infrastructures, tools and tasks need to be carefully underpinned by design ideas and purposes in order to support particular enactments. In addition, due attention should be paid to the fact that formal education practices need careful alignment, support and conscious re-negotiation of roles, responsibilities and expectations. This, in our interpretation, calls for a more explicit outlining of the epistemic and social design, i.e. expected roles and responsibilities, but also a clearer outline of the 'genre', 'content' and 'interactional patterns' expected.

In this study, it also seems that the creation and running of a (somewhat successful) peer-driven learning network was heavily intertwined with the hybridity of the course and the particular designed mixture of online and onsite engagements and activities. The set, epistemic and social design did not adopt a sharp distinction between e.g. lectures and then online discussions. Rather these were woven together through in-class and online experiments with technology that were also embedded in class presentations and discussions, further interwoven with the online reflections and dialogues. We do not mean to privilege the physical or material as the 'true or real' locus for learning and interaction, rather we see it as a social arrangement and a set of designed 'comings together of activities' that could equally take place online. We would emphasize the particular rhythm and mixture of engagements that, however, require a certain level of co-presence (online or offline).

Related to the social design, we experienced an overlap between the primary peer learning persons and resources in class and those in the online networks. The students use their understanding of familiar social relations when they begin to engage in the new and challenging online peer-driven networks. The students' social relations and the social design of groups can thus be seen as an enabler or affordance for the network; but also be somewhat exclusionary and problematic (students tending to interact with, or follow, perceived 'good' or 'popular' students). We also found that the transparency created online can adjust these perceptions among students. It does seem that the social – together with the set and epistemic – design could more explicitly address such potential inequalities. These are particularly worrisome if, for example, the number of interactions is taken as an indicator or judgment of the quality of students' work (which it was not in this case). The use of social media such as Facebook and Twitter can potentially further aggravate such tensions, as content in news feeds and hash tagged lists are sorted and filtered by inaccessible algorithmic and social rules. (For example, people who have more overlapping friends may have a higher probability of seeing each other's content; most-liked posts may be more salient, etc. The lack of transparency of the proprietary sorting and filtering rules can therefore be a constraint on good educational design.)

Our study suggests that the creation of a peer-driven learning network within higher education, aiming at supporting more student control and student-managed initiatives – paradoxically – seems to be afforded by being embedded within a structured course design to gain the drive and legitimacy needed. This is particularly visible from the students' needs for teachers to provide quality assurance and commentary, but also from the insecurity and hesitation experienced with the online discussions. Creating peer-driven learning networks within the frames of a structured course design featuring particular co-present 'comings together of activities' provides a number of different ways to address these needs or insecurities. For example, anxieties may be reduced by: mixing the forms of engagement, discussing the output of the online activities in the lectures, or by creating a social design that causes or encourages students to work together. The notion of structure might seem to contradict a peer-driven network, but in the context of a formal course within higher education we would argue that structure and design can be an important enabler or prerequisite for such a network. Structure should not be taken to mean prescription or detailed management of all activities, but rather a frame within which students have the social, pedagogical and technological support to develop a peer-driven learning network.

References

Barge, S., 2010. *Principles of problem and project based learning – The Aalborg PBL Model* [online]. Available from: http://files.portal.aau.dk/filesharing/download?filename= aau/aau/2010/~/pub/PBL_aalborg_modellen.pdf

Bennett, S., Maton, K. and Kervin, L., 2008. The 'digital natives' debate: a critical review of the evidence. *British Journal of Educational Technology*, 39(5), 775–786.

Clark, W., Logan, K., Luckin, R., Mee, A. and Oliver, M., 2009. Beyond Web 2.0: mapping the technology landscapes of young learners. *Journal of Computer Assisted Learning*, 25(1), 56–69.

Dirckinck-Holmfeld, L., 2002. Designing virtual learning environments based on problem oriented project pedagogy. In: L. Dirckinck-Holmfeld and B. Fibiger, eds. *Learning in virtual environments*. Frederiksberg, Denmark: Samfundslitteratur Press, 31–54.

Jones, C. and Shao, B., 2011. *The net generation and digital natives: implications for higher education*. York, UK: Higher Education Academy.

Kolmos, A., Fink, F. K. and Krogh, L., 2004. *The Aalborg PBL model – progress, diversity and challenges*. Aalborg: Aalborg University Press.

Luckin, R., Clark, W., Graber, R., Logan, K., Mee, A. and Oliver, M., 2009. Do Web 2.0 tools really open the door to learning? Practices, perceptions and profiles of 11–16-year-old students. *Learning, Media and Technology*, 34(2), 87–104.

Nicolajsen, H. W., 2012. Changing the rules of the game – experiences with Web 2.0 learning in higher education. In: V. Hodgson, C. Jones, M. De Laat, D. McConnell, T. Ryberg, and P. Sloep, eds. *Proceedings of the Eighth International Conference on Networked Learning*, 2–4 April 2012, Maastricht, Maastricht School of Management, 551–558.

6

PROFESSIONAL LEARNING AND A NATIONAL COMMUNITY OF PRACTICE FOR TEACHERS LEADING LOCAL CURRICULUM CHANGE

Lynn Robinson and Jaime Metcher

Overview

Leading Curriculum Change (LCC) is a Flagship Professional Learning Program commissioned by the Australian Institute for Teaching and School Leadership (AITSL). It is an online learning program incorporating a community of practice. Its purpose is to provide those classroom teachers who have key roles in curriculum innovation and change in their schools with the skills and confidence to lead local curriculum change initiatives. The context in which the program was commissioned was the introduction of an Australian Curriculum, a curriculum change challenge itself, the adoption of which is occurring at different rates in different Australian states. The LCC program was designed and developed by a team at the University of Queensland, with the School of Education providing the LCC curriculum and content expertise and the Centre for Innovation in Professional Learning (CIPL) providing the educational architecture and program design expertise.

The operational life of the Leading Curriculum Change program is anticipated to be close to two years with a reach of 2,000 teachers. The number of active participants averages between 700 and 800 at any time. They come from a range of school contexts; from government, religious and independent schools and all stages of schooling from early childhood to the end of secondary. To participate in the program, teachers are either nominated by their principals or self-selected with the approval of their principals. They undertake the program on the basis that they will apply their learning as leaders of local curriculum change projects, both during their involvement in the program and beyond. No prerequisite level of skill or experience with curriculum change is expected from participants. These two assumptions – that participants will be expected to take a lead role in planning and implementing change projects but that they may also have significant knowledge and skills gaps in this area – drive the design of the program.

The program has a number of innovative features. First, it is almost entirely online, and for many participants this is their first experience of online learning. Second, it is highly flexible, allowing participating teachers to set their own learning objectives, create their own learning pathways, set their own timetable and sequencing, and dip in and out of the program as it suits their professional and personal circumstances. Third, the educational design of the program reinforces to participants the importance of an iterative approach to planning and implementing curriculum change.

Participants begin the program by undertaking structured learning through a range of modules on topics related to curriculum innovation, leadership and teamwork, and change management techniques. In one particular module participants are also exposed to the vision and background behind the development of the Australian Curriculum. The scope, content and learning objectives of all of the modules were developed in consultation with stakeholders and representatives from the target participant group.

The program design anticipates that, through the completion of their chosen modules, participants will acquire the necessary knowledge, skills and problem-solving techniques to formulate a project plan for their local curriculum change initiative. It is expected that the plan will have been developed in conjunction with a local team in the participant's workplace. The draft plan is then subjected to review by two randomly selected peers (other program participants who have also drafted a plan). After reviewing the feedback from their two peers and an opportunity to make amendments, the plans are made available to all participants by means of a searchable projects database.

The sharing of plans is one of the ways the program design encourages participants to see themselves as members of a national community of practice. A further feature that supports the fostering of a community of practice is the inclusion of a community forum where participants have an opportunity to generate sub-communities around special interest areas. A few participants (about 80) have had the opportunity to meet face-to-face at a national learning convention.

Participants receive a Certificate of Completion if they complete all the elements of the program. This would take the typical participant as many as 60 hours of effort. Half of this time is attributed to completion of the online activities and the other half to workplace activities. For those who are interested, there is an opportunity to complete an academic portfolio, based on the program activities, for credit towards university postgraduate programs.

Leading Curriculum Change is designed to provide a professional learning experience for teachers, but its ultimate goal is national capacity development in the profession as a whole. Its underlying design intent is to facilitate the dissemination of ideas and approaches beyond the immediate learning experiences of registered participants (Figure 6.1). While the program content and activities explicitly address the development of teachers' own skills and confidence as curriculum leaders, the program design emphasizes the importance of participants' application of learned knowledge and skills to their workplaces and broader school communities. These design goals drive the architecture of the network and its designed elements.

Set Design

The set design anticipates that participants will act in their physical workplaces as well as in the designed digital space. In the digital space the designed elements are conceptualized as workspaces: spaces for learning, for project planning and action, and for seeking support from and supporting others in the program. A 'dashboard' home page brings together the designed elements of the program. Here, form follows function, and there are four main areas that reflect the four main modes of participant action in the program. They are:

1. structured learning (acquiring the knowledge and practicing the skills underpinning leading curriculum change);
2. working on the curriculum change project both in the online space and in the teacher's workplace;
3. participating in the networked community of practice (exposing project work, reviewing the work of others, and sharing resources, issues and solutions); and
4. administration (business processes and support services).

The set design assumes that participating teachers will have a PC or tablet and web browser with which to access the program online. No other specific tools are assumed. It is a requirement of participation that teachers have a sponsoring school principal and that they are in a position to collaborate with colleagues in their school to plan and later execute a curriculum innovation. A shared space for working with this local team is also assumed but no specific requirements are assumed for this space. Unless they also register with the program (which is not expected), the local team does not have access to the online community directly.

1. Structured Learning Space Design

The online learning space operates as a typical e-learning space, with structured sequences of designed tasks based on a toolkit of text and multimedia presentations, quizzes and polls and discussions. The link between the online learning spaces and the offline learning spaces occurs in the form of the downloadable tools and resources. These are provided for participants to share and use with their teaching

FIGURE 6.1 Program workspaces

colleagues back in the workplace. As the aim of Leading Curriculum Change is to support national capacity development and local action, the facilitation of the free exchange of resources and tools between the networked community and the workplace, in both directions, is considered to be an essential feature of the program design.

The online learning space goes beyond just assembling pieces from a fairly standard toolkit, however, as it also incorporates some critical behavioral and social enablers. Some features of the learning space are dedicated to enabling incremental engagement and easy re-engagement. These include fine-grained recording and display of where the user is up to, and grouping of activities by learning objective rather than by modality. For example, a discussion is enabled by a single discussion thread embedded in the activity sequence rather than appearing as a component of a multi-topic, multi-threaded discussion board.

Modules are made up of a sequenced set of tasks (units) each of which takes between 5 and 20 minutes to complete. The designed tasks may be expository material (e.g. reading or lectures), case- or problem-based scenarios (i.e. requiring the exercise of professional judgment and group discussions), tasks designed to enable translation to practice/action, and group discussion and problem-solving. Wherever possible, tools and templates for future action are included.

Each of the 12 modules, if experienced as a whole module, takes an estimated two hours to complete.

All parts of the design, including the set design, were informed by a consultative process that engaged and analyzed the target professionals. Representative teachers from the target group came together with the design team to workshop the learning objectives for the program and the scenarios and hypothetical characters for the case-based learning, as well as to advise on the authentic language and attitudes of the target group. Subtle set design elements, such as the 'look and feel' of the interface and the rendering of the cartoon personas of the hypothetical characters, depend on this process. This co-design process is part of a standard development methodology used by the CIPL design team. The rationale for this approach is that professional learning (for system capacity development) should be deeply embedded in context and directly applicable to practice. Without the collaboration with target professionals, at the very least in these aspects of the design, the program may not be impactful.

In addition to the internal relationships within the learning group, the learning space embodies the relationship of the group to the subject matter or practice challenge the education is trying to explore. The collaborative design process identifies entrenched attitudes and predispositions within the profession and these are then challenged or exploited in the set material. Thus the framing and phrasing of the static (in the sense of being statically published) subject material is guided by much more than the bare facts of the material. Case studies are played out by hypothetical characters that transcend the realistic to approach the status of archetypes, often provoking a visceral sense of recognition in the learners.

The overall result is to produce a set design that, when experienced by the target learner, promotes connectedness to the subject matter and puts the learner into a collaborative mental stance from the outset. An interesting side-effect of this design approach is that these design features can be almost imperceptible to an observer who does not share the sensitivities and concerns of the target group.

2. Design for Project Action

The space for project planning and action is conceptualized as both being within the program and in the workspace of the local teams led by the participating teacher. There is a personal project planning and reporting workspace, which is a private space for the participant. This workspace has a structure consistent with the project planning techniques taught in the program modules. Each step of the planning process also has a space that has links to the related learning materials, standards and guidelines. The separate steps or components of the project planning and documenting can be displayed as one whole document and converted to PDF format for sharing with others. The resources and tools can be downloaded for sharing and working with local colleagues.

3. Design for a Community of Practice

Steps to foster and facilitate a community of practice occur from the very beginning of participants' engagement with the program. Welcome discussions, polls and specific issue discussions are incorporated throughout the structured learning modules. Via the program dashboard, participants also access the Community Forum and relevant spaces for emergent community activities as they start to apply their learning to specific curriculum change initiatives.

At the outset, the Community Forum was the most experimental part of the design, and as such it was designed with only very basic structures and tools, using Drupal. It commenced with only one general forum space, itself comprising instructions, lists of participants, a discussion board, a library of resources (to be provided by the community) and the profile of the moderator. The design approach assumed that further spaces and features could be deployed by the program management team as the community activities emerged.

On the same sub-dashboard as the personal project workspace, participants also have a workspace for providing peer reviews to colleagues, and can view the project library that contains all of the completed project plans from the participant community.

4. Design for Administration

The last space linked to the dashboard provides participants and the program management team with the information and tools to support participants' progress to completion. It includes helpdesk contacts, progress reports, transcripts and business processes to apply for and receive various levels of certification.

Epistemic Design

The program is fundamentally an opportunity for action learning, supported by a community of practice, and opportunities for up-skilling in specific professional competencies that underpin leading curriculum change. The reflective learning/ action learning loop operates at all scales within the program. At the largest scale, the whole program is the initiating step of an action learning loop that will complete its cycle long after the program is finished, that is, when the real curriculum change project has been implemented and evaluated. At smaller scales, an action learning loop around formulating, reviewing and revising a project plan exists entirely within the program, and reflective learning loops exist down to the module and individual case study levels.

The richness of the set design somewhat blurs the boundaries between set and epistemic designs. A key part of the facilitator model, as described above, is that the facilitator 'speaks' through a set of pre-populated on-screen messages that vary by context and by the learner's state. Much of the task coordination load is taken

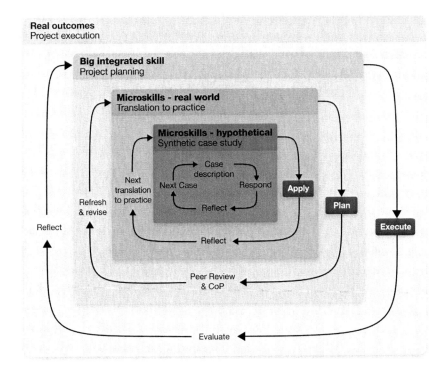

FIGURE 6.2 Action/reflective learning loops

up by these messages. In addition, the elements in the set design described above set the scene for the epistemic design and prime the participants for engagement in action learning in three ways:

- First, the set design recruits them into the learning group, at an almost subconscious level, by strongly identifying the learning group with their existing professional peer group.
- Second, the problems being addressed are 'their' problems. This is achieved first via highly resonant archetypes whose hypothetical practice problems are presented for group solutions, then later by their 'own choice' of translation to practice activities and, finally, by the real-world curriculum change project.
- Third, by putting the participant into a relational stance from the outset ('There are real people – *my people* – in my computer'), invitations to collaboration, such as discussions embedded in the structured learning activity sequence, are rarely refused. Discussion participation rates are about 85–90 percent.

While there is a great degree of flexibility, the success of the program depends on large numbers of participants engaging in all three ways of acting – learning, doing and supporting others. Hence, the first task, and the only mandatory task, is an orientation module (about an hour to complete) in which participants have the program explained and their commitment to the three ways of acting sought. About one-third of all people who register do not proceed further with the program after exploring the orientation module.

The tasks within all the structured learning modules, but particularly the first four modules, were designed to reflect the three ways of working in the program. Each module includes reading, listening to or watching expository material to scaffold learning. This is essentially an individual activity. Each module also includes one or more group tasks in which a scenario or issue is explored and discussed. Participants have to make individual professional judgments and are exposed to the views of others. Group members are able to discuss issues arising, or contribute solutions and personal experiences as reflection. Finally, each module closes with a specific challenge to each participant to reflect on and document how they will use their learning in their professional practice. This is called the 'Translation to Practice Activity'. Some of these tasks are drafts of components of project planning while some are less closely linked to the specifics of project action. All, however, are direct links to a form of local action.

The group work embedded in the structured learning modules is the partici-pants' earliest experience of the community of practice. In the group activities within the structured learning modules, the specific task is set by the learning designer and group discussion is kept on task. In contrast, outside the modules, the community activity is co-designed with and by the participants and is much more free ranging as a result (more on this later).

The other two epistemic tasks for participants revolve around the individual curriculum change project. As most participants have had no previous experience in project planning, one structured learning module is devoted to this technique. The task at the end of this module is to attempt a very rough first draft of a project plan using a short form template. Almost all participants do this module before attempting to draft a plan in the project online planning workspaces. The online project planning workspace includes online writing tools in the form of project planning templates and peer review criteria linked to the relevant modules, resources and tools, together forming a visible reference framework for the knowledge and skills surrounding leading curriculum change. Participating teach-ers are encouraged to draft their project plans in the workplace in collaboration with the team of colleagues who will be involved in the execution of the plan. In order to facilitate this local collaborative activity, tools to work locally, and also downloadable versions of the project plan as documented in the online project workspace, are provided for program participants to share with colleagues.

Once a good draft of the participant's local curriculum change plan has been completed, it may be submitted for peer review. Two other participants who have successfully completed a plan are then randomly allocated to provide feedback anonymously to the author. All project authors are allocated two reviews in return. This task is structured by means of a criteria-based score sheet with free comment sections for each criterion. Feedback from participants indicates that reviewing the plans of their peers against the criteria is the task that most underpins participants' confidence in their own new skills of project planning. The workflow of peer reviewing is managed by the system so that participants know by email when they have a peer review in their project workspace 'in tray' and, in turn, the project author can track the progress of his or her reviews. The system reallocates project plans to other reviewers if the review time frames are not met.

All tasks in the program are voluntary beyond the orientation module. Knowledge of how to optimize the learning experience and completion of the project planning objectives come from the designed tasks and instructions that are embedded as closely as possible to each of the working spaces. Beyond the individual's personal knowledge and actions, the group is invited to form a community. Many teachers already know what this means and already participate in local learning communities. For many others, this is a new experience. To facilitate the development of this community of practice, and in addition to the orientation module that exposes participants to the set goals, tasks and roles of participants in this particular community, there is a structured learning module that teaches the core concepts of learning communities. The participating teachers are then invited to co-design the Community Forum space and set specific tasks for their community of practice. A general forum is provided as the starting point. It is very simple – a threaded discussion area, a moderator and some instructions on how the tool/interface works. The moderator initiated the first discussions, which took the form of troubleshooting about the program and the work of participants within the program. Everything else that currently exists in this space has emerged during the life of the program.

Social Design

The basis for all of the social design in the program lies in the *Essential Eight* design pattern for groups used by the design team since 1998 (Robinson *et al.* 2011). The *Essential Eight* are explicitly incorporated into the design of all aspects of the Leading Curriculum Change program at both program level (i.e. the whole community of practice) and at each of the collaborative subgroup levels (i.e. structured learning modules, special interest groups).

According to the *Essential Eight* design pattern, the design to enable functional productive groups should include:

1. a visible, active leader or leaders
2. a means of knowing who is included in the group
3. an explicit mission, aim or objective shared by the group

4. a shared view of the 'rules' of engaging to achieve the objectives
5. appropriate (shared) resources
6. common spaces in which to conduct the business of the group
7. an understanding of the timing of the activities
8. some social capital (shared language, culture or experiences) on which to build.

Some of the *Essential Eight* are inherent in this group at its commencement. For example, participating teachers are aware of the criteria for participation and can infer that all members of the community of practice are teaching professionals, satisfying design element 2, membership, above. In relation to 8, social capital, it may be assumed that teachers share a great deal of professional language, culture and experience. According to the *Essential Eight* design pattern, the designers must, however, supply any of the eight that cannot be relied upon as being a given, while augmenting any that are implicit or inherent. This is the reason for the extensive consultative process and collaborative design methodology described earlier.

At the whole-of-program level, Leading Curriculum Change, as a national community of practice, is a very large online group to which the *Essential Eight* has been applied. The shared purpose is to inspire, engage and support teachers to lead curriculum change in local contexts. The leadership role is taken by the Program Director, whose persona and dynamic messages appear on the dashboard and other 'plenary session' spaces elsewhere in the program. The Program Manager is a support leader whose role is administration and logistics. Both the Program Director and the Program Manager are able to make announcements from spaces within the program dashboard and also email the participants. Participants are members of the community and formally sign up to the rights and responsibilities of membership – these being to share professional experiences and knowledge, and to support each other by providing a formal peer review on request. There is also an explicit commitment to standards of professional conduct covering respect, privacy and guidelines for not identifying or referencing people or situations without express permission.

At the structured learning level, the design of the modules is analogous to a set of small group workshops within the larger community. Again, the *Essential Eight* design pattern is the basis of this social design as it is at the program level. Each module has explicit learning objectives set for the groups' achievement.

Having been elucidated from the consultative phase of the design process, parts of the social design are already fixed into the set design. Participants are greeted and guided at all times by an on-screen facilitator, a real person carefully chosen not just for their personal qualities, but also for the place they occupy in the 'tribal society' of the group of learners. Depending on the group, a peer, an elder or (on rare occasions) an external expert might suit best. Common language, in-jokes and scenarios that resonate with the practitioner are all used to place the learner into a relationship with the learning group, well before any explicit collaboration is called for.

The experts' contributions are considered resources rather than leader-like instruction. The sequence of activities and steps within each activity, as designed by the learning designer, flows smoothly from screen to screen, with group work integrated into the flow. Instructions are provided by a facilitator on every screen. While the Facilitator is a real person, the facilitator's script and likeness or persona is pre-loaded into most screens. Analysis of the role of any small group workshop leader will show that much of their contribution is logistic advice, context setting, encouragement and instructions. This is the part of the Facilitator's role that can be anticipated and pre-loaded into the module screens. The script varies based on the 'state' of the user looking at the screen. For example, if a participant is viewing a discussion to which they have not yet contributed, they are exhorted to do so, but if they have already contributed they are asked to reflect on the responses and the discussion generated.

The Facilitator has training in online facilitation and in their role and responsibilities. He or she contributes personally in the group discussions, responding to the emergent issues in the discussion and keeping the group on task. The Facilitators are the first line of contact if participants are struggling with the learning or the tasks, but they do not act as expert tutors. Program issues are posted into the community forum and dealt with as a group concern with responses coming from other group members including subject matter experts.

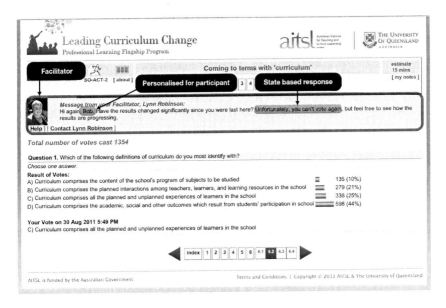

FIGURE 6.3 Facilitator at work – poll result

The cohorts are determined entirely by timing, in that each discussion thread is limited to 10 entries displayed (with the previous ones all available as an archive) so that participants experience the group activity of other participants whose contributions are roughly coincident in time with theirs. From the perspective of the Facilitator this is experienced as 'rolling cohorts'. The first group discussion in the program is in the orientation module and asks participants for an introduction and reflection on what they hope to learn from the program. This is an important part of group formation and making explicit who is a member of each 'rolling cohort'.

In the less structured community-of-practice workspaces, a moderator leads the Community Forum. The moderator is drawn from the leadership group (i.e. Program Director, Program Manager and peer Facilitators) and changes occasionally. Subject matter experts drop in regularly, and at the request of the moderator, to respond to emergent issues. All participants are members of the Community Forum and can contribute and start new threads or topics. Members can add resources to the community library by attaching them to the discussion.

Set, Epistemic and Social Co-creation and Co-configuration Activities

Before the online program is open to participants, the only content in the structured learning modules of the program is the expository material, the stimulus material for the case discussions and the instructions on pathways and administrative processes. In the project space and community forums, there is only the starting advice, the supporting resources and instructions. Once the program is peopled by facilitators and other leaders, and by the participating teachers, the environment comes to life. Case-based learning relies on the participants providing candidate solutions and discussing options at decision points. The participants vote on options, post justifications about their choices and critique the judgment of others. They reflect on the expository material and its application to their schools using stimulus questions posed by the Facilitators. Then they create their own plans of action in their notes and translation to practice activities, which are recorded. The participation rate in discussions is very high, with almost all participants contributing to discussions in the structured learning modules.

In the Community Forum participants pose problems, provide advice to other members and seek the input of the expert mentors who respond to questions posed by participants. They add links to useful resources or attach files that are listed in the community resource library. This process of interacting and collaborating, sharing and critiquing builds a common and extensive body of knowledge available to all members of the community. Catalogues and search engines facilitate resource discovery and retrieval. The most sophisticated product available to all members of the community of practice is the database of curriculum change project plans authored by participants in conjunction with their local teams. After the first year of operation, approximately 10 percent of the active participants had published a project plan into the community library, with about 30 percent in the process of drafting one.

As the designers anticipated, some necessary skills for leading curriculum change are more foreign to the participating teachers than others. As part of the planned architecture, augmenting material has been created in response to the demands of the community. Some of this has been informally provided through the forums, some has been integrated into the modules or resources and one additional topic has been created in the community space to assist the community to improve the standard of project plans and reviews. More confident participants have been co-creating this material informally alongside formally produced material from the subject matter experts.

The general forum has spawned five separate special interest groups, each of which has a membership of approximately 10 percent of the whole active community. These special interest groups were anticipated in the designed architecture and sit within the community-of-practice workspace. They are rather less active than the general forum, possibly due both to lower member numbers and to a less disciplined approach to design – some design parameters have been left in the hands of the emergent groups. So, for example, while the *Essential Eight* design pattern has informed the design of the space and some elements have been included, such as leadership (there is a moderator) and the explicit membership listing, the goals and expectation of members are left to each group to define and are much less clear than for the general forum. The overall rate at which participants contribute at least once to the community of practice forums, not including case-based learning, is about 4 in 10 active participants. There are some indications that some participants are starting to attempt to form some offline networks with face-to-face meetings in local areas. There is also an emerging trend for groups of teachers who are working together in a school on a curriculum change initiative to join up as a group and do the program together.

One of the interesting observations about the learners' behavior is the way they infer more structure or rules from the architecture than was intended by the designers. The most striking example of this is in the learning pathways that the participating teachers follow. The set and epistemic design of the structured learning activities are that each participant will exercise his/her judgment to determine which modules will be most useful, and at what time, in relation to drafting a project plan. The orientation module and the dashboard design both attempt to emphasize this. The dashboard, however, includes a tab under which there is a list of modules so that participants can quickly access any one of these and see their progress status for each module. Analysis of the pattern of usage shows that, in about 90 percent of cases, participants do the modules in the specific order of this catalogue list, rather than following the task direction to personalize their learning pathway.

Finally, some of the most important co-creation activities occur outside the program and will continue beyond its lifetime. In addition to the local study groups referred to above, every teacher in the program has a sponsor in their school hierarchy. Participants are explicitly guided by the program towards setting up local project teams and stakeholder groups, and to engage their local communities. Not all participants will do so, nor are they expected to, but even those who do not are better informed and prepared to participate in others' efforts. As a relatively large-scale intervention, the program is intended to have a ripple effect well beyond its direct participants. In addition to an intense engagement with a small group of committed change agents, a direct effect of the program is the creation of a larger second tier consisting of less committed program participants, and an even larger third tier of indirectly affected non-participants. In this sense, as well as producing valuable learning outcomes for its participants, the program is also working towards a system-level intervention aimed at the whole teaching profession.

Growth, Development and Evolution

Almost all of the emergent issues have been related to the way the design facilitates participants moving between modes of operating and between workspaces. The structured learning spaces and activities work well for online learning and group work, but many participants wanted more flexible modes of undertaking personal learning. (That is, they wanted the flexibility offered by mobile devices, rather than flexibility in the order in which they took the modules.) Mobile device solutions were not part of the original design but have since been deployed because of demand. Many participants also wanted to work offline with printable notes in addition to audio with slides as their preferred mode of learning, so these are now also provided.

The experience of participants integrating learning into project planning showed that better links between the learning resources and the project workspace were required, so these were embedded in each section of the project planning workspace. Even more usefully, printable versions of the key resources, such as the standards for each section, were added so that participants could work in the screen-based workspace, while referring to the printed guidelines on the desk beside them.

In order to bridge the gap between the online workspaces for project planning and the workplaces in which participants collaborate with their curriculum change project teams, the original set of designed tools and templates has also had to be augmented. Most of these are very simple, such as blank forms and templates in Word format, and the facility to make print files of project plan drafts from the online workspace. While these objects are simply reproductions of the web-based working spaces and tools, participants report that these simple resources have significantly improved their experience and productivity overall.

Abstracting and Synthesis

Professional learning is social, embedded in context, and focused towards practical action. The success of the Leading Curriculum Change program as a learning and productive community is largely due to the use of design patterns that have emerged from dozens of professional learning program designs over 15 years of experience by the CIPL design team. The *Essential Eight* design pattern, as described earlier, informs the architecture of the program at all levels. This design pattern calls for the explicit setting out of the key social, epistemic and spatial elements that support successful, productive groups. A major driver of the design was the understanding of the learners derived from a methodologically rigorous consultative process. This provided a rich insight into the participants, not just as generic learners or even adult learners, but as specific professionals (teachers) engaged in this specific problem (leading curriculum change) in a variety of local settings.

Critical to the success of this program is the integrated design approach to social, epistemic and set design. There are many examples of this, but the carefully selected and then largely pre-programmed facilitator is perhaps most emblematic of this integration. Another example of the integrated approach is that the set, epistemic and social design runs as seamlessly as possible across online and local workplace settings. For example, structured learning is followed by translation to practice activities and then local project action. Workflow is designed in. For example, learning modules flow in tabbed steps with pocket discussions embedded in the flow. The importance of this integrated design approach is underscored by the effect when it goes wrong – in this case, when the subtle visual clue of a list of modules influenced the behavior of the participants more than the instruction to personalize the sequence based on learning needs.

Because there are three main modes of working for participants in the program – learning, planning for action and acting in the workplace, and participating in a national community of practice – there are three main sub-architectures with an integrating dashboard. However, each of these proposed tasks is intimately related to, and indeed is intended to be integrated into, the other. The challenge inherent in this complexity was how to provide separation of tasks and spaces for clarity and focus, while facilitating movement between spaces and work modes. There were two design approaches used to address this problem. One was provided by the design of the dashboard and workspaces, which attempts to both separate and cross-link, minimizing any distraction from task, while keeping useful resources close at hand. The second was practical and sometimes overlooked in online design – providing portable tools and resources that can be exported and deployed in ways that are practical to participants in personal and workplace settings. Common office file types and printable artifacts have proved invaluable to the teachers participating in this program.

Overall, the key success factor in this case study is that there is a discipline and methodology of design that drives the technology and tools, rather than the other way around.

Acknowledgments

The authors wish to acknowledge the Australian Institute for Teaching and School Leadership (AITSL). *Leading Curriculum Change* was developed by AITSL in partnership with the University of Queensland and with funding provided by the Australian Government.

Reference

Robinson, L., Bianco, N., Hendy, R. and Metcher, J., 2011. A design pattern language for effective professional development programs for clinicians: a decade of design-based research. *Design Principles and Practices*, 5(4), 553–570.

7

ONE LAPTOP PER CHILD (OLPC)

A Small Computer to Serve a Big Cause

Martin Parisio, Kate Thompson, Tracy Richardson and Rangan Srikhanta

Overview

The One Laptop Per Child[1] (OLPC) Foundation (2013) is a not-for-profit organization originating from research conducted at the Media Lab (Papert 1980, Kay and Goldberg 1977) at the Massachusetts Institute of Technology (MIT). At the heart of the OLPC program lies the desire to provide rugged, low-cost, low-powered, connected laptops with customized software to the children of the developing and disadvantaged regions of the world. It is hoped that the program will both stimulate and encourage collaborative, joyful and self-empowered learning for all children, everywhere.

OLPC Australia[2] (2013) is a branch of the worldwide OLPC Foundation that manages the implementation of the XO laptop program, open to all Australian schools with children between the ages of 4 and 15. The program involves the distribution of XO laptops and the provision of ongoing support to Australian teachers, as they implement and use the laptops in classroom activities. The XO laptops are designed within a tight budget to provide reliable Internet connectivity in a robust casing, and are preconfigured with specialized software that enables social collaboration via the Internet and laptop to laptop. XO software consists of tools for exploring and expressing, rather than tools for instruction. Children and learning are at the heart of this network.

This chapter discusses the OLPC Yammer network, an online environment created to support the XO laptop program by nurturing exchanges amongst teachers about their experiences with the program, the laptop and related classroom activities. The XO laptop (Figure 7.1) needs to be seen as a significant element in the OLPC Yammer network and aspects of its use are the focus of this discussion.

In the digital space, the OLPC Yammer network is supported by the Yammer platform and initiation into the network is facilitated through the One Education Program (2013) (see Figure 7.1), which provides compulsory training leading to OLPC certification for school leaders, teachers, technicians and teaching assistants, and voluntary training for parents and students. The One Education Program addresses a range of topics, including pedagogy and technical support, and formally introduces teachers to the OLPC Yammer network. This training course takes 10 to 15 hours to complete and is delivered via a Moodle-based learning management system. Once teachers have completed the training course, they are expected to create a Yammer account and join the OLPC Yammer network as part of their continued learning and as a way of connecting to colleagues around Australia. Completion of the One Education Program is a pre-requisite for the distribution of the XO laptops. *In the physical space*, elements in the classroom environment and the XO laptops comprise the setting for the teacher's and students' activities, and provide the subject matter that enables the social interactions between network participants. As indicated in Figure 7.1, and as will be further discussed in this chapter, most elements in the set design of the network are tied to the Yammer platform and the XO laptops, whereas its epistemic design is tied to the One Education Program.

The OLPC Yammer network has been running since 2011, and currently has more than 300 participants. Most are directly involved in teaching, overseeing

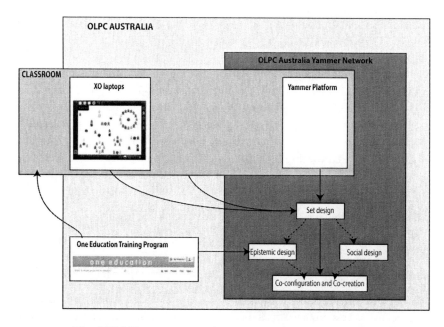

FIGURE 7.1 The OLPC Yammer Network

the use of XO laptops in their respective educational institutions. The 'off-the-shelf' Yammer platform is designed to mediate social activity in professional settings, and is optimized for file sharing, project management and team productivity. The OLPC Australia instance of Yammer customizes the platform to provide a supportive environment for community building, sharing of experiences around the XO laptops, including implementation, and ongoing educational practice in Australian schools.

The network offers local and regional communication and an opportunity to connect to teachers at a national level. In Australia, public (school-level) education is a *state* responsibility, though there have recently been moves towards a national (Australian) curriculum. At present, state governments, each with their own education department and curriculum, are in charge of state schools. In addition to this, there is a sizable Catholic Education Office, organized nationally, and many independent or private schools administered by autonomous school boards under state and national guidelines. While the OLPC Australia program is open to any school, the initial focus of the program was on schools in remote, rural and/or disadvantaged communities. The advantages of participating in the national OLPC Yammer network are perhaps of higher significance to those in isolated communities, however all participants could derive benefit from joining the network. At its heart, the network provides a platform for communication: a shared space for Australian teachers to connect and exchange experiences, irrespective of the type of school in which they work or the region in which they are located.

In this chapter, we analyze the OLPC Yammer network, drawing on qualitative data collected during interviews with an OLPC Australia representative, a teacher, a State education department representative and a computer specialist. All of these participants contribute directly to the OLPC Yammer network. Pseudonyms are used in all cases. Our analysis also takes into account our observations of the members' activities and the network environment.

Set Design

The set design of the OLPC Yammer network includes elements in the physical (e.g. the XO laptop) and digital spaces (e.g. the Yammer platform and online resources). The material elements are found in the classrooms of participating schools and in the physical space where network members work and learn. The XO laptops play an important role because their use is the 'object of discussion' of network participants; the laptops are what (initially) bring these individuals together. They enable the exchange of information and creation of resources and knowledge, related to pedagogy and learning through the XO laptops. Internet connection and XO software tools enable students and teachers to access visualizations of peer group configurations and activities (see Figure 7.1). Through these visualizations XO users can identify other users with similar interests for future collaborations. This particular design intention, of identifying and bringing together people with similar interests, is also the focus of the OLPC Yammer network.

As with many social networking platforms, Yammer software may be downloaded as an application for desktop computers, smartphones and tablet computers for use with various operating systems including Apple MacOS and iOS, Google Android and Microsoft Windows. Once installed these applications connect to the Yammer web server, allowing users to access the same content from a fixed desktop computer or a mobile handheld computer via subtly different interfaces and subsequent system processes. These different options for accessing the network enable flexibility and allow participants to choose their preferred device and location for connection. As a result, participants can, for example, customize the degree of visibility the network will have for them. The passage below, extracted from an interview with a teacher, illustrates her appreciation of this design element:

> It does help if you install the desktop version of Yammer on your computer because then if you have it set up so that it starts when you ... start your computer, it pops up and it tells you if there's been any activity on the network. So I find that that's helpful, rather than having to go to the website and check whether anything has happened. If it's on your desktop you're more likely to check and use it.

The rationale behind the selection of Yammer, as the social networking platform for the program, was to reduce potential barriers to participation. Its simple interface and similarity to other platforms, such as Facebook, was seen by the OLPC organizers as an advantage. The interface provides a profile, newsfeed, instant messaging and 'who's online' sections. The 'familiarity' of these features is acknowledged by the OLPC Australia representative, and is seen as a factor that contributes to an undemanding user experience: 'You post something and something gets responded to'. Features that support the setup of membership (e.g. the profile page, and being able to 'follow' members), ongoing communication with other members (e.g. the newsfeed, and the synchronous chat tool) and the identification and retrieval of knowledge stored on the network (e.g. tagging digital artifacts) are all part of any Yammer environment. Each of these supports and enables collaboration, communication and learning amongst participants. Of interest is the way in which these elements of the set design relate to the epistemic and social design intentions, specific to the OLPC Yammer network, and how these, in turn, enable and support the activities of network participants.

When a participant first joins the network, they complete a profile page with their name, affiliations, skills, interests, experiences and a photo. The profile page acts as a digital representation of the member, who may customize 'their space' by uploading digital artifacts. Other network members may view a profile via a link on the participant's name. The ability to 'follow' other participants enables each member to choose whom he or she connects with, and in doing so, to form smaller personal networks. When a participant posts to the newsfeed or shares a file, all 'followers' receive a notification, which can be delivered in a variety of forms, but most commonly via email.

The newsfeed is the primary means for keeping up to date with network activity. Similar to the 'tweet' feed in the Twitter system, or the 'update status' feed that is part of Facebook, the Yammer newsfeed facilitates the speedy turnaround of a reply to a comment or question posted to the network. The Yammer system also pushes popular, or 'trending' posts. A participant may start a conversation by posting a general message to the newsfeed, visible to all members. A list of all posts is created on the webpage, with the most recent positioned towards the top. Participants can comment on any post, and these comments, or other interactions (such as 'liking' it) are displayed under the original message. As new posts are created the older ones move towards the bottom of the page, and are eventually no longer displayed, but remain accessible through archive and search features. Provision is made for synchronous communication through a chat tool housed on the bottom right of the web browser channel, giving participants the opportunity to maintain one-to-one conversations alongside asynchronous group conversations. This flexibility, which allows participants to communicate in various ways, and with low barriers to entry, is discussed further in the 'Abstracting and Synthesis' section of this chapter.

Another interesting element in set design is the tagging of both posts and replies to the newsfeed, and other digital artifacts. Tagging is useful for the identification and retrieval of knowledge created in the network, for example allowing teachers to search for ideas on how others have dealt with an issue they are facing, or for inspiration, by topic, on task design. Tagging relies on participants assigning one or more keywords to a digital artifact, creating categories, which enable the search function and facilitate data management for archival purposes. In addition, it simplifies the process of downloading and moving digital artifacts from one computer system to another, providing portability across platforms. Furthermore, as the network grows, members generate a framework of tags (keywords) in which knowledge and digital artifacts are stored, and this framework shifts according to the needs of the participants, contributing to flexibility in the network.

The OLPC Yammer extends beyond the technical specifications of the Yammer system itself, complementing its use with other online resources such as YouTube, Facebook, WordPress and Moodle. Through either the embedded or link feature participants can connect with other systems. The ease with which participants can access other online resources reinforces, once again, the value placed on flexibility.

Social Design

Individuals can customize the social groups they join (in the groups section), and choose other members to follow (in the newsfeed), or whom they interact with (via the chat tool). A pop-up window is displayed on the bottom of the screen, revealing the members who are 'online now', with a green dot indicating those who are available for chat. *People you may know* are suggested, as are *groups of interest*. The newsfeed allows members to reply to the status updates, resulting in a discussion more closely related to a traditional discussion forum. However, members can also 'like' a posting, or share it with their own personal network. Members have the option to add topics, and keep up to date via messages sent to their inbox, viewing a conversation, bookmarking the collection or requesting an email from the author of the post. These design elements once again enable flexibility in use, and the ability for each person to configure their preferred types of interactions with others in the network. These elements realize OLPC Australia's design intention of providing a space for shared conversations about the program. As voiced in an interview with an OLPC Australia representative: 'We really needed a way for teachers to talk to each other'.

Participants in the network include OLPC pedagogical and technical experts, representatives from State education departments, researchers and teachers. Subgroups tend to be a space for focused conversations, such as 'community engagement' or 'XO teaching resources', on topics that vary from technical and pedagogical issues to personal experiences and educational resources. Teachers often join the network in the role of a 'learner' as part of their activities in the One Education training program. This initial role, however, tends to change over time as a result of the accumulation of expertise, so the boundaries between being 'a learner' or 'an expert' eventually become blurred.

The variety of professional backgrounds ensures peer support for a broad range of problems and provides many opportunities for learning, in a social context that values open channels of communication and facilitates just-in-time help. The social design of the OLPC Yammer network fosters participants' easy access to OLPC organizers, educators and technicians involved in the program, besides the teachers participating in the program. As a result, the posting of a particular problem may, for example, prompt advice from technical staff at the same time as it raises awareness of that particular issue to OLPC organizers. Feedback may also be gained from other teachers who have had similar experiences within their own schools. Such a structure of communication allows teachers to receive quick feedback, from peers and/or from technical staff, and also helps OLPC staff in monitoring and evaluating the ongoing development of the program. Organizers are able to follow how teachers are using laptops and collect technical and pedagogical feedback to enhance the XO program itself. Technical staff also use the network to gather ideas for new developments in terms of XO software and other resources. And these, in turn, inform the development of improved resources and pedagogical strategies (Figure 7.2). The passage below, from an interview with a representative from an education department, illustrates the value placed on the openness in the lines of communication within network:

> It [the network] provides direct access to the One Laptop per Child organizers, so directly to the people that work with the teachers, the people that run the training courses, you know, their executive director is regularly on there, the technical director as well. So in some ways, you know, probably even easier than picking up the phone. You know that if you put a message in there, those key people will see it and that they'll respond.

Thus, the social space is grounded on a structure of communication that enables connections, sharing experiences and learning from each other. This is particularly important for those teachers in remote communities for whom information and resources may not be immediately available in their physical setting. For example, an XO laptop technician can help teachers troubleshoot when there is no one physically present to help. In addition, teachers in isolated areas can connect with teaching staff both locally and in other states. Although there are many other networks available to teachers, most are open only to those employed by their State education departments. The *national* reach of the OLPC Yammer network, and the inclusion of many professional groups, are distinctive aspects of this network.

Community building and social presence are of utmost importance to the OLPC organizers, and they take great care in providing support when it is needed. As the OLPC Australia representative noted, it 'takes some time for relationships to develop' and therefore it is important that relationships are continuously nurtured. Essentially, its social design aims to encourage fluid communication while fostering participation. Organizers of the OLPC Yammer network are mindful of the difficulties in sustaining ongoing conversations, and use several strategies to stimulate interactions, for example by personally encouraging members to post to the newsfeed, by frequently contributing to posts themselves, by commenting on milestones achieved or pointing out interesting ideas. As in any learning network, however, some members still prefer to remain less active.

Epistemic Design

The epistemic design of the OLPC Yammer network aims to encourage members' knowledge building. At the micro level this relates to classroom activities using XO laptops, and involves the storing of knowledge, resources and information about the many ways of practically implementing the program within the classroom setting. At this micro level, the focus is on knowledge and artifacts that would be of most value to teachers including practical pedagogical resources and classroom activities that may be subject matter specific, or grade specific and so on. At other times, these resources may be technical in nature, such as 'what one should do if x occurs'. At a macro level, however, knowledge building involves gathering ideas, information and requirements for the production of resources that may be used more broadly, as a way to guide the development and implementation of the XO laptop program. Examples include gathering information about difficulties teachers encounter with the implementation of the laptops, or about the types of software teachers would like to have in their classrooms. As a result, OLPC organizers are able to identify areas for future improvement and new resources. These changes are incorporated and, over time, contribute to a more effective implementation of the XO laptop program.

Most of the formal tasks that teachers are expected to complete are part of the One Education training program. Once the One Education training program is complete, teachers are encouraged to continue using the network to share pedagogical ideas and strategies, and as a way to request technical advice. The transition from the training course to the OLPC Yammer network is formalized through tasks that are part of the One Education training program – teachers are expected to sign up to the Yammer network, create a profile page and contribute an introductory message to the online community. These tasks formally introduce participants to elements of the set, epistemic and social design and mark the changeover from formal instruction to ongoing independent learning. The rationale behind these tasks is to give teachers an opportunity to experience the activities and interactions within the Yammer environment and to consider their potential value so that they can make an informed decision about whether or not they would like to make participation in the network part of their daily routine. These tasks, at the end of the One Education training program, aim at initiating conversations beyond formal training, as reported in an interview with an OLPC Australia representative:

> What we're trying to do is promote those conversations all the way through, right from the beginning of training, and beyond training because once they've finished in the Moodle course, we don't expect them necessarily to come back to it. But we do hope that they will come back to Yammer.

Pedagogical knowledge, which is the focus of this network at the micro level, is valued only insofar as it contributes to workplace knowledge. On the home page, one can always find the newsfeed latest posts, and members also have the option to respond to the question prompt: *What are you working on?* This set design feature, common in many social networking platforms, is appropriated and modified to fit a conversation about work-related subjects, thereby meeting an epistemic design intention of the network: the exchange of knowledge about work practices. As mentioned earlier in this chapter, questions can be posted to the newsfeed and to groups, and range from pedagogical ideas to specific just-in-time technical troubleshooting. These questions act as stimuli for discussion and are answered by other teachers, OLPC Australia experts and OLPC technicians. Seed questions from the organizers are often used to guide discussions and shape the online conversations, as highlighted in this quote from an interview with an OLPC Australia representative:

> It's very difficult, I think, to get teachers to talk about what goes on in their classroom because they just don't have the time, or necessarily the motivation to get online and really tell their stories. . . . really the best way for teachers to learn is to hear about what other people are doing and 'steal' their ideas . . . it's hugely powerful as a training tool for us.

In addition to asking questions, participants are expected to contribute their own knowledge by sharing ideas, pedagogical strategies, and tips and tricks via the newsfeed. Pedagogical knowledge draws upon teachers' experience in their current educational contexts. Teachers are encouraged to share successful and unsuccessful classroom practices. While contexts are often different, value is gained from exposure to teachers' practices generally, as well as to the specific use of the XO laptops and the resources available to support their practice, such as government funding.

As the material environment includes a variety of elements (such as the XO laptops, classroom configuration and location, as well as the XO laptop software and the OLPC Yammer platform), topics discussed in the network also vary. Some of these are concerned with the technical components of the XO laptop, and so the Yammer network has to facilitate easy access to troubleshooting in a safe environment. The teachers frequently move between the digital OLPC Yammer network, and the physical network of XO laptops, the classroom, students and group classes. Network participants are often able to switch between discussion of the material and digital environment, and tools, with clarity and precision.

Set, Epistemic and Social Co-creation and Co-configuration Activities

The core purpose of the OLPC Yammer network is to facilitate knowledge building in order to support the use of the XO laptops in classrooms all over Australia. This is enacted through the interplay of elements from the set, epistemic and social design. The simple act of one member posting to the newsfeed, and a second member commenting, incorporates an element of the set design (the newsfeed) with the expectation of the epistemic design that knowledge be created and accessible, and that requires social involvement, of members talking to each other. The network facilitates one-to-many and one-to-one style question-and-answer with participants building on each other's ideas and making

Jake Matthews
I just programed Lego with an #olpc XO! using Scratch - super easy
http://bit.ly/NW6r1P

Like · Reply · Share · More · July 26 at 1:45pm from IFTTT

Kitti Sonny: Next step - getting the students to do it!
August 2 at 8:07pm from Desktop · Like · Reply · Share · More

Write a reply...

FIGURE 7.2 OLPC: building an idea

recommendations drawn from personal experiences. The collective exchange of knowledge through conversation leads to new ways of knowing about technology and pedagogy, and new ways of understanding the relationship between the two. The conversation threads become digital artifacts (resources) accessible to all members, at any time. Figure 7.2 shows an example of this interplay.

Elements of the set, epistemic, and social design support the interaction that is revealed in Figure 7.2. The original post is from Jake Matthews (a teacher), and it appeared in the newsfeed. In the post, Jake shared an achievement and a link to a resource: a Scratch program that he wrote. By including a link he kept the status short and added valuable information, allowing easy access to the resource. The tags associated with the post (#olpc) appear in the message and also below the post. Both of these tags link to a collection of posts that include the same keyword. Two members replied to the post, the first (not shown here) congratulated Jake on his achievement, and included some humor. This first reply was 'liked' by two other members, including Jake, who posted the original comment. The second reply (shown in Figure 7.2) was encouraging, and added to the original idea. If uploaded, members' photos are shown next to their name (not included in Figure 7.2), as is the type of access mode. For example, 'from IFTTT' in Jake's post and 'from Desktop' in Kitti's reply indicates that the 'desktop' version of Yammer was used. Finally, the times and dates of the responses were recorded. This short excerpt demonstrates the way in which the elements of the set design facilitate social communication and how they provide insight into the location of the member posting, as well as their photo. Figure 7.2 illustrates design elements that blend aspects of set, social and epistemic design with the provision of a link to the newly created artifact, and searchable knowledge attached to that artifact using the #olpc tag.

Organizers from OLPC Australia identified the facilitation of friendly interaction as being an important objective in their design of the network.

The example shown in Figure 7.2 illustrates how these friendly interactions are realized within the environment, and it is the combined effort of many who together provide quick technical tips, useful learning tasks and important announcements. This notion is also referred to in the interview with an OLPC Australia representative:

> In this network I think people are actually really asking questions and getting personal responses, you know, particularly the people who post more regularly, and then post with each other are developing those relationships and I think, you know, if we were to bring them all together at a conference, they'd be like oh, I know you – and get on with each other quite well because it is a relationship, they've established a relationship with each other.

Many members are located at remote communities, and so one purpose of the network is to provide members with opportunities to connect, and to share their experiences, knowledge and skills. Figure 7.2 illustrated an interaction between participants in which a sense of ease and a connection between members was achieved. The punctuation of the final remark also indicates a sense of excitement, of ideas moving towards something valued. It is difficult to achieve a connection via one-sentence posts but the inclusion of members' photos next to each post, as well as the use of the 'like' feature, do establish a positive tone.

Request for technical help is also a central activity among network participants; an example is shown in Figure 7.3. In this excerpt, Sam Samson (an OLPC Australia representative) asked for examples of tasks and games that could be developed for XO laptops. This excerpt illustrates the bridging between technical and pedagogical knowledge. Kitti Sonny (a teacher) replied with an idea, 'liked' by Mark Mason, and George Pak added to the discussion thread by identifying existing tools to solve the problem. This final post was also 'liked' by Kitti. Activities in the network rely as much on members contributing to discussion threads as on relevant questions being asked in the first instance. Through such exchanges members share knowledge about their work practices, which may be of value to both teachers and XO laptop software developers.

Part of the co-creation and co-configuration activities also reveal the adoption of implicit norms and social rules for communication. In a typical request for support the initial post is often short. The member who posts the original question may also post the first reply, which expands on the initial post, explaining the issue in more detail. The details of the issue are important, but the implicit social rules of the site seem to suggest that they are not appropriate in an original post. A participant may then tag the post and reply, using existing tags such as 'XO support' or 'activities', or create their own. Members who have signed up to receive notification of activity related to these tags are subsequently notified, often by email. Unlike the example in Figure 7.3, replies to requests for technical

Sam Samson

⑦ Hi Everyone. We're wondering what kinds of Activities you would like to see developed for the XOs? Do you have any examples of other games or activities that would translate well?

Like · Answer · Share · More · January 16 at 3:01pm

Kitti Sonny : A simple image editor for cropping screenshots would be nice - that way students can create more 'professional' memorise games etc.
January 16 at 7:44pm from Desktop · Like · Reply · Share · More
👍 Liked by Mark Mason

George Pak : Hi Kitty

I use Paint to crop images. I use the select tool to copy the cropped image to the clipboard and then save the clip to the Journal

George

January 17 at 6:24am from Email · Like · Reply · Share · More
👍 Liked by **Kitti Sonny**

FIGURE 7.3 OLPC: technical help

information tend to be quick, often measured in minutes rather than hours or days. All replies share the tags allocated to the original post and so become part of the structure of knowledge shared on the site.

Growth, Development and Evolution

As this network grows, its potential to support teachers' use of XO laptops in teaching strengthens. The conversations become longer and more detailed but, importantly, the knowledge and expertise contributed to the discussion are more diverse and dense. The OLPC Yammer network only began in 2011, so it would be fair to describe it as a network in its early stages. Further customization is ongoing in the set, social and epistemic design, based on the observations of the co-creation and co-configuration carried out by the members of the network. The ability to tag posts and search for them is an important element in this ongoing development. As participants code digital artifacts, they are categorizing content for subsequent searches. Thus, the network becomes increasingly dense with knowledge relevant for all its members. Another addition to set design is the branding of the network. Across the top of the OLPC Yammer home page, the title 'One Education' has replaced the original 'XO Connect', so that the importance of the relationship between OLPC Yammer and the One Education training program is clearer. This shows the change from a community formed around the technology (the XO laptops) to one in which the pedagogy and practice are at least as important as the laptops themselves.

Abstracting and Synthesis

There are two key design features that contribute to make the OLPC Yammer a productive learning network. The first is flexibility. Discussed throughout this chapter is the interplay between fixed elements of the set and social design that enable flexibility in the epistemic design. The choice to use the Yammer platform in the first instance locked in a number of elements such as the newsfeed, profile pages and tagging, as discussed, but careful epistemic design prevents these from being barriers to entry or to participation in the network.

Teachers require flexibility in the way they participate. By providing multiple methods of access (e.g. smartphone, desktop computer, tablet computer), participants can more easily integrate knowledge gained through their activities in the network into their existing work practice. Teachers need similar flexibility in their classroom practice around the use of the XO laptops. The design of the network facilitates flexibility in practice within a fixed structure. Flexibility enables engagement in conversations, asynchronous or synchronous, and in one-to-one or one-to-many arrangements. Members choose who to follow, which groups to use and the tags to use when posting. Flexibility is also apparent in the roles participants play over time. They enter the network with a fixed role related to their work practice, such as teacher, software developer, or administrator; however, their role often shifts from knower to learner and back again.

The second significant design feature is the focus on knowledge building, and this is most strongly indicated through the change in the network title from 'XO laptops' to 'One Education'. Discussions revolve around specialized knowledge, whether it is about students' learning in the classroom, or teachers' or professionals' learning in practice. Every participant has the potential to assume the role of novice or expert, and to move fluidly between the two. While this is supported by the nature of teachers' introduction to the network via the One Education program, and the brief question-and-answer posts on the newsfeed, it is most strongly supported by the leadership of OLPC Australia. Their attitude towards learning from teachers' experiences in the program, and the encouragement of technical developers to ask members what they want, means that teachers are empowered to naturally assume the role of *knower*, and are provided with an opportunity to demonstrate this. This is evidenced in the social design that includes the seed comments and questions posted by OLPC representatives to the network. The creation, sharing and recording of *relevant* knowledge, comprising practical, pedagogical and technical knowledge, is important. The knowledge work of *all* participants is valued equally.

It was reported by the teacher interviewed that OLPC Yammer is 'useful for wider exposure to the educational community' and this touches on another reason why we consider this network productive. As discussed earlier in this chapter, participants who would otherwise be isolated are connected via a strong support network, including OLPC administrators, technical experts and other teachers. People who have an effective personal learning network are able to seek help, make suggestions, share ideas and learn from others quickly and easily. Domains of knowledge, which are specialized, tend to be well supported by these types of learning networks. The OLPC Yammer is one such environment that supports the creation and sharing of knowledge specific to a unique subject domain.

The flexibility in use within a fixed structure, and a focus on knowledge building, are two key design components of the OLPC Yammer network. The network not only provides essential knowledge and connections for teachers in disparate communities, as well as technical developers and administrators, but for all members it reinforces participation in the culture of the one-laptop-per-child program itself.

Notes

1 Accessed at http://one.laptop.org. Please note that the network as described in this chapter may have evolved since the time of writing.
2 Accessed at http://one.laptop.org.au. Please note that the network as described in this chapter may have evolved since the time of writing.

References

Kay, A. and Goldberg, A., 1977. Personal dynamic media. *Computer*, 10(3), 31–41.

OLPC Australia, 2013. *Mission* [online]. Available from: www.laptop.org.au/mission [Accessed 2 January 2013].

One Education Program, 2013. *One education* [online]. Available from: www.one-education.org [Accessed 2 January 2013].

One Laptop Per Child Foundation, 2013. *About the project: mission* [online]. Available from: http://one.laptop.org/about/mission [Accessed 2 January 2013].

Papert, S., 1980. *Mindstorms: children, computers, and powerful ideas.* New York: Basic Books.

8

DISEÑA EL CAMBIO

Helping Mexican School Children to Design a Better World

Crighton Nichols and David Ashe

Overview

In the autumn of 2010, a group of school children from the rural town of Tepanzacoalco, Ajalpan, in the state of Puebla, Mexico, organized the local community to help repair the toilets at their local school. The toilets were in such a bad state that many of the local girls did not want to attend classes. As part of the initiative, and to ensure its longevity, they also promoted general practices of good hygiene within their school and the wider community. Although this demonstration of initiative, creativity and sustainable social impact by the children is remarkable, it was far from an isolated or spontaneous incident. That year, in Mexico alone, around 1,500 similar projects were organized as part of what has become the world's largest school-based competition: 'Design for Change'. The contest, known in Mexico as 'Diseña el Cambio',[1] was run again in Mexico over the summer of 2011–2012 and demonstrated remarkable growth, resulting in approximately 4,500 new projects for change, all initiated, designed and led by school children. Similar stories can be found from all over the world, from raising awareness about, and working to prevent, child marriages in India, to redesigning a children's ward in a hospital in Australia, by making it more colorful and child-friendly.

'Design for Change' was conceived in India by Kiran Bir Sethi, who firmly believed that by enabling the children of the world to design local solutions to problems, and by empowering them to take action, the world could become a better place. The core idea behind the program is transforming the question 'Can I?' into the positive affirmation 'I can!' From modest beginnings, Design for Change (2013) has rapidly grown into a global network of over 40 countries, reaching an estimated 25 million children, along with their families and teachers.

The network has been designed to provide a mechanism for school students to consider issues in their communities and to create and implement ideas about how things could change, making their community a better place. In carrying out these plans the network relies on existing school infrastructure, teachers, family members and the wider community to assist the students to implement their ideas for change.

The primary means of spreading the program has been in the form of national competitions, involving school children and their teachers. These competitions involve working through four steps of a simplified design-thinking process (Brown 2008): Feel, Imagine, Do, and Share. Through these four stages, students are encouraged to engage with problems they identify in their world, to generate ideas about how they could improve the situation, to act on those ideas and to share the story of their achievements with the rest of the networked community. In this way, students are encouraged to explore their desires for a better future and, with the guidance provided by a simple yet powerful design process, consider ways of acting to bring a better future into reality. By informing others about their successes, students are able to inspire other members of the networked community to 'give it a go'.

While the program was developed and started in India, it has been used in various different localized forms in other countries. This chapter focuses on one implementation of the Design for Change network, Diseña el Cambio México. In the interests of clarity, we use the title 'Design for Change' to refer to the global initiative and its key ideas, and 'Diseña el Cambio', when referring to the specific implementation in Mexico. Diseña el Cambio is coordinated by EducarUno, a Mexican non-governmental organization that is responsible for coordinating Design for Change across Ibero-America. After the 2011–2012 challenge, EducarUno redesigned their website for Diseña el Cambio, to better facilitate the sharing of ideas, projects and experiences by participants and other interested community members, considering the core principles supported by the global Design for Change network. The participants in Diseña el Cambio include teachers, school children, parents, sponsors, partners and other community members. Through the Internet, as well as more traditional forms of media such as radio and print, EducarUno have been able to implement the program at scale across the country, reaching out to local communities and mobilizing a national audience, providing opportunities for school students to help make their world a better place.

The redesigned Diseña el Cambio website was launched in September 2012 with two main objectives. The first, in recognition of the crucial role played by teachers, was to support them in learning how to implement the program in their schools. The second was to support the growth of an online community, through the provision of a platform for participants to view and provide feedback on the projects undertaken by children from around the world.

The Diseña el Cambio platform has been designed in a modular way with features that address internationalization (such as supporting multiple languages), making it possible to create new instances of the platform to be used in other countries. The web platform evolves as participants move through their particular design challenge, providing features and tools to support them at each stage, from simple instructions for registering for the contest to tutorials on how they can share their completed projects. When the projects are ready for sharing, teachers are able to upload a video or slide presentation of the project in which they have been involved, so the wider network can view, comment and vote on individual projects. Over 3,000 projects from previous years are already available, providing many inspirational stories of positive social change to motivate students and teachers participating in the current year.

Although the global Design for Change network provides a number of general guides and tools to help each country establish a national competition, each country's local implementation of the network is unique, requiring specific tools and strategies for the needs of local communities. EducarUno have constructed

FIGURE 8.1 Diseña el Cambio: home page

a learning environment that is suitable for the specific needs of schools and teachers in Mexico. This chapter explores the Diseña el Cambio network, investigating how EducarUno have reconfigured and implemented the global network, and how it extracts ideas that could be considered when repurposing existing learning networks.

Set Design

Diseña el Cambio provides a number of digital tools and resources to help participants run the 2013 challenge in their schools. To make use of these tools, and fully participate in the program, there are also a number of physical tools and resources that participating schools need, such as classrooms, materials for brainstorming ideas and managing projects, and Internet-enabled devices with a connection to the Internet. One of the initial points of entry into the program for many participants is viewing completed projects by other schools. Seeing what others have managed to achieve provides both ideas for new projects and also encouragement that real change is achievable. The final part of the challenge is for the participants to upload a presentation or video about their progress through the challenge. Although this content is only uploaded at the end of the challenge, it is necessarily created throughout the challenge. Many schools will document their progress using some form of diary, with photographs and video. This combination of digital tools (web-based) and physical tools (school-based) is essential for the successful implementation of the program.

The Diseña el Cambio challenge typically starts with potential participants (usually a teacher or principal) discovering the program and becoming a champion for the program within their school. For this to be successful, potential participants need to know of the existence of Diseña el Cambio and to understand what participating in it could mean for them and their community. In many parts of the world, social media and the Internet can be relied on to inform and encourage people to get involved; at present, however, many Mexican schools do not have reliable Internet access. As a result, EducarUno have partnered with a number of government agencies to help disseminate information about the competition. These include the national ministry of education (SEP), programs to improve school quality (PEC) and security (PES), the Indigenous schools program and CONALITEG, who are responsible for the delivery of textbooks and other printed literature to all schools. These partnerships have facilitated the provision of information packs, detailing the 2013 challenge and the registration process, to 230,000+ schools in Mexico. These strategic partnerships have been critical in helping Diseña el Cambio reach so many schools: in terms of the number of participating schools, it has become the largest implementation of the Design for Change program in the world.

In order to sustain a program of this size, EducarUno have employed a number of dedicated full-time staff to manage and support the program. Their salaries are dependent on sponsorship from corporations and local businesses, though some sponsors provide prizes to the winning schools instead. Attracting sponsorship to a social program is always difficult, but the advantage of Diseña el Cambio is that – primarily due to the 'Share' stage – the outcomes of the program are highly visible. Many of the projects initiated, designed and led by the school children are extraordinary in their creativity, scope and impact. As a result, the social return on investment is easy to demonstrate. Furthermore, sponsors are acknowledged in a prominent place on the website, in recognition of the fact that their continued funding is essential to the sustainability of the program.

Having discovered the Diseña el Cambio challenge, potential participants are directed to the Diseña el Cambio website. The site contains information about the competition and over 3,000 examples of projects that have been completed in the past. These projects have been tagged with category labels, such as health, environment and bullying, so that examples from particular areas of interest can easily be located. Examples are further classified by other criteria, such as: school type (private or public); participation in other programs (such as school quality, school security or Indigenous programs); student level; and whether the program was a winning entry from a previous competition year. Geographical filters to the state and city/municipality are also provided, though strict care is taken never to reveal the personal information of any of the students. The range of different filters helps interested users find projects of specific interest, and the details of the projects are available on a map to help facilitate spatial searches. The visual

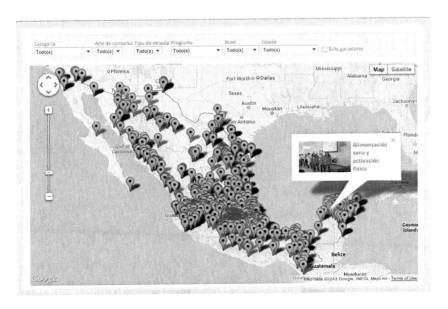

FIGURE 8.2 Diseña el Cambio: projects map showing filters and example of selected project

representation of thousands of projects on a map also effectively illustrates the scale of the impact of the program, which helps demonstrate a form of accountability to sponsors and partners.

The website also provides support materials and resources for the teachers in both digital and physical formats. The digital materials and resources include interactive video guides, case studies and tutorials, whereas physical materials and resources include general information sheets, registration forms and posters to display around the schools. This combination of both digital and physical elements provides multiple access points to the information for teachers and students. To take part in the challenge, teachers need to register with EducarUno. This is achieved either by filling in an online registration form, or completing a paper-based form and returning the form either electronically or physically to EducarUno.

Once signed up to the Diseña el Cambio community, participants are encouraged to play an active role within the online community by following their favorite schools, providing feedback on comment walls, messaging or chatting with their friends and joining or creating discussion groups.

Epistemic Design

The Diseña el Cambio platform has been designed to support a number of specific learning goals, some of which relate to the children who are involved in the design projects, some to their teachers and some to the community more broadly. A primary goal is for all participants to understand the Design for Change challenge, including the four stages through which participants will progress. Second, teachers need to gain an insight into how the program can be implemented within their particular school, classroom and curriculum. Coupled with this is a desire to explain how the web platform can assist the teachers in setting up and running the program in their school, taking into account the fact that many of the teachers may have limited access to technology or limited IT skills, or both. A third goal is to disseminate information about the project to the wider community. This incorporates the passing on of ideas and successes as well as initiating communication between individuals and groups in the form of discussions and feedback.

To help meet each of these objectives, the EducarUno team structured the program so that the learning tasks and the participants' activities are aligned as much as possible. Within each project, as part of the challenge, there are specific tasks that need to be completed within defined time frames. These tasks range from registration to the main part of the challenge, where participants are asked to Feel, Imagine, Do, and Share. EducarUno are aware that many participants may not be familiar with the web technology and have worked hard to emphasize this as an experience about the Diseña el Cambio competition, and not simply a technological challenge. For example, the initial task that potential participants are faced with is registration. The web design team at EducarUno designed a special registration process that takes into account the fact that many teachers in Mexico are unfamiliar with registering details in an online environment. Although inspiration was taken from other social networking sites so as to be familiar to those teachers who were often online, the main goal was to capture all of the details required to register the participant in the system and the school for the competition in a single step. This was important, as there was a risk that participants may have thought they had registered their school for the competition when they had only personally registered their details in the system. Guides on how to register were also made available. Despite the efforts to simplify the registration process as much as possible, for many participants even the task of checking emails to verify registration details can be difficult. Consequently, the staff managing the Diseña el Cambio program at EducarUno established dedicated telephone support to help people through each step of the process.

The main part of the challenge is for participating students to create ideas that can be acted upon to make their world a better place. However, EducarUno recognizes that properly trained teachers are critical to the success of the program. To help the teachers learn about the program, the Diseña el Cambio platform provides a number of 'friendly' video resources for both teachers and students. These use a conversational style to explain the process and the stages the participants should pass through to achieve their goals. By breaking the challenge down into the four key stages, and then splitting up each of these into smaller video sections that discuss the 'Why?', 'What?' and 'How?' for each stage, EducarUno have created a system that leads novice users through the learning materials, providing adequate scaffolding for each of the various stages of the challenge. Furthermore, teachers are asked to consider reflective questions in order for them to experience the core aspects of the program for themselves. For example, 'What problems or issues do you face in your community that you would like to change?' and 'How do you imagine addressing these issues?' It is hoped that the teachers are then able to facilitate similar reflective processes in their classrooms. The video materials also provide a number of examples, showing how other teachers have implemented each stage in their classrooms, which teachers can use to help relate the program to their own students.

While the web platform provides teachers with access to a step-by-step process, there is also significant flexibility in access to these resources, which allows teachers to move off the prescribed path. This flexibility enables moving through the design process in such a way that the needs of particular students, and particular situations, can be accommodated.

The epistemic design for any website with learning objectives requires that the web design team ensures the relevant pedagogical theories and models are understood and meaningfully incorporated into the design of the platform. Software developers may be well versed in user-centered design, software design patterns and various creative processes and practices to ensure the website is

FIGURE 8.3 Diseña el Cambio: video guide for Mexican teachers

pleasant to look at and the information architecture is intuitive to follow, but even if all of the best practices for website design and development are followed, the resulting online platform may not meet the learning or pedagogical objectives. In other words, the website may look and feel intuitive and engaging, but the users may not achieve the desired learning goals through their interactions with the website and other people using it.

One strategy considered by the EducarUno web design team was to combine user-interface design patterns and pedagogical patterns to increase the probability that the desired learning goals would indeed be achieved. This approach has been pioneered by Fiona Chatteur (2011). The training process for web designers to learn how to incorporate pedagogical patterns in their designs (as outlined by Chatteur) is quite demanding, so due to time constraints a simplified strategy was adopted – one in which a senior member of the web design team was responsible for reviewing and incorporating pedagogical aspects into the designs with the rest of the team.

Shifting focus to the global Design for Change program, during the four stages of the competition participants experience working on a *design challenge*. Research has shown that design challenges can lead to powerful learning (Bamberger *et al.* 2011, Kolodner *et al.* 2003), providing opportunities for collaboration on a task that has an immediate purpose and is, therefore, intrinsically engaging. The design task is complex and may require many iterations before its completion. Each stage of the process provides a number of learning opportunities for the various participants. All participants (students, teachers and parents) become co-designers and each takes on a number of responsibilities, solving problems that matter to them and their community. Learning through a design challenge can bring about the learning of a variety of skills, which include problem-solving, communication, and collaboration. For example, each project revolves around 'problem-solving'; students identify an issue that has an emotional basis and are required to find a solution to that issue. The students move through an experience that is both personal and action-oriented. Through the projects, students begin to consider issues in their community and focus on how their actions can affect the wider community. As all projects are self-funded (there is no access to a central fund), participants are required to generate their own ideas and work with their community to meet all costs. This provides a sense of ownership of the project, which is likely to create a stronger basis for sustainable change.

Participants are faced with multiple learning opportunities as they progress through the four stages. For example, in the 'Feel' stage, they are asked to identify possible projects by empathizing with others in their community; this may involve fact-finding and discussions. In the 'Imagine' phase, students are required to think creatively, to work collaboratively and refine ideas. The 'Do' phase is more practical: students are required to perform operational tasks associated with their projects; and the 'Share' phase involves summarizing and communicating the project to a wider audience. Each phase presents its own challenges and, as a whole, the project requires a wide variety of skills.

Social Design

The Diseña el Cambio competition is rooted in social activity. Taking part in the contest requires participants to consider the conditions in which they live from a problem-solving perspective, to identify problems and then, through social interactions, take action to find and implement solutions to the identified problems. For this to happen, a strong social network needs to be in place. From the start, students and teachers are exposed to other participants' projects and are encouraged to comment and question others' work. This takes place in the 'Feel' and 'Imagine' phases of their challenge; they are encouraged to view, provide feedback on and comment on other participants' projects. This is facilitated in the online platform with commonly used social networking tools, such as online chat, private messages, groups and comment walls, which have been implemented at different levels within the program. For example, participants are able to comment on, and provide feedback to, individuals, groups, projects and schools. This method of providing feedback also works as a conduit for effective communications between participants and between participants and organizers. These social interactions provide valuable information and feedback, which further enhances both the effect and reach of the program.

In order to help facilitate communication between network participants, the web design team at EducarUno has ensured that there is a clear distinction between the different 'entities' and 'roles'. The four main 'entities' are the users (either participants in projects, or other interested parties contributing in some way to the projects), projects, schools and groups. Users also have clearly defined roles in order to encourage them to take responsibility for the different types of content associated with the schools and the projects. This is achieved by providing appropriate tools for each 'role' to help individuals perform tasks. For example, in Mexico, each school has to specify a 'Maestro Guia' (Guide Teacher) who is responsible for registering their school to participate in the competition and for sharing the projects that their school undertakes. The Maestro Guia is provided with instructions that clearly lay out the information required to perform their tasks, displaying a step-by-step guide to each phase, which includes sample discussion questions and a list of suggested activities. The Maestro Guia's initial task is to complete the school's registration and once this has been completed, other participants, such as teachers, students, parents and community members, are able to share their ideas and experiences on the school's (and project's) comment walls. This also enables further comments and feedback from participants. The site has been designed to reflect the best practices of existing social networking sites, enabling participants who have some familiarity with other online tools to understand the system quickly. The Diseña el Cambio platform also allows individual users to 'follow' a particular school so they can stay informed of the latest developments with minimal effort.

In addition to individual roles, the system also encourages 'group' participation. Groups can be created at any time and bring together participants with common interests. They take the form of online discussion walls, where participants exchange ideas about a particular topic or issue of concern. Groups can be public, meaning anyone can view and join in the discussion, or private, enabling the group leader to invite specific people to participate in the conversation.

The social interactions described thus far tend to be asynchronous in nature; however, the platform also offers support for synchronous communication via an online chat module. This allows participants to communicate in real time with other participants, using a familiar social networking practice of requesting individuals to become 'friends' before being able to initiate chat sessions. Initially participants are assigned one 'friend', the Soporte (Support) user, who is available to answer support questions via chat. While this helps inexperienced users to understand the chat system, it has been recognized that novice users may initially struggle even with this level of online interaction. To ensure that participants can access necessary support, help is also available via telephone.

Throughout the competition, but especially during the 'Do' phase, schools are communicating with a wider community. Some of this communication can take place in the online platform, but the vast majority will happen offline through face-to-face meetings and phone calls with interested family and community members, including local businesses and government representatives. Through these communications, community links are created and students become agents of change within their communities. There are examples of projects where the challenge has given students a voice to obtain assistance with their projects by petitioning local businesses and government representatives. Therefore, in addition to empowering students to effect change within their communities, the Design for Change program is also designed to encourage imaginative and creative thinking skills, communication skills, teamwork and project management.

Set, Epistemic and Social Co-creation and Co-configuration Activities

The Diseña el Cambio program is designed to empower and enable students to make changes for the better in their local community. The starting point for any group of students is to identify a project and design an activity that will ultimately result in beneficial change. This process of design, followed by action, allows students to work together to create not only the activity itself but also a web-based presentation of their activity, thereby informing others outside of their community about their activity. This collaborative creation and dissemination to a broad audience is at the heart of this networked learning environment. As projects come to an end, it is easy to see that the participants have indeed been creative. Unlike many learning opportunities, the creation of artifacts in this program is not limited to the learning process itself. Once change has been implemented, there is an ongoing process of creation as participants continue to effect change in their local communities. In this way, the effect of the Diseña el Cambio program extends beyond the boundaries of the challenge itself.

In the Mexican implementation of the global Design for Change program, there are specific needs that have required a significant reconfiguration of the existing international programs. It is easy to assume that repurposing a learning network only requires copying the structure from one program to another with minimal localization; however, the Diseña el Cambio example shows that there are times when much more needs to be taken into consideration. An example of this is that EducarUno had to acknowledge that many schools in Mexico are not yet connected to the Internet. This presented a challenge to the EducarUno design team – to ensure that participants were not disadvantaged if they only had limited access to the online materials. By reconfiguring the support materials and providing physical as well as digital tools, EducarUno were able to expand the network throughout their region. EducarUno found many examples of teachers accessing the Diseña el Cambio website from Internet cafés or from private home connections rather than from schools. Therefore, by using multiple forms of communications (such as a dedicated telephone system and printed resource materials) they were able to help teachers implement the program in their schools.

The way in which Diseña el Cambio has divided up the challenge into entities (participants, projects and schools) and roles (with pre-defined activities) enables the system to be extended and changed as and when the need arises.

The current plan is to extend the network into neighboring countries and, when implementing the expansion, to take into account the varying needs of those different countries and communities. The different needs can be reflected in the program by adjusting the entities and the roles of the participants. The design will allow for the delegation of responsibilities; the equivalent of the Maestro Guia could be allowed delegate the creation of projects to other teachers or students. Once key participants have been identified and a trusted relationship has been established, those participants would be able to create their own network of participants and grant roles within their network with the ability to perform other tasks. As the network of trusted participants expands, so does the number of people who can create primary content, such as schools and projects.

Abstracting and Synthesis

This networked learning environment is based on the idea that students can design their own solutions to problems they identify and that this is helped by the sharing of ideas. Diseña el Cambio uses a website to disseminate information about both the program itself and about the projects that participants have created. It uses a wide variety of tools to achieve this idea-sharing, and these tools are both robust and scalable. By using discussion forums in the form of comment walls, Diseña el Cambio enables participants to share their experiences among themselves (regardless of age), between schools and between countries, bringing together ideas and participants. While the program has been set up as a 'challenge', and there is a form of voting for favorite projects with prizes, the motivation to take part in the program does not appear to stem from the extrinsic rewards. Rather, the students and teachers, along with their local communities, are inspired by the fact that they believe that change is possible; that they can make it happen.

This intrinsic motivation, generated by participants seeing what others have achieved, appears to have played a major part in the success of the program. The outcomes can be seen in the videos and presentations uploaded on the Diseña el Cambio website, which show successful implementations of students' ideas. In addition to working on the observable 'change', participants are also exposed to other learning opportunities, such as reflection, collaboration and problem-solving, as they embark on a design activity that is intrinsically engaging, locally grounded, self-selected and therefore deeply relevant to their context.

The program and its supporting materials were made available to the participants in multiple appropriate formats. This flexibility can be seen in the way in which EducarUno integrated digital material with physical print-based materials, and digital (web-based) practices with physical (telephone) support mechanisms. The key to its success lay in developing a platform that was able to adapt to both the conditions and needs of local participants, whilst foregrounding the stories of change, which in and of themselves generated the impetus for positive social change.

Note

1 Accessed at www.disenaelcambio.com. Please note that the network as described in this chapter may have evolved since the time of writing.

References

Bamberger, Y., Cahill, C., Hagerty, J., Short, H. and Krajcik, J., 2011. Learning science by doing design: how can it work at the middle school level? *Journal of Education, Informatics and Cybernetics*, 2(2), 41–46.

Brown, T., 2008. Design thinking. *Harvard Business Review*, 86(6), 84–92.

Chatteur (née Kerr), F., 2011. *Design for pedagogy patterns for e-learning*. Thesis (PhD). University of Sydney. Available from: http://ses.library.usyd.edu.au/handle/2123/8737 [Accessed 20 May 2013].

Design for Change, 2013 [online]. Available from: www.dfcworld.com [Accessed 22 February 2013].

Kolodner, J. L., Camp, P. J., Crismond, D., Fasse, B., Gray, J., Holbrook, J., Puntambekar, S. and Ryan, M., 2003. Problem-based learning meets case-based reasoning in the middle-school science classroom: putting Learning by Design(tm) into practice. *Journal of the Learning Sciences*, 12(4), 495–547.

9

BIEBKRACHT: LIBRARY PROFESSIONALS EMPOWERED THROUGH AN INTER-ORGANIZATIONAL LEARNING NETWORK

Design Principles and Evolution

Marlies Bitter-Rijpkema, Steven Verjans, Wim Didderen and Peter Sloep

Overview

The Biebkracht learning network (BLN) is an inter-organizational learning network for geographically distributed public library professionals in the Dutch province of Gelderland. The librarians' profession is changing drastically in a context of disruptive social and technological changes and changing cultural policies. In BLN, library professionals work together to design, develop and implement innovation at a local and regional level, in face-to-face workshops and online collaboration. This chapter describes the architecture and the design of the Biebkracht ('librarians empowered') learning network.

The Biebkracht network is the result of a two-year effort by library professionals, researchers and learning technologists, who co-created the network. BLN builds on three main learning network components: (1) users and their knowledge profiles, (2) self-managed user communities and (3) knowledge artifacts, made accessible through a mechanism of self-regulation and self-categorization. The interaction between these three components affords not just knowledge sharing but also knowledge creation.

The Biebkracht learning network builds on existing practices of in-service professional development, but extends those practices by adding specific function-alities, facilitation and moderation roles to the learning network. It rapidly became an integral part of professional practice within the Gelderland public libraries. At the time of writing, a national knowledge network is being developed, inspired by BLN.

Biebkracht's Organizational Background and Context

Biebkracht was initiated by the provincial service organization Biblioservice Gelderland (BSG), and is the result of a co-creative process with the academic support of the Open University of the Netherlands (OUNL), more specifically researchers and technology developers from the Learning Networks research program at the Centre for Learning Sciences and Technologies (CELSTEC). BSG initiated the Biebkracht network as it anticipated that the role of library professions would change radically in the current information age. It felt that public libraries worldwide need to continue to be important and accessible cultural institutions. However, due to (a) the diminishing importance of paper books and the services related to them, (b) changing demographics and (c) changing policies regarding public cultural services, BSG saw that the future role of public libraries is under debate. Major cutbacks in funding, paired with the advent of modern media, question the very existence of traditional public libraries in many places, including Gelderland. BSG therefore challenged the libraries to actively reconsider and redefine their mission: New services needed to be designed and implemented that take the upcoming digital media into account and new sustainable business models needed to be developed. Each public library organization in the Netherlands is an independent legal entity (most often a not-for-profit foundation), and its task is to serve its regional community. All changes therefore take place at the regional level, although there will be significant similarities of approach across regions. Indeed, the disruptive social and technological changes and changing policies call for major changes in the role of all libraries, and thus among library professionals generally. It is no exaggeration to claim that the public library sector needs to reinvent itself and find new roles for public libraries and librarians (Bitter-Rijpkema et al. 2012a, 2012b).

In the Netherlands, this situation led to numerous professional development initiatives, with two of them explicitly building on networked learning conceptions. The first, the Library School initiative (Bitter-Rijpkema et al. 2012b) focuses on a tailored professional development track for in-service library staff, centered on an innovative learning-network-based, one-year academic curriculum. The second consists of the inter-organizational learning network Biebkracht, which is the topic of this chapter. To provide some context, we will briefly describe the Biebkracht project's history and background.

The association of public libraries in Gelderland encompasses 22 municipal public libraries. Together they serve a population of over 700,000 people, geographically distributed over 5,000 km^2 (Figure 9.1). In 2006, this association, together with the provincial service organization 'Biblioservice', launched community workshops to facilitate dialogue on the future of the Public Library System in this region. Library staff met in small working groups, and collaborated for a period of time. Common tasks included discussion of such questions as:

- How can we, as front desk professionals, behave in a more entrepreneurial and proactive manner with library visitors?

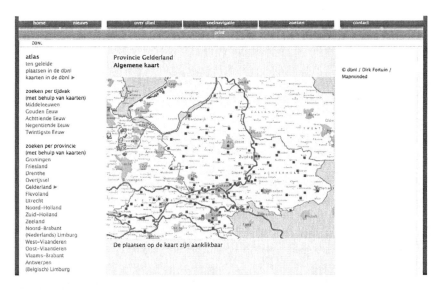

FIGURE 9.1 Map of the local libraries and satellite libraries in the Dutch province of Gelderland

- Can we define a common policy for dealing with e-books?
- How do we see our role in relation to youth, schools and education?
- How do we define our local strategies in relation to local stakeholders and local politics?

At the time, information exchange and dialogues among the workshop participants were limited to five to six face-to-face workshops a year, supported by email and a static information webpage. In 2009, the partners to the project started to realize that these face-to-face workshops were not sufficient to achieve the desired large-scale, sustainable innovation required, and that an online supplement was needed for the workshops. Inspired by the research on networked learning at OUNL, an effort was made to collaboratively design, develop and grow a suitable and sustainable learning network for the public library community in Gelderland.

Set Design

The Biebkracht learning network thus built on an already established practice of inter-organizational collaboration between the local libraries and BSG. Library staff would meet in small working groups with a common task, and collaborate for a period of time on this task. This way of working was inspired by Wenger's concept of 'communities of practice' (Wenger 1998). The working groups would meet on a regular basis for brainstorming sessions and discuss first drafts of working documents. They felt that an online platform was needed in order to continue their work in between face-to-face meetings, i.e. they wanted to share document drafts, but also to continue discussions and share online links or external documents relevant to the work at hand. The social dynamics of these closed face-to-face working groups were regarded as an important aspect of the success of the collaborative practice, so the online platform should allow for the continuation of these closed groups, but extend them into the online realm. The first version of the learning network BLN was designed to support at least the current collaborative practice. BSG – as the driving partner behind Biebkracht – had some preliminary ideas of what the learning network should and should not support. These ideas were inspired by our research efforts (Sloep 2008), but also by existing online platforms.

At the start of the Biebkracht project in 2009, a number of knowledge-sharing initiatives emerged in the public library field. The largest one was Bibliotheek2.0 (meaning Library2.0), an open, bottom-up knowledge network hosted on the Ning.com platform (online platform for social websites). In 2009, the network had more than 1,000 members, and kept growing exponentially. At the end of 2011, the number of users of Bibliotheek2.0 was about 6,000, with well over 400,000 page clicks per year. The network is used to share information about new events, new policy decisions and technological innovations that may (or may not) influence the library sector, and thus the work of the library professional. It has different subgroups and forums related to specific topics, where focused discussions and information sharing takes place. Yet the BSG partners judged that the information and the debate on Bibliotheek2.0 remained at a level that was too superficial to allow real changes in the profession; it mainly focused on sharing tidbits of information, and not enough on shared knowledge building. According to BSG, this was mainly due to (a) the lack of differential access rights within the Ning platform, (b) the lack of sufficiently concrete common goals and (c) the absence of a social dynamic.

Inspired by the pros and cons of such examples, and with the lessons learned from their face-to-face collaborative workshops, the BSG and OUNL teams began a co-creative design and development journey, which resulted in the Biebkracht learning network. The preliminary requirements were translated into the following design choices:

- In view of the initial under-specification of functionality and the expectation that many design changes would have to be implemented on the go, a very flexible architecture was needed, one that could easily be adapted to changing user wishes and changing contexts-of-use. This called for a modular platform architecture.
- Moreover, although the OUNL was responsible for informing the design of the BLN and for building the prototype, they were not going to be the 'hosting' party for the operational BLN. Therefore, a mainstream platform

was chosen as the basis for the design, one that could be easily transferred, and later hosted, maintained and updated by a commercial provider outside the original research partnership.
- Analysis of the existing practice and the BSG requirements – both at the outset and at later stages in the life of the BLN – showed that an intricate system of access rights was needed.

As Sloep and colleagues argue (Sloep *et al.* 2011, Berlanga *et al.* 2009), self-organization and self-regulation are important guidelines in order to foster sustainable online communities. Users of the BLN have to be able to determine in detail who they want to have access to the knowledge that is developed and shared. It needs to be possible, therefore, to set access rights at the group, artifact and person levels. Although the majority of mainstream content management systems have role-based access rights, a more intricate and flexible system was deemed necessary. First, the requirements for a very open and flexible platform ruled out a commercial, licensed system. Therefore an open source approach was needed. Second, only a small number of ICT staff could be assigned to the project. Therefore a mainstream system was required, with a large online developer community and a proven track record in flexible solutions, one that did not need extensive modifications.

All these arguments led to the choice of the open source content management system Drupal as the platform that would host the BLN. The standard Drupal was extended with functionalities that allowed document management, decentralized group creation and management, user profiling and aggregation of external content, for instance from Bibliotheek2.0, Twitter or other social media platforms. The platform can be further extended with multimedia functionality, such as video or photo sharing, but thus far these functionalities have not been implemented. The first version of the BLN included modules such as calendar, blog, groups, document library, tagging and aggregation.

Epistemic Design

The functions of the modules described above are related to the different types of knowledge and knowledge artifacts in the BLN and were designed to build on existing knowledge sharing and creation practices, within both established working groups ('communities') and new ones. The following types of knowledge and knowledge artifacts are at the core of the BLN, and were implemented in its first version.

- User knowledge profiles (inspired by Berlanga *et al.* 2009) are a key aspect of the BLN. They are needed as Biebkracht supports a network of geographically and organizationally dispersed members – over 300 users, who do not know each other personally. Profiles allow individuals to present themselves to all members of the network, not only with their contact information and educational background, but more importantly with information about the library organization they work in, their current role in the library, expertise and knowledge they have to offer to the network and topics they are mainly interested in.

- Network members can upload documents (draft and final versions) with descriptions, and add them to a structured document library.
- Members can inform each other about relevant events.
- News items are messages that are highlighted on the front page, or are given a prominent place within a certain community.
- Questions are a specific type of contribution that network members can use to query other network members, when they are searching for specific information.
- Contributions are the standard information items that users can contribute.
- Blog posts are personal reflections or contributions from network members.

Each of these knowledge artifacts can be targeted to the various communities within the BLN, to the network as a whole, or even to the general public of non-registered visitors. This mechanism follows Berlanga *et al.*'s (2009) guidelines of self-regulation: 'Allow participants to control the level of privacy of (their) contributions'. Network members can label their own contributions by means of tags. By using thematic tags, they could categorize their contributions as belonging to one or more themes. Network members could also add tags to other people's contributions, again following the suggestions of Berlanga and colleagues (2009) on self-categorization: 'Help participants to classify and evaluate their own contributions but also those from others'.

The Drupal platform visually structures knowledge according to (a) themes and groups ('communities of practice'), but also according to (b) types of artifact, i.e. documents, questions, blogs, etc. In the background, however, all knowledge artifacts use the same set of tags and categories, which causes them to appear independently of their point of entry. For example, searches for 'media literacy' will not only yield all contributions with this tag, but also the user profiles of people who have tagged themselves as interested in this topic. Selecting the thematic entry 'media literacy' from the home menu will present not just an overview of blog posts, documents, questions, but also users related to 'media literacy'.

The BLN not only supports knowledge sharing and creation within the platform itself, but also aggregates information from external sources, such as Google news, Google alerts or from Twitter (through hash tags). This notifies the network members of relevant external information and allows them to keep an eye on the 'outside world'.

Table 9.1 summarizes the epistemic design of the BLN. The three main knowledge functions relate to documents, (user) knowledge profiles and communities. The columns in the table signify the different knowledge activities

TABLE 9.1 Biebkracht: epistemic design

	Knowledge activities			
	1. Reading and learning	*2. Action*	*3. Interaction*	*4. Creation*
Documents/ contributions	Searching/finding documents Using documents	Uploading/sharing documents	Reacting to documents	Making connections between and summarizing documents and reactions
User knowledge profiles	Searching/finding colleagues 2.0 Filled out basic fields in own profile	Filled out all fields in own profile	Making use of profiles	Finding/making connections between profiles
Communities	Reading blogs and discussions	Posting blogs and questions	Reacting to blogs, discussions and polls	Making connections between and summarizing blog posts, discussion and polls
Goal	Information sharing $\longrightarrow$			Knowledge creation
leadership	Facilitator $\longrightarrow$			Moderator

associated with the knowledge functions. Biebkracht differs from, for instance, Bibliotheek2.0 by actively supporting activity at level 4, knowledge creation, through intensive moderation activities, both online and offline, during the face-to-face workshops. Community moderators actively stimulate interaction and knowledge creation by summarizing debate and comments, and connecting knowledge atoms across time, themes and communities. The community moderators thus play a crucial role in the social design of the learning network, as described in the next section.

Social Design

The social design of the BLN has been based on two principles. First, the network was not designed as architectural support for a static knowledge organization, but as support for the organic growth and development of professionals within a knowledge ecology. This approach follows scientists like Orlikowski who look at organizations and learning networks such as the BLN as living organisms, as 'self-evident' productive parts of the organization (Orlikowski 2010, Cummings and Worley 2009). Burns and Stalker (1961) argue that an open organic system approach is appropriate for organizations in transition because of its characteristic fluid definition of functions and interactions, both lateral and vertical. This organic perspective influenced not only our initial design approach but also matched with the aforementioned conceptual inspiration and the overall innovation management strategy of the BSG network library organization at that time.

From a social design perspective, this implies that the design efforts do not end when the first functional design has been implemented, a working platform has been created and learning activities are underway. The key to sustainable success of such learning networks requires a continuous design, focused on providing enhanced support and recommendations to the network members. The aim of the continued design efforts is for such a network to ultimately become a self-sustained, self-supporting part of the organization's entire habitat (see below). So, after the initial implementation, co-design activities start to differ in nature and scale. The emphasis shifts to:

- completion and enhancement of functionalities (rendering them more sophisticated);
- structural enhancement of types of collaboration;
- knowledge creation for the future of the organization;
- dedicated facilitation of network-based group work;
- embedding learning processes in daily work;
- support for emergent future network activities aimed at engaging employees in innovation.

In short, in our case, the educational design focus shifted from the provision of basic functionalities to the implementation of intervention strategies to support collaborative project work.

Second, typical of Biebkracht-like learning networks, aimed at organizational learning of adult working professionals, is that their educational design seeks to support expected but in essence unpredictable learning needs (Fischer and Sugimoto 2006, Goodyear and Carvalho 2013). This is the more so as the aim of the learning network is to change current organizational practices. While current organizational practices shape the development of the learning network, the learning network also shapes the development of new organizational practices (Giddens 1984). Therefore the design methodology of such a learning network necessarily shows a high level of improvization or 'bricolage' (Ciborra 1992, Orlikowski 1996). While staying focused on the ultimate ambition – i.e. to empower self-organization of networked learning through structured (moderator-led) activities, a set of flexible educational support tools needs to be at hand for use by network participants (Callon 2004). Since, typically, such networks start as a new element in the organization's daily routines (Orlikowski 1996, 2002), educational design has to provide enablers for new ways of knowledge sharing (Berlanga *et al.* 2009). Developing these in collaboration with the organization's existing ways of knowledge sharing ensures that they blend into repertoires that become part of the organization's natural routines.

These two principles informed the social design of the BLN. As discussed, the starting point of the social design of the BLN was to enable self-organization. However, asking groups right away to assimilate new technologies and new ways of working, and additionally demanding them to self-organize their work, is asking too much too quickly. Based on the research of Vrieling and colleagues (Vrieling *et al.* 2010) into self-regulated learning of prospective teachers, one can argue that the design of the network needs to contain a scaffolding process in which the network gradually moves from moderator control to learner control. The design team therefore decided to work on an emergent social design. They first focused on supporting the optimization of group processes, varying from agenda setting, collaboration and knowledge sharing to result dissemination, and on stimulating knowledge sharing at the organizational level. These needs led to specific moderator roles (alongside pure technical and administrative roles). The moderator was to take care of a community as the person who (a) stimulates and facilitates discussions, guides collaboration processes and (b) lifts dissemination of results, issues and questions to the level of the BLN. In addition to local community moderators, two or three moderators were appointed who had to take care of forging connections at the level of the network as a whole, by monitoring overall activities across communities and artifacts and taking action when needed. After a short period with dedicated moderators, moderation was rotated amongst various community members. One of the moderating tools that emerged in the course of the project was the Biebkracht knowledge spotlight, a clearly visible element of the website that flags important results to trigger attention and engagement with all colleagues.

The second element of the emergent social design was the users' (knowledge) profiles. As mentioned before, Biebkracht is intended to support a network of geographically and organizationally dispersed members, so the network members are at the heart of the learning network. An important question is how to find – in such a distributed organization – the right person to answer a specific question or to join a new project. It is essential that the members of the BLN are aware of their colleagues' qualities and connect to the right professionals for a specific request or job. The importance of profiling in virtual networks is well known. However, the standard profile options in popular social networks are too generic for the professionals' needs and for the all-important organizational trust building (Berlanga *et al.* 2009). Therefore, based on scientific heuristics, the team designed a personal profiling service tailored to the network's individual and organizational needs. It resulted in a dedicated profiling service with contact information, providing just the relevant expertise and work experience directly related to someone's current work and ambitions. The profile included information on participation in networks other than BLN.

Co-creation and Co-configuration of a Growing Learning Network

Looking back at the various design activities, the BLN design team has tried to address two different design challenges in a new way. The first was to design a professional learning network that supports productive work collaboration and knowledge sharing amongst about 700 knowledge workers spread across 22 organizations and even more geographical locations. The second was to involve this whole community of professionals to collaboratively reshape the organization for a radically different yet sustainable future. As described, these two challenges initiated a deliberate participative process. Its ambition was (a) to rapidly fulfill the request of the BSG organization and develop an operational learning network able to support actual operational collaboration and knowledge sharing needs and (b) to facilitate strategic activities for the exploration of future ways of working.

It was clear that these challenges could only be met by a profoundly participatory approach and the development of a flexible architecture. A solid foundation for the learning network would have to be developed, fit for direct use and matching the organization's needs. But the design would also have to be capable of evolving to meet future needs. A strong and productive collaboration was needed between the stakeholders of the BSG organization, the network's prospective users and the learning and technical designers, which would allow them to integrate their respective expertise (Fischer 2012, Callon 2004). The collaboration had to translate crucial individual and organizational requirements adequately into learning network affordances and functionalities fitting the organization (Bitter-Rijpkema andVerjans 2010, Sloep *et al.* 2011).

The multidisciplinary Biebkracht team combined the expertise from BSG representatives with the educational design and technical expertise from OUNL. In our view, both the educational and technical design methods should be in line with the underlying organic conceptual approach: open, flexible, effectively capturing expertise from the participating members of the network, enabling rapid translation of design to practice, feeding back experiences into improvements and resulting in a learning network that would fit like a custom made suit. Therefore a rapid prototyping approach was taken. We developed 'BiebAS', our own agile method of project and software development, inspired by the popular SCRUM (2013) method but dedicated to BLN's learning network development. Agile software development methods work through iterative and incremental development cycles instead of linear sequential process organization. The SCRUM method (Takeuchi and Nonaka 1986, Schwaber and Beedle 2001) offered inspiration with its ideas about intense multidisciplinary collaboration, iterative development and short sprint development cycles with feedback loops. For the BLN design and implementation, it meant that design ideas were defined in the multidisciplinary team, structurally encompassing BSG stakeholders and representation of future users, the educational and technical designer and usability specialist. Within the overall conceptual framework, ideas were made concrete via small design results, open for testing, evaluation, improvement and renewal, and informing the next steps in the iterative design process. This design process did not stop when the BLN was launched, but is still ongoing. In essence, the social design approach was similar to the Multiview2 multi-contingency framework (Avison *et al.* 1998), as represented in Figure 9.2.

The Biebkracht design team (represented in the diagram by the change agents) interacted with the organizational situation, and interpreted the situation from multiple perspectives, with the ultimate goal to develop a self-organizing learning network. The interpretive scheme that guides the emergent design can be characterized as follows (Verjans 2003, p. 16):

(a) The organizational analysis component is concerned with understanding the organizational needs for an information system, and tries to find out which purposeful activity the new information system aims to support. This 'purposeful activity' concept is not limited to existing practices within an organization, but tries to analyze and describe potential future activities and events.

(b) The information systems modeling component aims to develop a representation of the information system in technical terms, using modern analysis and modeling techniques.

(c) The sociotechnical analysis component is concerned with analyzing the interplay between personal, social and technical interpretations of the situation.

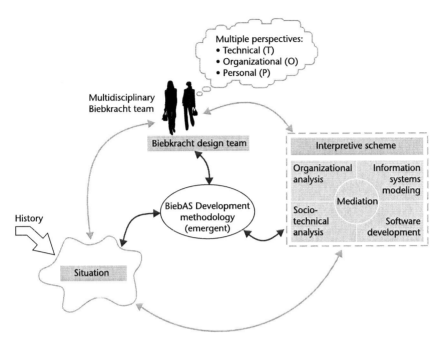

FIGURE 9.2 Multiview2 framework for Information Systems Design (adapted from Avison *et al.* 1998, p. 136)

(d) The final component is the software development, i.e. the design and construction of information technology (hardware, software and communications), focusing on both the internal functional part and the external human–computer interface part of the development.

The mediation process that governs these four components is inspired by actor-network theory (e.g. Callon 2004), where the information system developers are directors and translators who move between the different components of the framework and try to achieve a stable configuration.

In the case of the Biebkracht project, a small operational version of the learning network was developed in a short time frame (2009–2010), ready to be used in practice by the collaborative project workgroups (version 1.0, cf. Figure 9.3). Network members (predominantly adults aged over 35) started using the environment for their project work. Rapidly, other groups started asking for their own community on the BLN. When (top) management also decided to use the BLN for their meeting results, the network rapidly moved to a larger scale in 2011/2012. Design team members monitored the BLN live, discussed experiences with first users and iteratively realized small improvements.

A mid-term reflective evaluation was organized after one year of operation. The ambition was to evaluate the scientific and conceptual basis of the BLN, as

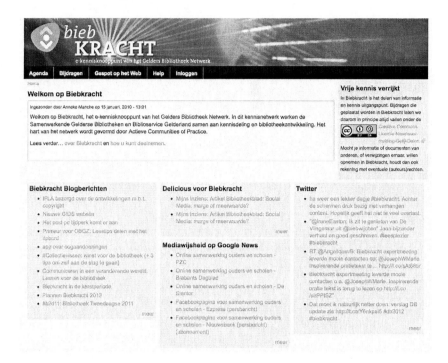

FIGURE 9.3 Biebkracht 1.0

well as to assess how it functioned in real life. Fifteen experts from academia and public libraries were invited to the meeting and, under the guidance of a coach, evaluated the specifications and achievements of the first version as well as its potential to become an effective and sustainable learning network for the entire target group. Based on the recommendations from this expert meeting (Bitter-Rijpkema *et al.* 2012a), along with direct feedback from participants, the platform was updated (see Figure 9.4). In the meantime, the Biebkracht initiative has been instrumental in triggering service, at a national level, for all public libraries in the Netherlands.

Concluding Remarks

Biblioservice Gelderland (BSG) started Biebkracht in 2009 when it realized that its current amalgam of face-to-face project meetings, *ad hoc* contacts and connections via the personal learning networks of its professionals was not adequate to meet the need for structural knowledge-based innovation. BSG and the local libraries needed a learning network that was able to cope with uncertainty and change, one that could meet the specific needs of non-formal, social learning of individuals in the workplace but also could support the whole organization, empowering current and future learning.

FIGURE 9.4 Biebkracht 2.0

It became clear that working with conventional learning scenarios, based on pre-defined, fixed goals was not adequate, but that the situation called for a 'permanent beta' learning network. The learning network needed to be well designed, stable and sustainable for operational use but at the same time flexible and permanently open to necessary change so as to be able to absorb new ways of working collaboratively in the future. The design team needed to design for unpredictability and flexibility. This was achieved by taking a fundamentally participatory design and development approach, in which the network participants contributed from the outset, and increasingly so over time. The educational and technical designers were very active at the start of the project but gradually retreated, leaving the continuous network configuration in the hands of the network administrators and moderators. To achieve this, a flexible design methodology was used, a participatory co-creation approach that allowed improvization in the design – inspired by agile SCRUM-like development methods – resulting in rapid concept collaboration, prototypical realization and iterative improvements.

Technically, the learning network needed to afford organic growth and development of self-managed learning communities. This inherent reconfigurability is technically implemented through a system of highly customizable access mechanisms, allowing network members to create and develop self-managed communities, where access restrictions are determined by the network members. Regarding the network members' access to knowledge artifacts, a similar publication mechanism was implemented, allowing authors to determine in detail which individuals, of what communities, were allowed access to their artifacts.

The results – at the time of writing – are the BLN implementations 1.0 and 2.0 as examples of informal professional networks, where professionals learn in collaboration with their colleagues, in the context of their daily work (Bitter-Rijpkema and Verjans 2010). From January 2010 www.biebkracht.nl has been in use as a virtual learning network. While the prototype was initially developed for a few project communities, it quickly evolved into a permanent beta version. At the time of writing (November 2012), there are approximately 400 active participants. As expected and predicted by the experts at the mid-term evaluation, it takes time to evolve into a large self-sustainable living network embedded in the organization. Its growth is an organic process that is still ongoing.

Note

1 The multidisciplinary, multi-stakeholder design team consists of people from Prof. P. Sloep's LN program, namely: Dr. M. Bitter-Rijpkema, K. Pannekeet, W. Slot, W. Didderen, H. Hermans (Hermans (OUNL-Celstec), Dr. S. Verjans (OUNL-LOOK) and ir Air A. Manche, I. Meuleman, MA, Drs. A. van Betten (BSG/GBN organization). Hosting and technical realization of the mid-life update to Biebkracht 2.0 were done by Ivo Hermans (Betawerk).

References

Avison, D. E., Wood-Harper, A. T., Vidgen, R. T. and Wood, J. R. G., 1998. A further exploration into information systems development: the evolution of Multiview 2. *Information Technology & People*, 11(2), 124–139.

Berlanga, A., Rusman, E., Bitter-Rijpkema, M. and Sloep, P., 2009. Guidelines to foster interaction in online communities. In: R. Koper, ed. *Learning network services for professional development*. Berlin: Springer.

Bitter-Rijpkema, M. and Verjans, S., 2010. Hybrid professional learning networks for knowledge workers: educational theory inspiring new practices. In: L. Creanor, D. Hawkridge, K. Ng and F. Rennie, eds. *ALT-C 2010 – Conference Proceedings into something rich and strange – making sense of the sea-change* (pp. 166–174). September 7–9 2010, University of Nottingham, UK.

Bitter-Rijpkema, M., Didderen, W., Sie, R., Rajagopal, K., Manche, A. and Van Betten, A., 2012a. *Biebkracht expertmeeting: from prototype to workpractice*. Arnhem Internal Report.

Bitter-Rijpkema, M., Verjans, S. and Bruijnzeels, R., 2012b. The library school: empowering the sustainable innovation capacity of new librarians. *Library Management*, 33(1/2), 36–49.

Burns, T. E. and Stalker, G. M., 1961. *The management of innovation*. London: Tavistock Publications.

Callon, M., 2004. The role of hybrid communities and socio-technical arrangements in the participatory design. *Journal of the Center for Information Studies*, 5(3), 3–10.

Ciborra, C. U., 1992. From thinking to tinkering: the grassroots of strategic information systems. *The Information Society*, 8(4), 297–309.

Cummings, Th. G., Worley, Ch. G., 2009. *Organization development and Change,* 9th ed. Mason, OH: Thomson South-Western Cengage Learning.

Fischer, G. (2012) Co-Evolution of Learning, New Media, and New Learning Organizations. In: *Proceedings of the Iadis International Conference "E-Learning 2012"* July, Lisbon, pp. xxvii–xxxiv. Retrieved from http://l3d.cs.colorado.edu/~gerhard/papers/2012/paper-IADIS-final.pdf.

Fischer, G. and Sugimoto, M., 2006. Supporting self-directed learners and learning communities with sociotechnical environments. *International Journal Research and Practice in Technology Enhanced Learning (RPTEL)*, 1(1), 31–64.

Giddens, A. 1984. *The constitution of society: outline of the theory of structuration.* Berkeley: University of California Press.

Goodyear, P. and Carvalho, L., 2013. The analysis of complex learning environments. In: H. Beetham and R. Sharpe, eds. *Rethinking pedagogy for a digital age: designing and delivering e-learning*, 2nd ed. London: Routledge.

Orlikowski, W. J., 1996. Improvising organizational transformation over time: a situated change perspective. *Information Systems Research*, 7(1), 63–92.

Orlikowski, W. J., 2002. Knowing in practice: enacting a collective capability in distributed organizing. *Organization Science*, 13(3), 249–273.

Orlikowski, W. J., 2010. The sociomateriality of organisational life: considering technology in management research. *Cambridge Journal of Economics*, 34(1), 125–141.

Scrum Alliance, 2013. Available from: www.scrumalliance.org [Accessed 1 June 2013].

Sloep, P. B., 2008. *Netwerken voor lerende professionals; hoe leren in netwerken kan bijdragen aan een leven lang leren* [*Networks for learning professionals; how networked learning can contribute to lifelong learning*]. Heerlen: Open Universiteit Nederland. [Retrieved from http://hdl.handle.net/1820/1559]

Sloep, P. B., Van der Klink, M., Brouns, F., Van Bruggen, J. and Didderen, W. eds., 2011. *Leernetwerken; Kennisdeling, kennisontwikkeling en de leerprocessen.* Houten, Netherlands: Bohn, Stafleu, Van Loghum.

Schwaber, K. and Beedle, M., 2012. *Agile software development with Scrum.* Upper Saddle River, NJ: Prentice Hall.

Takeuchi, H. and Nonaka, I., 1986. The new product development game. *Harvard Business Review*, 64(1), 137–146.

Verjans, S. M. E., 2003. *Harmony and stress in information systems development and implementation: a multilevel theory and some empirical work on the crossroads of work psychology, organisational theory and information systems research.* Unpublished Thesis. University of Southern Denmark – Odense University.

Vrieling, E. M., Bastiaens, Th. J. and Stijnen, P. J. J. 2010. Process-oriented design principles for promoting self-regulated learning in primary teacher education. *International Journal of Educational Research*, 49(4–5), 141–150.

Wenger, E., 1998. *Communities of practice: learning, meaning and identity.* Cambridge: Cambridge University Press.

10

QSTREAM

Learning in the 'In-between'

David Ashe, Pippa Yeoman and Tim Shaw

Overview

Reaching professionals with education programs that can improve their application of evidence-based practice can be extremely challenging. This chapter looks at one example of a networked learning environment that has been designed to provide flexible and effective learning for such professionals.

Qstream,[1] developed by academics at Harvard Medical School, is the product of research into the neuroscience of memory. Using a question-and-answer format, the environment integrates the delivery of information with the testing and tracking of each learner's progress. It brings together learners, teachers and professionals in a learning environment, which is designed specifically to improve the retention and recall of critical information when and where it is needed. Based on the research of Dr. B. Price Kerfoot, Qstream went online in 2008 and is used in diverse settings by thousands of people, from scholars to medical practitioners and from hi-tech industries to those of retail and sales. Qstream takes a 'spaced' approach to learning and is based on two premises: that small amounts of information repeatedly presented over a spaced time frame, and repeated testing of that information, produce better learning outcomes. The design of the environment evolved to support learning in this way and has the added benefit of mitigating the time constraints associated with learning when actively engaged in practice. That is, rather than presenting training in blocks or units delivered in either a fixed location or at a particular point in time, Qstream uses ambient technology to enable learners to make use of 'in-between' times in order to master critical content.

Interaction within the Qstream environment is facilitated through questions in which knowledge is tested, followed by feedback to clarify answers and discussion to promote a sense of collegial support. Creating a Qstream account gives the learner access to browse courses on offer. On signing up, learners are able to specify both the frequency of question delivery and the number of questions they will receive with each release. Having submitted an answer, the learner is provided with material elaborating on the answer and a space in which they can ask questions or make comments. This feature encourages discussion amongst learners, and between learners and subject experts. As the environment provides a way to structure and deliver content and not the content itself, it can be described as being content neutral – fit for use in many fields. Of the current courses on offer, it is the Continuing Medical Education (CME) programs that are most popular, with some having thousands of learners enrolled. The examples used in this chapter come from the CME learning programs.

This chapter analyzes Qstream's design for learning. We explore how the environment combines the administrative function of question delivery with the social aspects of discussion forums to bring about sustained and effective learning (Kerfoot et al. 2009, 2010a). In line with other chapters in this volume, our analysis covers four key areas; the set, epistemic, and social design; and the co-creation and co-configuration activities of learners. Bringing these dimensions together, we look at how the environment is being used from a learner's perspective and how individual learners reconfigure their learning environment. We explore some of the ways in which learners take charge of their personal learning trajectories, becoming knowledgeable in their subject and passing on that expertise to future learners. We note the blurring of lines between expert and novice, and learner and teacher, and in conclusion we hope to identify some key elements within its design that may be applied to other learning networks.

Epistemic Design

There are occasions when it is imperative that individuals quickly recall previously learned information with speed and accuracy. For example, medical practitioners are often required to rapidly recall critical, context dependent information and research has shown that this ability diminishes over time (McKenna and Glendon 1985). In a study conducted amongst nursing staff who had taken an advanced cardiac life support examination, it was shown that of those who passed the initial training, only 30 percent passed when resitting the test three months later, and only 14 percent did so at the 12-month mark (Kerfoot et al. 2010a). Results like this prompted Kerfoot and colleagues to pursue the development of a learning environment that could harness the benefits of spaced education. Qstream, the product of their research, has been shown (in numerous randomized controlled trials) to improve learners' ability to recall previously learned information and skills across multiple contexts (Kerfoot 2008, Kerfoot et al. 2007, 2009, 2010a, 2010b, Kerfoot and Baker 2012a, 2012b).

Designing a course that can target this type of learning presents difficulties, not least of which is coming to a firm consensus of what needs to be learned and then being able to present that knowledge in a well-articulated way. Qstream provides an environment that assists authors in ways of communicating the knowledge to be learned and assists learners to aggregate that knowledge and pace their learning experience. Qstream differs significantly from other online training courses in that it provides learners with a framework within which to interact with learning material, reminds them to take part in the activity, but allows them to decide when and where the learning will take place.

The design of Qstream is based on two major research findings in psychology, 'the spacing effect' and 'the testing effect':

- *The spacing effect.* It has long been recognized in memory research that it is easier to remember items if they are presented multiple times over 'spaced' periods of time (Ebbinghaus 1913). More recently these ideas have been extended by Sisti *et al.* (2007), who describe this effect as an increase in retention when the same information is presented repeatedly over spaced intervals, rather than being presented at a single point in time. In the case of a learner being required to recall specific facts in a given context, learning a response repeatedly over an extended period of time is more likely to be effective than learning it at one particular point in time, say for a single test. Qstream builds on this research by incorporating into its design features that enable information to be presented to learners repeatedly over a carefully calculated time frame, thereby creating opportunities for increasing both the acquisition and retention of knowledge.
- *The testing effect.* The testing effect, first reported by Gates (1917), suggests that the process of testing alters the learning process itself to significantly improve knowledge retention. This effect was further demonstrated by Carrier and Pashler (1992), who show that increasing the number of tests that a learner has to go through results in longer-term retention of information. They state that 'learning should include a large number of test trials' (p. 641). More recently it has been demonstrated that testing not only assesses mastery but also alters the learning process in ways that are beneficial for retention (Karpicke and Roediger 2008, Roediger and Karpicke 2006). Qstream has been shown to be effective in increasing retention and in changing behavior in a number of randomized controlled trials (Kerfoot and Baker 2012b, Shaw *et al.* 2012, Kerfoot *et al.* 2009, 2010a, 2010b). The design of Qstream implements the testing effect practically by presenting learners with ongoing tests, recording the results of those tests and repeating the tests until the learner has accurately demonstrated the knowledge a requisite number of times. In addition, learners are presented with succinct feedback about their performance and this has been demonstrated to further enhance the retention of knowledge (Larsen *et al.* 2008).

By addressing these psychological findings within the design of Qstream, Kerfoot and his team set out to help learners participating in continuing medical education to acquire and retain critical, context-specific knowledge. By considering the impacts of these findings broadly as they relate to all learning, Kerfoot and colleagues have designed and provided an environment that can be used in a similar fashion by those in other fields.

The task design supported by Qstream is based on learners answering one or more questions in a short session. This is achieved (in the set design) by using multiple-choice questions, with either one correct answer using a radio button response, or multiple correct answers using check boxes that allow for the selection of more than one answer. As the point of entry into a course is a question, not the presentation of content, there is an assumption that learners have already been exposed to the material under review. Learners are presented with a question and are required to answer it as best they can. Once an answer has been submitted, feedback is immediate and clear. A table is presented listing each answer, a red cross to the left of incorrect answers, a green tick next to each correct answer and a blue marker indicating the choice of the learner. Alongside this information is a bar graph showing the percentage of learners who answered each question. Regardless of whether or not the response was correct, the learner is presented with material elaborating on the correct answer (Figure 10.1). Results from studies have shown that this method of questioning followed by revealing both the answer and supporting details is effective in enabling learners to access information when and where it is needed (Kerfoot *et al.* 2007).

Current research conducted on learners using the Qstream environment has shown an improvement in long-term retention and recall of clinical and surgical skills and changes in clinicians' diagnostic behavior (Shaw *et al.* 2012, Kerfoot *et al.* 2010a), in addition to promising indications of transfer of learning across contexts (Kerfoot *et al.* 2010b).

These recent studies build on research conducted by Entwistle and Entwistle (2003) about students' preparation for examinations. Entwistle and Entwistle (2003) found a connection between memorizing and understanding; observing that students used memorized information to create 'knowledge objects', which in turn assisted them in the process of deeper thinking. As such, the design of Qstream can be said to encourage learners to reflect on their own practices and provides them with an opportunity to consider complex issues within their field.

Set Design

The Qstream learning environment is hosted online, delivered via mobile technology, and is accessed by learners at a time and place that is convenient to them. 'Reminders' to complete questions are sent via email or RSS feed. Queuing reminders in this way leverages the benefits of using the learner's current email

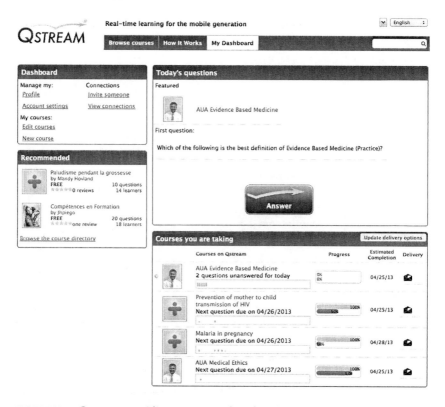

FIGURE 10.1 Qstream: providing answers and explanations

system, giving them the freedom to answer questions as a part of their daily routine. In the current interface, a new learner is presented with an array of different learning materials. Browsing through courses on offer, prospective learners will find brief summaries of each, including the number of learners enrolled and an estimation of the level of commitment required in terms of the total number of questions. Once a selection has been made, the learner is taken to the course home page, which provides further details including reviews and a brief biography of the author. Some courses are mandatory for particular cohorts; an example of this is *Surgical Ethics and Professionalism*, which is a requirement for final-year medical students at the University of Sydney, Australia. In these cases, the author retains significant control over the operational parameters of the delivery and timing of questions throughout the duration of the course.

Where learners are given more flexibility, enrolment includes either accepting the author's recommended parameters – governing the number of questions per delivery and the space between each release – or tailoring them to suit their particular circumstances. For example, the recommendation may be that a learner should accept two questions per release and receive a delivery every day

FIGURE 10.2 Qstream: specifying operational parameters

(Figure 10.2). A learner enrolled in more than one course may elect to complete four questions every second day in order to accommodate other commitments. In this way, the design of the learning environment has some flexibility, allowing learners to customize the 'set' according to their individual needs and preferences.

Underlying this flexibility are the designed elements that make it possible to structure courses in a question-and-answer format, and to break down testing and teaching into manageable chunks. This structure, when combined with the benefits of mobile technology, enables learners to accommodate course work within everyday routines. It does this by 'pushing' information to the learner in the form of a question, as opposed to relying on the learner 'pulling' content from a static environment. On reading an email that includes the question, the learner is invited to respond by clicking an 'answer now' button, which links directly to that question on their Qstream dashboard. While it is relatively easy to ignore an email, and not take part in the day's delivery, unanswered questions are not 'missed' but return to the pool from which the next release is drawn. This does, however, delay the time to course completion. In this way, the learner has the ability to control the pace of his/her own learning, within an environment structured to facilitate choice: to continue with the course that day; to leave it until another day; or to withdraw from the course altogether. In practice, however, the burden in terms of time and cognitive effort is low, making it easy to deal with the request and move on. The ease with which learners can respond to individual questions makes this environment both attractive to learners and successful in terms of training.

It is the 'push' of the question-and-answer format that provides simplicity at the micro level; however, it is the personal dashboard that provides cohesion at the macro level. Each learner is provided with a bird's eye view of how they are traveling on all their courses. The dashboard (Figure 10.3) consists of six fields including today's questions, a list of all courses the learner is enrolled in, a list of those they have created, recommendations for other courses, a general settings manager and updates from people and courses the learner is linked to. The graphical representation of progress towards completion is striking. A horizontal bar

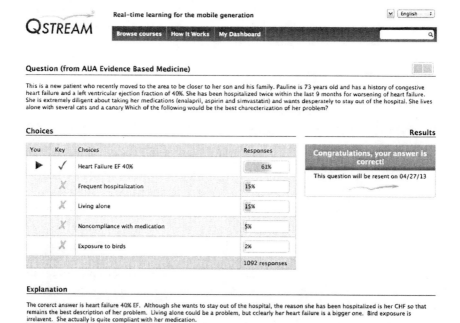

FIGURE 10.3 Qstream: a personal overview of progress

graph in red immediately flags a course in which the learner has fallen behind. Where a learner is on track, a green bar indicates the percentage of questions attempted, and underneath this bar, a gray one illustrates the percentage of questions that have been 'retired'. The course is completed when either a minimum threshold of retired questions is reached or all questions have been retired depending on the parameters established by the author. For example, the course may require that for a question to be retired it should be answered correctly three times, with a space of a few days between the first two correct answers and a space of a number of weeks between the second and the third correct answer. As the date of completion depends on whether the learner is keeping up with the pace set for the course and whether the questions are being answered correctly, the personal dashboard includes a current estimated completion date. Linking the micro actions of the learner in answering each and every question with the graphical representations of progress towards completion at the macro level illustrates how the designed elements of the environment support the underlying epistemic design of Qstream.

Social Design

Qstream is a learning environment designed to leverage the cumulative effect of multiple short encounters. As such, the intention is not to draw learners in for extended periods of time but to facilitate the delivery, answering and tracking of questions with the least amount of disruption to daily life. This being noted, Qstream does include designed elements that foster both competitive and relationship-building social interactions amongst learners.

The environment, while designed with the individual in mind, always provides low-level ambient feedback that depicts the learner in relation to all other learners. Each time a question is answered, participants are given immediate feedback including what percentage of their peers have submitted each answer and how many have successfully retired that question from their list of possible questions. This type of information, while giving the viewer a visual representation of their performance compared with that of their peers, is still personal; it aggregates 'the rest' and is not public. At this level, 'social' interaction may be deemed to be competitive rather than concerned with relationship building. However, it has been shown to be effective in terms of motivating learners (Kerfoot and Baker 2012a, 2012b). On a more public level the design of the environment includes elements such as the de-identified dynamic leader board that allows participants to see how they are performing compared with their peers. This can be extended to include groups of learners, such as nurses on a given ward or teams of nurses across multiple wards. While still largely competitive in nature, this element has been instrumental in fostering social camaraderie within groups.

To support relationship building, space for asynchronous dialogue is provided in the form of comment boxes at the level of question, course review and within personal networks. While there is a sense that cohorts move through courses and do not return to individual questions, they do leave traces of their participation in these spaces. Some questions become mini discussion boards that are added to by different people over extended periods of time. This asynchronous social interaction appears to foster a sense of professional collegiality without the demands of real-time social networking sites and often evokes a more collegial response from learners or mentors who offer support for those who are preparing for examinations that mark the passage from novice to expert. It is in these message threads that one can see evidence of an asynchronous relationship-building element within the site. This simple, non-intrusive mechanism facilitates the sedimentation of peer mentoring over time.

Dialogue at question level offers learners the opportunity to discuss content, whereas dialogue at the course level is facilitated through a simple review mechanism. Learners past and present are encouraged to provide a 'star' rating for each course, by highlighting any number of stars from one to five, along with a short text-based review to justify their rating. These reviews operate as an informal referral system for learners and as a means of feedback for the authors.

Following a link to the introductory page of a course takes a learner to a dashboard, which functions at the course level. Here learners will find an 'about me' field, which is used by authors of courses in varying degrees. Through this element of set design, authors and learners are able to customize their social profile: some choose only to include basic biographical details while others choose to publish qualifications, publications and references in a way that actively seeks to establish their credentials within the environment. This set up mirrors the learner's profile page, and together these 'about me' spaces provide both learners and authors with the opportunity to express their identities in ways that suit them. Where a cohort or community of peers actively participates in a Qstream course, individuals have access to an activity feed that provides updates on the comments and courses of those with whom they are connected. The feed can be found on the bottom left-hand corner of the dashboard, and hyperlinks make following the ongoing commentary and introductions to the new courses of one's peers very easy. It contains only the most recent information and operates as an aside, rather than part of the core information flow. Thus, the learning environment is designed to maintain the focus on multiple short interactions with current course content, while making further connections within the community in a simple and undemanding way.

This subtle balance between ease of access and a sense of collegial competition has seen 70 percent of all learners completing the courses for which they enroll. Other evidence of Qstream's success can be demonstrated in the fact that 75 percent of learners enrolled have elected to take more than one course. Current research amongst physicians shows that this model is preferred 3:1 over other web-based training (Kerfoot 2008, Lennox and Kerfoot 2012) and anecdotal evidence that echoes these findings can be found amongst the reviews posted by a broad cross-section of learners within the Qstream learning environment.

Leader boards, feedback, comments and reviews form a network that fosters social interaction within the Qstream learning environment. Connecting Qstream to the wider world is achieved at a corporate level through various social media outlets. These links serve to disseminate new research, highlight upcoming conferences and training sessions and loosely connect current learners to the wider Qstream network.

Set, Epistemic and Social Co-creation and Co-configuration Activities

Qstream is at its core a way to orchestrate learning over a spaced time frame for large cohorts not connected by shared learning times or learning spaces. What starts out as an administrative hub, once colonized, becomes a supportive and collegial learning environment, through the joint sharing of professional knowledge and personal experiences.

Central to this metamorphosis is the role of asynchronous message threads that build over time to inform, encourage and correct those who follow. To a new learner it is the course reviews that provide an initial point of access into the environment. Reviews left by others guide course selection, giving both practical and theoretical feedback on different aspects of individual courses. Once enrolled in a course, learners are prompted to add comments to questions and exchange ideas about course material. These interactions, which are asynchronous and often entail responses to individuals who have already finished the course, leave a digital trail for future learners. In this way, material created by learners may not be of immediate benefit to them, or even their cohort, but over time becomes a valuable resource for future learners.

A recent addition to the Qstream environment is the ability for authors of a course to create questions with open text answers. The emergence of this format has increased the potential for learners to make a significant contribution to learning material for future use. As these types of questions have no fixed right or wrong answers, the ensuing discussion often provides participants with valuable opportunities for reflection on complex issues within the field. This has been shown to be particularly effective in the course *Surgical Ethics and Professionalism*, where learners are asked open-ended questions such as the following:

> *Bob is an elderly man who has been admitted from a nursing home and has been placed under your care. It is clear early during his admission that an escalation of his care would not provide any medical benefit. The family are insistent that* 'everything is done for Grandpa'.

How do you manage this situation?

Learners are invited to respond in a text box with a limit of 140 characters. Once an answer is tendered, learners are presented with a selection of alternative answers, proposed by past learners. They are then required to select a final answer, choosing either their original answer or one of the alternative responses provided. In this way, the learning environment is designed to accumulate a case library of sorts, which exposes learners to a wide array of opinions. A facility for comments built into the feedback learners receive encourages lively discussion around differing interpretations of the scenario or case presented. These threads grow in an organic way that reflects the interests and concerns of the learners within the environment. The discussion actively engages some, but persists in a way that informs others, and generates debate into the future.

In many cases, those who use the Qstream environment work towards the completion of a course on their own, albeit with assistance from the author and other past and present learners; however, the environment is equally able to support teams. This is well illustrated by a recent quality improvement program for nurses on *Patient Safety and Infection Control*. For this course, members of the nursing staff were put into ward-based teams and each team was asked to compete, as a team of individuals, by answering a set of Qstream questions. Nurses taking part in the program were assigned pseudonyms that allowed them to track their performance across the course, compared with their peers, on a de-identified dynamic leader board. This addition to the learning environment has been very popular amongst nursing teams and has led to an increase in discussions about patient safety and infection control on the wards in which it has been used. Although in some cases the team challenge resulted in a pooling of resources amongst the individuals on a team, B. P. Kerfoot argues that it has contributed to an increase in learners' understanding of key aspects of the course and to their awareness of associated issues (personal communication, October 12, 2012).

Qstream's design provides a structure for learning in fields where the ability to recall information, or react in a particular fashion in a given context, is crucial. The appropriation of this design by learners in other fields can be observed in the diversity of courses currently on offer via Qstream. What these fields have in common is the use of examinations for accreditation or advancement, a need to master specific critical content that governs behavior and a high representation of professionals who work either in shifts or in decentralized teams. It appears that the Qstream learning environment acts to connect learners over time and space.

Abstracting and Synthesis

Whether it is the underlying epistemic design, the efficient appropriation of mobile technology, the clear visual representation of one's passage through a course, the presence of collegial competition or the slow accretion of shared knowledge and experience, it is clear that Qstream provides a learning environment that is sufficiently effective and malleable to be used across many fields. The designers of

Qstream have managed to achieve something quite remarkable: to interrupt without interrupting. The persistent delivery of short questions at calculated intervals via email sees learners answering their 'daily dose' on the train, in the queue or over a coffee. Coupled with the dashboard, which illustrates the aggregation of all these 'bits', ranking the individual learner amongst all other learners results more often than not in course completion.

The rapid recall of previously learned information central to a discipline, profession or subject, while critical to learning, has somehow lost its appeal. Mastery based on repetition and drill, while acknowledged as necessary, is not often explicitly designed for. Qstream was developed in response to this need. Acknowledging that memorization is linked to understanding, and that understanding prepares learners to engage with the complex issues within their field, reveals what lies at the core of this learning environment. For an epistemic perspective that values spacing, repetition and administrative automation, asynchronous mobile communication is a perfect match. To unpack the success of Qstream one must surely focus on its ability to penetrate the physical, digital and social lives of learners already engaged in practice and on how these practices intersect in time and space.

Note

1 Accessed at www.qstream.com. Please note that the network as described in this chapter may have evolved since the time of writing.

References

Carrier, M. and Pashler, H., 1992. The influence of retrieval on retention. *Memory & Cognition*, 20(6), 633–642.

Ebbinghaus, H., 1913. *Memory: a contribution to experimental psychology*. Trans. from German, Ruger, H. A. and Bussenius, C. E., New York: Teachers College, Columbia University.

Entwistle, N. and Entwistle, D., 2003. Preparing for examinations: the interplay of memorising and understanding, and the development of knowledge objects. *Higher Education Research and Development*, 22(1), 19–41.

Gates, A. I., 1917. Recitation as a factor in memorizing. *Archives of Psychology*, 6(40), 1–104.

Karpicke, J. D. and Roediger, H. L., 2008. The critical importance of retrieval for learning. *Science*, 319(5865), 966–968.

Kerfoot, B. P., 2008. Interactive spaced education versus web based modules for teaching urology to medical students: a randomized controlled trial. *The Journal of Urology*, 179(6), 2351–2357.

Kerfoot, B. P. and Baker, H., 2012a. An online spaced-education game for global continuing medical education: a randomized trial. *Annals of Surgery*, 256(1), 33–38.

Kerfoot, B. P. and Baker, H., 2012b. An online spaced-education game to teach and assess residents: a multi-institutional prospective trial. *Journal of the American College of Surgeons*, 214(3), 367–373.

Kerfoot, B. P., DeWolf, W. C., Masser, B. A., Church, P. A. and Federman, D. D., 2007. Spaced education improves the retention of clinical knowledge by medical students: a randomised controlled trial. *Medical Education*, 41(1), 23–31.

Kerfoot, B. P., Fu, Y., Baker, H., Connelly, D., Ritchey, M. L. and Genega, E. M., 2010a. Online spaced education generates transfer and improves long-term retention of diagnostic skills: a randomized controlled trial. *Journal of the American College of Surgeons*, 211(3), 331–337.

Kerfoot, B. P., Kearney, M. C., Connelly, D. and Ritchey, M. L., 2009. Interactive spaced education to assess and improve knowledge of clinical practice guidelines: a randomized controlled trial. *Annals of Surgery*, 249(5), 744–749.

Kerfoot, B. P., Lawler, E. V, Sokolovskaya, G., Gagnon, D. and Conlin, P. R., 2010b. Durable improvements in prostate cancer screening from online spaced education: a randomized controlled trial. *American Journal of Preventive Medicine*, 39(5), 472–478.

Larsen, D. P., Butler, A. C. and Roediger, H. L., 2008. Test-enhanced learning in medical education. *Medical Education*, 42(10), 959–966.

Lennox, D. and Kerfoot, B. P., 2012. *Sales force effectiveness insights in 3 minutes a day* [online]. Qstream. Available from: http://qstream.com/resources/articles/sales-force-effectiveness-insights-in-3-minutes-a-day [Accessed 20 May 2013].

McKenna, S. and Glendon, A., 1985. Occupational first aid training: decay in cardiopulmonary resuscitation (CPR) skills. *Journal of Occupational Psychology*, 58, 109–117.

Roediger, H. L. and Karpicke, J. D., 2006. Test-enhanced learning: taking memory tests improves long-term retention. *Psychological Science*, 17(3), 249–255.

Shaw, T. J., Heit, J. J., Co, J. P.T., Ghandi, T., Pernar, L. I., Peyre, S. E., Helfrick, J. F., Vogelgesang, K. R., Graydon-Baker, E., Chretien, Y., Brown, E. J., and Nicholson, J. C., 2012. Impact of online education on intern behaviour around joint commission national patient safety goals: a randomised trial. *BMJ Quality & Safety*, 21(10), 819–825.

Sisti, H. M., Glass, A. L., and Shors, T. J., 2007. Neurogenesis and the spacing effect: learning over time enhances memory and the survival of new neurons. *Learning & Memory*, 14(5), 368–375.

11

ISQUA KNOWLEDGE

Fostering a Sense of Community for the
Emerging Field of Quality in Health Care

Dewa Wardak, Paul Parker and Tim Shaw

Overview

In September 2011 the International Society for Quality in Health Care (ISQua
Ltd.) launched ISQua Knowledge, a collaborative learning platform that was to
operate independently of the parent organization. The platform was designed
to connect individuals with an interest in improving quality and safety in health
care, through an environment that facilitated sharing, with the intention of
developing a global knowledge base. In October 2012, prompted by both user
feedback and the changing priorities of the organization, the environment was
redesigned and launched from within the website of the parent organization,
ISQua Ltd. Although ISQua Knowledge is no longer a distinct entity, several of
the most successful features of the original platform have been retained. The
analysis presented in this chapter is based on the first version of ISQua Knowledge.

ISQua Knowledge was designed to meet the needs of a broad cross-section
of individuals with an interest in quality and safety in health care. Participants
included students and educators, researchers and professionals, experts in key
topic areas, government and/or policy representatives and consumers. Collective
knowledge creation and professional networking were facilitated through access
to information and resources, online learning activities and collaboration with
peers and experts in areas of common interest. Participation brought with it
the opportunity to develop a professional profile and become part of one of
many dynamic communities formed around key topics in an emerging field of
medical practice.

The discipline of safety and quality in health care has grown over the past
15 years. With the release of the report *To Err is Human*, by the Institute of
Medicine in 1999, the impact of adverse events on patient care has become more
visible. The pivotal role played by this report was the revelation that as many as a

million patient injuries and 98,000 patient deaths resulted from adverse events in health care annually in the United States alone (Kohn *et al*. 1999). It was within this context that ISQua Ltd. launched ISQua Knowledge as a platform to facilitate change in safety and quality in health care through education, collaboration and research, and by the dissemination of knowledge worldwide. To this end, ISQua Ltd. collaborated with a number of internationally recognized organizations such as the Canadian Patient Safety Institute (CPSI), United States Agency for International Development (USAID), Health Care Improvement Project (HCI) and World Health Organization (WHO). The aim of these partnerships was to contribute to global knowledge in health-care quality by organizing resources, and by allowing interested stakeholders to connect with expert convenors and professional leaders through the ISQua Knowledge platform.

ISQua Knowledge benefited from these partnerships by gaining access to a large number of individuals (an estimated 90,000) with an interest in quality and safety in health care. Wide recognition of the activities and services offered through the website saw the number of registered users increase to over 1,200 people. The ISQua Knowledge web environment was designed to stimulate these users to contribute to activities on the website and to promote participation in the Salzburg Global Seminar. The Salzburg Global Seminar is an annual event that brings experts and leaders from around the world, together with key organizations and agencies involved in improving health-care quality and safety, to discuss current issues and plan improvements in health-care quality in developing countries.

ISQua Knowledge provided its users with options to participate in various online activities such as online debates, expert-led discussions, online workshops, ISQua talks, blogs and webinars; all focused around key issues in health care related to quality and safety. Other resources provided by the environment were real-life stories from people working in this area, interviews with experts and opportunities to network with those in leadership positions. ISQua Knowledge provided links to external resources such as information reports and current research outcomes in the area. Resources were carefully selected and aimed at offering high quality, evidence-based information that would benefit the work practices of its members. Another strategy to attract greater involvement and collaboration from individuals in this area was to offer an ISQua Fellowship to registered users. The fellowship, which remains the cornerstone of the redesigned environment, is a professional qualification awarded in recognition of an individual's contributions to research, quality improvement, teaching and knowledge translation, including an active involvement in ISQua Knowledge. The social value associated with the ISQua Fellowship is that it provides international recognition for professional development and achievement in health-care quality and safety for selected individuals.

Quality and safety in health care are relatively under-researched, particularly in developing nations, and ISQua Knowledge addresses this, by offering access to resources and opportunities for collaboration and learning from experts in the field, which helped to bridge these gaps. As interest grew amongst users, concerns about the sustainability of the ISQua Knowledge model prompted the redesign of the platform. The redevelopment was guided by users' feedback and in consultation with partner organizations with the intention of providing access to larger numbers of experts in the area, and a unique professional development program. Under the new plan, the redesigned site will focus on developing the fellowship program to encourage participation and as a means of generating a potential source of revenue.

Set Design

Our analysis focused on the digital space represented by the ISQua Knowledge platform between September 2011 and October 2012, supplemented by an interview conducted with a member of the ISQua Steering Committee.

To support wide participation and ensure access by health professionals from developing countries, it was important to avoid specialized hardware or software in the design of the ISQua Knowledge platform. As such the site could be accessed via a web browser on any device with Internet connectivity. While some features, such as video, required Adobe Flash player, this is available free of charge for most browsers. The site contents could be viewed publicly. However, to contribute, post comments and take part in some activities, users were required to register as members. Registration was free of charge but required the users to share some of their personal contact details.

At first glance, the ISQua Knowledge site appeared busy (Figure 11.1). On closer examination, three main sections were used to display information: the header, the footer and the main contents. The home page was slightly different from the main content pages and all content pages shared the same layout. The global navigation system was displayed in the header with the website name and logo on the far left-hand side. Within this configuration the logo also acted as a link back to the home page from any point in the site. On the right-hand side of the header were seven main navigational links: Home, ISQua (ISQua Ltd. website), About, Contact Us, Feedback, Register, and Sign In. The section housed within the footer displayed the copyright sign on the right, and links to Home, Privacy Information, Terms of Use and FAQs (frequently asked questions) on the left. Both the header and the footer remained consistent throughout the website, displaying the same links on each page.

The middle section of the home page was divided into two horizontal panes. The upper pane was dedicated to promoting current news and events, displaying either two or three items at a time, while the lower pane, which was divided vertically, housed to the right a link to the latest Spotlight – a series of interviews with experts in quality and safety – as well as links to sponsors and information

FIGURE 11.1 ISQua Knowledge: home page

on the benefits of ISQua membership. On the left-hand side of this pane were links to the values underpinning the site: Activities, Communities and Fellowship. Clicking any of these links took the user to the corresponding page, where they would find further information.

On the content pages, the global navigation of the header and footer remained the same. However, a secondary local navigation appeared above the main contents, which provided links to additional features and resources related to that topic. In addition, the content pages also displayed a breadcrumb trail below the local navigation. Breadcrumb navigation acts as a visual aid that displays the user's location within the website. In terms of usability, breadcrumbs are an important feature of large websites (Vora 2009), like ISQua Knowledge, which has content organized in a hierarchical manner. The main content sections were divided into two vertical spaces (Figure 11.2). The left-hand side displayed contents directly related to the topic; and the right-hand side provided additional information, such as suggested readings on the topic, links to external resources, details of the activity of conveners or, on some pages, current news and events. The Activities page contained links to several collaborative tasks available through ISQua Knowledge.

FIGURE 11.2 ISQua Knowledge: contents page

These links provided opportunities for various types of user involvement. The first deployment of the platform included links to the following:

- *Social media series* were a series of blog posts aimed at educating the users about the benefits of social media for health-care professionals.
- *Members' stories* provided a space where ISQua Knowledge members could tell the stories of their professional development and express their opinions about quality and safety in health care.
- The *Debates* activity was generally chaired by one ISQua member, with four other members debating 'for' or 'against' a pre-defined motion.
- The *Spotlight on Salzburg* activity enabled the users to participate remotely in this seminar by contributing to the discussion before, during and after the seminar.
- *Expert-Led Discussions* included links to webinars and online discussion forums convened by experts in the area.
- *Online workshops* provided links to learning materials on related topics, generally in the form of videos and additional recommended reading and resources.

- *ISQua talks* replicated the same format as TED talks. These were short videos of influential leaders in the area discussing controversial topics in health-care quality.
- *Meet the author* contained a series of interviews with authors who had recently published research in the area of health-care quality.
- *Blogs* featured a list of blog posts by members sharing their personal reflections, opinions and stories about key topics in health-care quality.
- *Spotlight* featured a series of short interviews with professionals working in the area of quality and safety in health care from around the world. Each interviewee was asked the same set of questions – aimed at providing a quick introduction.
- *Leaders' networks* provided opportunities to connect with influential leaders in the area. This section provided links to ISQua Knowledge members' profiles pages, blogs, posts and other contributions to the site.

The Fellowship page contained information on the fellowship program and asked users to register their interest in order to receive notifications about application and related procedures. The Communities page had links to three communities: Patient-Centered Care, Research and Accreditation. Each community was moderated by one or two experts. The Patient-Centered Care and Research communities had links to a knowledge base containing reports on the latest research in the area, community news, tools and useful resources, examples and best practices, authors and leaders in that community and educational links such as external courses and workshops. Most of the activities detailed above were related to one of these three communities. For example, the Accreditation community mainly provided opportunity for debate in that area, while Expert-Led Discussions had links to four activities related to the Patient-Centered Care community and three related to the Research community.

Epistemic Design

One of the design intentions underlying ISQua Knowledge was to provide access to a pool of learning resources to help individuals learn and implement strategies related to quality and safety in health care. As such, the platform did not target a specific audience, so the visitors to the site included professionals and experts as well as students and other people with an interest in the area. Intended for a broad base, the desired learning outcomes for ISQua Knowledge users primarily related to one of the following three central goals:

1. First, raising participants' awareness of strategies and practices for improving the safety and quality of health care.
2. Second, building participants' capacity for critical reflection on their practice as related to the growing body of evidence on safety and quality.

3. Finally, in building self-confidence to practice differently and lead change in practice amongst others to improve safety and quality in health care.

Participation was voluntary; therefore, the site organizers had to think carefully about how to engage the users in the activities of the site. This was in contrast to, for example, the Peep environment (see Chapter 4) where the participants are required to contribute and upload their work as part of their assignments. Regular email updates on existing and planned activities were sent to all registered users as a way to encourage contributions from members. ISQua Knowledge also utilized a Twitter account and a Facebook page to publicize the activities on the website. Users were also encouraged to explore its many sections, to take part in the activities, to contribute their ideas and to connect with other members. Several strategies were used to increase participation, and this chapter discusses some of the most successful strategies.

The starting point was to create a site where visitors would find relevant information on key topics in quality and safety in health care. The aim was to provide an environment that housed information that visitors could not easily find elsewhere. Furthermore, the resources and links to external materials were selected by experts in the area to make sure the materials provided succinct and relevant information of high quality that users could readily apply in their workplace. A second successful strategy was to provide users with a forum in which they could both ask questions of, and make connections with, high profile leaders and experts in quality and safety in health care. Safety and Quality is still a relatively new discipline and this made ISQua Knowledge one of a small number of environments where individuals could learn from the real-life experiences of experts in this field. For users in developing nations especially, the site provided a way of connecting with peers working in this area.

To encourage active participation in discussions, the site organizers often opted for raising controversial or 'hot' topics. For example, a discussion on Patient-Centered Care used the heading 'Is it cost-effective to kill patients?' as a way to attract members to the debate on the cost–benefit analysis of patient care. Similar strategies were also used to attract participation in debates, where callouts were intentionally phrased to sound controversial. The motion for one of the debates was, 'There really is no evidence that accreditation has improved the quality of care provided in hospitals or patient safety; in fact, the number of adverse events is increasing'. ISQua Knowledge members were then asked to vote for or against the motion. The members could also reply to the motion by posting their comments on the page. Another way to encourage participation was by introducing topics with short thought-provoking videos that acted as triggers. These videos were designed to challenge beliefs, opinions and biases and to stimulate thinking about issues from a range of different perspectives. Participants were then invited to respond to the video and share their opinions or experiences. ISQua Talks served a similar purpose.

ISQua Knowledge also provided opportunities for members to shape the knowledge practices of this emerging field by inviting participation in the decision-making processes associated with the running of discussions and the topics to be discussed in pre-seminar activities and in workshops at the Salzburg Global Seminar. In addition, participants in the pre-seminar were invited to contribute to the agenda for the seminar by posting their questions, comments and suggestions. The collated results were shared with those who participated in the workshop, after which they were made available to all members of ISQua Knowledge for further discussion and comment. Members could also read about and respond to the experiences of the seminar attendees who posted their daily deliberations and reflections on what was happening at the event.

Another feature that supported the underlying epistemic design of the site and proved very successful at attracting participation was live webinars. Participants were strongly motivated by both the immediacy and the afforded real-time interaction with professionals and experts in the field. Looking to the future, the introduction of the Fellowship, where participation in ISQua Activities is mandated, is also designed to increase participation for the benefit of all.

Social Design

On registering, members were asked to create a profile page, where they had the option to upload their photo and provide information about their background in health care, education and the current position that they held. The completion of these fields allowed for some flexibility in terms of the amount of information they chose to provide, and a member's profile would only become visible to others on the site once they had contributed to an activity. There was no search function on the site and no other method of gaining access to profiles. This feature encouraged members to contribute to the activities in order to become visible. Once a member had made a contribution, the member's name and photo appeared as a link to their profile next to the contribution. This feature enabled users to click on the name or the photo of the contributing member and see their profile, including their professional background information. In this way, users could check the professional background and qualifications of those who contributed to posts.

Even though the social design did not have a specific design feature to make members' hierarchy immediately explicit or visible on ISQua Knowledge, there were a number of design elements in the network that dealt with the visibility of members' 'knowledge status'. For example, members who assumed specific roles in certain activities were more prominently identified, such as conveners for communities, debates, discussions and other activities. There was also a list of 15 expert members in Patient-Centered Care available to all. This was known as the Leaders' Network. Users could find out more about experts in the area, reading the interviews with members on the Spotlight, Meet The Authors and

Member Stories pages. In addition, registered members could vote for their favorite contributions, by clicking on a small thumbs-up icon at the bottom of most contributions, posts and pages. This feature offered another way for members to gain prominence within the community. Furthermore, most member-contributed activities were moderated and the site had a full-time knowledge coordinator who scheduled events and activities, most of them either highly or semi-structured. The highly structured activities included debates, seminars, expert-led discussions and online workshops. These activities had a pre-defined structure for tasks and required certain types of participation from members, such as voting for a motion or responding to a question.

Important aspects of the social design of ISQua Knowledge, such as roles and divisions of labor, reflected the task structures and can be clearly seen, for example, in the Salzburg Global Seminar, expert-led discussions and online workshops. Organizing the online activities for the Salzburg Global Seminar required significant input from volunteers drawn from the membership base of ISQua Knowledge. Before the seminar, ISQua Knowledge invited a number of members, who were intending to attend it in person, to post a short video exploring key issues related to barriers, resources or leadership in quality and safety in health care. It was hoped that this would generate discussion amongst those members who were not attending the seminar. Once in session a number of members, who had been recruited earlier, reported on their daily activities, posting deliberations and summarizing key points discussed during the sessions attended. Others were asked to contribute with longer posts in the form of a daily diary, reflecting on events, analyzing their experiences and reporting key messages from the sessions. Towards the end of the seminar, the ISQua Knowledge committee reported back to members on the key outcomes and findings of the seminar.

The expert-led discussions were another activity that required the voluntary participation of a number of ISQua Knowledge members. These discussions took place synchronously as a webinar, or asynchronously as a discussion forum. On the forums, discussion was initiated with a short video by one of the members explaining the topic and deliberating on the challenges to quality and safety in health care. This was followed by a few key questions on the topic with an invitation to post a response to the forum. These task designs often require that volunteer members start responding to questions on the discussion board in order to encourage other members, and especially newcomers, to participate in the discussion. The webinars ran in real time with a live audience from around the world. Generally, the webinars had a convener who would set the context for the topic and invite experts to give presentations related to the webinar topic. Only the convener and the presenters were connected via a web camera. The attendees could view the live video presentations and post their questions and comments in the chat box.

The online workshops were also a highly structured feature of the site. They required a volunteer member, who was an expert in the area, to post videos discussing a key topic such as 'fundamentals of quality improvement'.

This volunteer also provided the workshop participants with a number of reading resources and links to other websites. These workshops were one of the few activities hosted by ISQua Knowledge that did not make provision for registered users to add comments to the page.

The design of ISQua Knowledge emphasized not only the value of learning from the experiences of others, but the ability to relate what one learned through the network with past experience, and to reflect upon current practices. The main aim was to help health-care professionals and managers understand the complexity of issues related to quality and safety in health care. This aim was reflected in the social design of the learning network and by the structuring of tasks as described above. The core tasks were designed to channel participation into various peer interaction and mentoring roles, and in many a member assumed the role of 'expert' or mentor. This peer interaction and mentoring function is an area where the social design of ISQua Knowledge intersects with its epistemic design, enacting the purpose of channeling participation into activities that connect recognized experts with members, to stimulate critical reflection, discussion and knowledge sharing on the site.

Set, Epistemic and Social Co-creation and Co-configuration Activities

In a sense, all the content on ISQua Knowledge was produced by its members. For example, five members were needed to run a debate activity and, although the architecture of the Debates page included a space for the moderator, four debaters, general members' comments and voting buttons, it was the ISQua Knowledge members who supplied the content. Similarly, other pages such as Blogs, Meet the Author, Spotlight, and Member Stories only came to life as members made their contributions.

One of the distinctive design elements of ISQua Knowledge was that tasks often required planning that took into account implementation at different stages. For instance, certain tasks involved scheduling and preparation, such as requesting members to present in a webinar, or to chair and moderate a debate, followed by a second stage where selected members would post their comments on the motion on the Debates page. Only once there was a motion, and four selected members had posted their comments arguing for or against a motion, could the general ISQua Knowledge members make their contribution. These examples illustrate how the design of certain tasks realized a specific sequencing, where general ISQua Knowledge members could not deliberately initiate certain activities on their own without the permission and co-organization of the site organizers. However, the environment had other spaces where tasks did not require such precise sequencing; for example, members did not need authorization to start a new topic on the discussion boards, comment on various activities around the site, vote for their favorite member contribution or on a motion on the Debates page, and have their say about what should be discussed at the annual global seminar.

Every contribution by a registered member became part of the rich content of the site, including past webinar recordings, which were provided as resources. In this way, participants derived benefit from the activities themselves and from the comments made by other members on those activities, which in turn reinforced the site's main objective of supporting learning from the experiences of professional peers. Comments by general members often provided a valuable contribution to the site and ISQua Knowledge had been successful in promoting the sharing of ideas, information and knowledge amongst its members. For example, in relation to a discussion on cost–benefit analysis in patient care, one member posted the question: 'Do you know of a framework or model for economic research in patient safety?' Only a few hours later, another member answered with a link to the abstract of a paper on the issue. Comments also included insight into the real-world and deeply human side of many of these issues. Posts included stories of personal loss, such as the death of a family member due to a lack of quality and safety in health care. These stories seemed to have a positive impact on the discussion boards, motivating interactions and thought-provoking contributions from other members. These stories and the resources shared by members, in turn, became part of the site content helping future visitors learn more about these issues.

Abstracting and Synthesis

Several of the designed elements of ISQua Knowledge, as described above, were fundamental to the operation of the network and to the productive professional learning it facilitated. The functions of these elements are highlighted in closing as strategies that could be of interest to the design of other networks for professional development. The first is the ability to facilitate the exchange of ideas between professionals in the field.

ISQua Knowledge provided its users with opportunities to connect with experts and leaders in the emerging field of quality and safety in health care. The platform's design and activities enabled health-care professionals to connect and share knowledge with national and international peers. Many professionals in this field lack the access to expertise in health-care quality and safety in their workplace, and so ISQua Knowledge provided a unique forum to ask questions and gain support from both recognized advocates and experienced peers. The platform was therefore particularly valuable for health professionals working in developing countries where access to relevant expertise and resources in this field can be very limited.

The second important intention was to maintain ongoing interactions after a major live event that is of great significance to a professional community. For ISQua Knowledge, this was the Salzburg Global Seminar. The seminar was promoted on ISQua Knowledge through activities that encouraged members to participate remotely in related seminar events. The platform offered an opportunity for selected members to contribute to the seminar and then, once the live event was over, members were able to continue their discussions and collaborations through the ISQua Knowledge platform, throughout the year, with a broader audience.

The third notable function is about stimulating participation, and this is enacted through the design of tasks that encourage members to contribute to the website by making them visible only after they post a comment or participate in an activity. Although ISQua Knowledge members could make their own profile page on the site, other members were only able to visit this page once the member had made a contribution. This strategy was used to initiate participation in the activities on the site. Similarly, another important design feature that aims at encouraging participation is the structuring of tasks to guide users in making contributions. When members are contributing to a highly structured activity, they know what is required from them. For example, in the debate activities members were asked to argue for or against a motion, and so these participating members knew where to make their contribution and what role they played in the activity. This helped reduce time commitments and provided a sense of direction and purpose.

Lastly, the use of a phased approach, including planning and implementation of strategies for highly structured activities in the design of tasks, is also of importance. For example, the administrators of ISQua Knowledge would often ask an expert to contribute to a discussion on a topic, providing an initial comment or statement for discussion. To spark the discussion, the expert would post a video on the topic, which would need to be in place before general members started their participations, posting comments and responses to the opening statement.

These key design elements, when combined, established an architecture conducive to distributed professional learning. With ISQua Knowledge, the society successfully applied this design to stimulate productive change in professional practice, engaging health practitioners with new knowledge and critical discussions in health-care quality and safety. Its design provided an online environment that overcame the barriers of distance and status that separate health professionals (in their place of practice) from the insights of experts and leaders in health-care policy and governance. Lessons learned from the first implementation of ISQua Knowledge have informed the architecture of the current ISQua Ltd. website and its associated networks and services.

References

Kohn, K.T., Corrigan, J. M. and Donaldson, M. S., eds., 1999. *To err is human: building a safer health system.* Washington, DC: National Academy Press.
Vora, P., 2009. *Web application design patterns.* Boston, MA: Morgan Kaufmann Publishers/ Elsevier.

12

THE SYNAPTIC LEAP

Open Science Combating Disease

Paul Parker, Beat Schwendimann, Kate Thompson and Matthew Todd

Overview

The Synaptic Leap (TSL)[1] is a web-based environment designed to generate collaborative research in biomedical science. The purpose of TSL is to enable anyone in the world with relevant expertise, resources or connections to contribute to biomedical research projects. The projects to date have focused on synthesizing or identifying affordable treatments for tropical diseases in developing countries. These diseases spread rapidly in communities with poor water quality, sanitation and access to health care, and include malaria and tuberculosis but also 'neglected' tropical diseases (NTDs) such as schistosomiasis. They continue to flourish in several low-income nations around the world and also in areas of high poverty in some wealthy countries. It is estimated that over one billion people, or about one-sixth of the world's population, are currently affected by NTDs (WHO 2012). Although medical means exist to effectively treat these diseases, assisting large populations in conditions of poverty requires the development of suitable low-cost medications. The research projects hosted by TSL are developing the chemical foundations for such medications by applying open source methods of online collaboration that avoid the commercial constraints of the pharmaceutical industry.

TSL was created by two people who are still key participants in the network. Due to a series of personal experiences, and with a background in software engineering, Ginger Taylor (now the executive director for the Board of Directors and the system administrator of the website) applied the model used by the *Tropical Disease Initiative* (http://sgt.cnag.cat/TDI/) to general biomedical research. Almost concurrently, Mat Todd (Chair of TSL and biomedical research adviser) became interested in the idea of *open source science*. The two were introduced in 2005, when *The Synaptic Leap* was also incorporated as a non-profit organization in the USA. Work on the first significant experimental project began in the lab in 2010, after funding was granted from the World Health Organization and the Australian Government in 2008. The second major project (in malaria) commenced in mid-2011 with funding from another NGO (the Medicines for Malaria Venture) and the Australian Government. The contributors have changed over the years and have included biomedical research advisors, intellectual property and policy advisors and a Web 2.0 advisor. All are part-time volunteers, and a list of past volunteers instrumental to the establishment of the network is provided on the website.

TSL is currently home to four disease-based communities. In each there are a number of sub-projects (17 in the schistosomiasis community, five in the malaria community, and one each in the toxoplasmosis and tuberculosis communities). Each sub-project has a range of members, usually about 20 people, although one of the schistosomiasis sub-projects has about 50 contributors. In some cases, the groups of active collaborators tend to be small, but the overall scale of participation has grown, with substantial recruitment undertaken through live events and social media.

In the sub-projects we examined, the *open science* approach to research and knowledge construction in biomedical science often involved cycles of evaluation and revision similar to iterative design methods like rapid prototyping. Our chief purpose in this chapter is to articulate how the architectural features of the network combine to facilitate and sustain such cycles of collaborative activity. In the description and analysis that follows, we draw on two main sources of data: an interview with Mat Todd about the origin and evolution of *The Synaptic Leap*, and our observations of online activity in the malaria research community.

Set Design

The set design of *The Synaptic Leap* interconnects physical and digital research environments. Many of the network's contributors work simultaneously in traditional biomedical laboratories around the world. It is in these physical laboratory environments that much of the research is developed that forms the major contributions to the network's communities. A single blog site, *The Synaptic Leap*, serves as the primary digital environment. Additional cloud tools and services have been enlisted to support, promote and extend the activities hosted within the primary environment. These secondary digital environments are deployed flexibly to suit the needs and collaborative practices that emerge within each research community. The selection of these digital environments reflects a key design imperative for this learning network. To facilitate open, honest and sustained knowledge sharing, it is essential to keep technical barriers to access and participation as low as possible. The network's developers and leaders have chosen a highly accessible technology infrastructure that is free to use, has relatively basic hardware and software requirements and incorporates mainstream online channels. The importance of facilitating productive participation is further reflected in the ways that tools and features have been deployed on the blog site, and in the ways that project communities introduce secondary digital environments to extend upon the functionality of the primary environment. Viewed as a whole, this technology infrastructure and its configuration for use forms an open science laboratory for distributed research in biomedical science that complements and enhances work conducted in physical laboratories.

The blog site is the coordinating hub and central forum for this distributed, open laboratory. It is primarily within this digital space that open science research projects are initiated and managed, and where much of the underlying experimental work is discussed in detail. Page layout, site structure, tools and functions have all been configured to facilitate productive participation from users. The layout and structure of the blog is simple and functional (Figure 12.1). The header

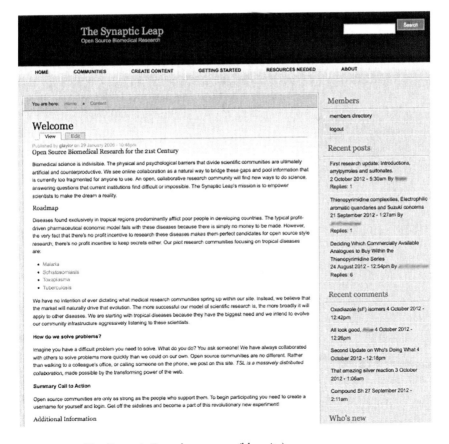

FIGURE 12.1   The Synaptic Leap: home page (blog site)

is understated, presenting the site title beside a small graphic that evokes online collaboration. The header also includes one important global function on the right: a search box that allows participants to search for blog posts and the profile pages of registered users. The central content area dominates the page and is divided into sections that provide background to the open science goals of the learning network (Home, About), information about current projects in each research community (Communities), guidelines for productive participation (Getting Started), requests for specific skills or resources required for a project (Resources Needed) and tools for posting new blog entries (Create Content). To facilitate free and open discussion, user comments are enabled for all content pages. A final significant feature of the blog platform is support for navigating new blog posts and accessing the profile of those who posted them. A right-hand side panel lists the latest community activity (Recent posts, Recent comments and a Who's new list of links to profiles of new members) and provides links to membership resources (account creation, login and, for registered users, a Members' Directory). While it is possible for users to create new blog posts and add comments without creating a site account, registration generates a searchable user profile (including fields for organizational affiliation and relevant expertise), provides access to profile tools for compiling the posts of registered users (Track) and emailing them from the site (Contact), grants editing privileges for blog posts and enables optional subscription to daily email notifications.

The secondary digital environments that comprise this learning network function to augment the community functions of the hub site by offering participants more specialized tools for communication and collaboration, and also by sharing access to activity through wider online networks. Three broad types of secondary digital environment can be observed. The first is the shared information and knowledge repository. This category includes open access Electronic Lab Notebooks (a form of blog) created to capture raw experimental data for review and discussion, a wiki site maintained by project leaders that provides a central record of project history and current status and an online reference manager (Mendeley) that allows collaborators to compile and share published research relevant to addressing the present research problem. Some of the activity of this learning network is enabled and/or extended by web conferencing technologies. Supporting different forms of synchronous online communication and collaboration, these platforms represent another type of secondary digital environment available to the network. They are called upon to overcome geographical barriers to participation in live community events that range in scale from public presentations and consultation meetings (Adobe Connect) to smaller collaborative working groups (Skype and Google+ 'hangouts'). The third type of digital environment to supplement the blog site is social media. In the malaria research community, for example, a YouTube channel has been created to archive recordings of live events in Adobe Connect for review and sharing across the network, while Twitter, Google+ and Facebook accounts provide a means for network participants to rapidly share access to online resources, live streams and updates on project activity through these more widely subscribed networks. Moreover, as a result of the accessibility and integrated media sharing affordances of Google+ and the mass user base of Facebook, the dedicated project sites on these platforms are quickly becoming alternative discussion spaces to the blog site.

These diverse components and features of set design equip participants of the learning network with an open and accessible set of tools for rapidly sharing, discussing and archiving project news, data and events in a variety of synchronous and asynchronous modes (Figure 12.2).

Epistemic Design

From an epistemic perspective, the design of the main blog site and the choice and configuration of its secondary environments reflect the knowledge creation activity undertaken by the informal, *open source* research communities they host. Their purpose is to generate productive collaboration in biomedical research, which to date has focused on addressing diseases prevalent in developing countries. This priority is evident in the differentiation on the main blog site (part of the set design) between four tropical disease research communities and one community for general (non-disease specific) open research projects. These research foci reflect the expertise and interests of the founders of *The Synaptic Leap* and of current project leaders, but do not represent a limit. Users are also invited to suggest and lead new open biomedical research communities and projects.

Upon entering a research community, users can choose to explore information about current research projects, links to associated research tools and prior contributions from the network community. Projects provide the primary framework for epistemic activity in *The Synaptic Leap*. The site's user guide, located in the 'Getting Started' section of the main blog site, offers a set of basic guidelines for creating new project pages. It is suggested here that any new pages should include:

- an aim or overview;
- identification of those who are already involved (including links to their profile pages);
- clarification of the current status of the project;
- links to existing support resources and tools (links, file attachments, etc.); and, importantly,
- details of how others can contribute, such as by donating data, materials or research skills.

Since clear and accessible information about how to contribute to projects is a fundamental prerequisite for the epistemic activity of the learning network, the

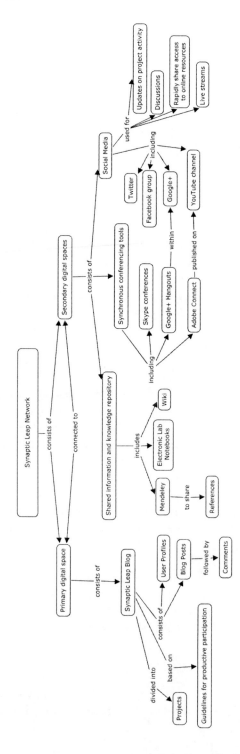

FIGURE 12.2 The Synaptic Leap: primary and secondary digital environments

user guide also suggests foregrounding this information on dedicated child pages. These pages can in turn be tagged to appear in the 'Resources Needed' section for direct access from anywhere on the site via the global navigation bar.

Another set design feature of the main blog site intended to stimulate epistemic activity among members of the disease research communities is an electronic form page for posting new blog entries. Located under 'Create Content' on the global navigation bar, this page incorporates a system for tagging new blog posts to particular research communities and subject areas. These subject choices can be understood to function within the learning network as genres of asynchronous epistemic interaction. The 'Request for Help' subject, for example, serves as the basic task unit whereby users invite others to work on resolving specific problems to advance an aspect of the larger project. Another common way epistemic interaction is triggered in this network is by tagging as 'Results' new blog entries that report the outcomes of experimental work. This classification prompts other participants to comment with interpretations or recommendations for future efforts. Other posting genres serve to provoke debate about controversial issues ('Rants') and project direction ('Project Fork'), or to invite more general discussion ('Technical Note', 'External News', 'Miscellaneous').

Conditions for transparency and peer review, important features of the epistemic design, and essential for open science, are produced by the convergence of elements that preserve the knowledge created (set design) and the explicit rules of the network (social design). Discussions are preserved, the history of blog and wiki edits is captured, webcasts of public meetings and presentations are archived and project leaders and their trusted lieutenants actively steward an ethos of transparency and open access. Together, these aspects of set and social design allow epistemic practices of peer review to develop across the network. Rather than use an explicit user rating or voting system, the quality of contributions to research projects hosted at *The Synaptic Leap* is managed by the community of project participants through a meritocratic process of open peer review. That is, the personal status of contributors is unimportant. What matters is the merit of the contribution itself, as judged by the project community. All contributions remain open to public scrutiny as a way of encouraging participants to maintain high standards. Those contributions judged by the community to lack merit are rejected from further consideration. Participants whose input consistently survives peer review stand to gain recognition and reputation within the network.

Social Design

The social design of the network is tightly tied to the epistemic design. Membership is open to everybody who has knowledge that can contribute to the problem that is the focus of the disease research community. The roles identified in this network can be mapped to those in other open source communities and, apart from some key roles, most of the structure is non-hierarchical. There are two important outcomes necessary to the ongoing success of the network and related to the social design: recruitment of new members (this helps to manage the high turnover and changing roles of participants), and ongoing productive contributions from existing members.

The social design of *The Synaptic Leap* allows members to join easily. The non-hierarchical, open science philosophy of the network encourages a breadth of potential participants, and the individualized contact given to specific members ensures the support of those whose contribution is considered essential. The philosophy of the network is that 'it's science which isn't behind closed doors anymore, and where anybody can take part' (Mat Todd). Academic titles and ranks are removed from the information displayed about members, and participants are identified by photos, real names or user names, although, in order to post to TSL, it is not necessary for a member to sign in. Rather than networks forming around qualified people, as one would normally find in traditional scientific models, in TSL networks are expected to form around the 'interesting' statements that members make in the first instance. An important part of the ease of joining the network is the variety of tools used, as outlined in the discussion of set design. There is a tension between this open science philosophy and the reality that there are different types of experts, and additional support is given for buy-in from identified experts (including Skype calls to discuss project requirements). For those who are referred through third parties, or recruited directly, Skype provides an efficient way to communicate the non-negotiable practices of the network. By using Skype, project leaders can discuss the concerns of potential members without making these public to the rest of the network and, in doing so, create a more personal connection with those who have been referred, and have not had this interaction before. These include the complete sharing of data (preliminary and final), as well as any uncertainty that is present around the project. It is important for entry to the network that all participants are considered to be of equal importance in the main blog site, and for any extra activity to take place away from this central site.

For open science to work, the expectations associated with key roles need to be communicated to the members who need to be able to contribute soon after joining and who may change roles as their involvement continues. In open source projects, such expectations are often managed by an authority figure, typically the founder and sometimes termed a 'benevolent dictator', who governs for the benefit of the whole community (Coffin 2006). In TSL, two members share this role: one specializing in the content (Todd), and the other focusing on the structure of the blog site (Taylor). These members both engage in activities around recruitment and management, as well as the work involved in adding to the set and epistemic design. One of these founders determined the rules that all other members of the network follow (discussed further below). The foundational members occupy another important role in TSL. These members are acknowledged on the website for the contributions they have made in these roles. Given that these members began the activity, they have helped to determine the rules and ethos of the network. Individual project leaders are a third role, as the members who lead specific research activities are often referred to as 'trusted lieutenants' in the field of open source software development (McConnell 1999). Project leaders play a pivotal role in initiating the work of participants. They carefully keep other participants on track in terms of their social obligations (posting to the group), coordination updates and hosting of the various configurations of users of the smaller networks. They also give explicit attention to motivate participants to complete unfinished work. The members, in their role, provide feedback, help new users, recommend the project to others and request new features. In addition, they undertake the equivalent of *testing and reporting or fixing bugs* in the development work that they do. As outlined above, they write papers based on the discoveries that they make and, as will be discussed below, update documentation and translation processes involved in the network.

Once people have decided to participate in *The Synaptic Leap*, there are many design features to encourage interaction between participants. Project leaders actively steward the network (Wenger *et al.* 2009), monitoring and encouraging engagement from all participants by sharing updates on project progress through the social media channels. There is importance placed on participants understanding what combination of tools to use, for what purpose, with which partners and for the appropriate project. Participation guidelines were developed during the course of one of the earlier projects and are explicitly stated on the blog site, termed 'The 6 Laws'. These pertain to expectations around roles ('Anyone can take part at any level of the project') and interaction ('Suggestions are the best form of criticism', 'Public discussion is much more valuable than private email'). Without such explicit rules, the meritocratic processes (discussed as part of the epistemic design) could not work. 'The 6 Laws' also support the open source philosophy that projects fail if a single person is responsible for fielding all inputs. The members fulfilling these roles have focused their attention where needed as the network has grown, and this shifts, along with the shifting needs. The two laws which state that constructive suggestions are the best form of criticism, and that interactions should be public rather than private, encourage a supportive culture using a scaffold that extends and fuels social engagement with and within the network. They highlight the importance of inclusiveness within this learning network. In addition, in linking to the set design, regular access to live events (links to webcast presentations and meetings) and their recordings (archived in YouTube) give the impression of a vibrant, active network. There is also regular sharing of content (see epistemic design) with immediate relevance to the purposes and concerns of TSL's research communities. This provides motivation for members to interact with each other, whether in relation to a particular event, or to move the project to the next stage.

The social design is important in terms of encouraging trust between members. One of the significant features of this network is that participants are willing to volunteer time and ideas, their intellectual property, to contribute to finding a solution to a larger problem. In order to do this, users have to trust each other and the coordinator. That all interactions occur in an open environment, that anyone can contribute to any part of the project, that suggestions are valued over solutions, and that these are regularly monitored, means that the difficulties often apparent in group activities are largely overcome.

Set, Epistemic and Social Co-creation and Co-configuration Activities

Having outlined the primary features of set, epistemic and social design apparent in *The Synaptic Leap* site and its extended environments, we now consider the ways and extent to which participant activity influences the evolution and configuration of this architecture. We argue that the possibilities for the co-creation and co-configuration of this network's design are governed by the basic pragmatism of the open science ethos that drives participant engagement. That is, the fixity or flexibility of architectural elements reflects what 'works' in practical terms for both project leaders and contributors, and so enables productive activity to continue and to grow.

To provide an open science laboratory for distributed research in biomedical science, a network needs certain elements to operate in ways that remain stable and familiar. First, the network needs a relatively fixed digital space where projects are initiated, research problems posed and contributions discussed, and project goals and resources iteratively clarified. As observed under set design, this 'hub' or 'home' site function is currently served by a blog site, the design and deployment of which has remained essentially the same since its inception. The activity of distributed science research also requires relatively fixed spaces in which to centrally capture and manage the ongoing work of knowledge production, ranging from the outcomes of experimentation (e.g. raw data on potential drug compounds that requires interpretation) to uncontested knowledge such as the history of project activity. Once the network began to generate a high volume of data, the main knowledge repositories (Electronic Lab Notebooks and wiki) therefore became permanent companions to the blog site.

A related criterion for sustained epistemic activity in this network is that the design of projects and tasks aligns with the expectations and knowledge practices of contributors, who possess expertise appropriate for engaging with novel research problems in biomedical science. In this network, the epistemic design currently centers on research projects within specific disease research communities. These drug discovery/synthesis projects are in turn composed of smaller tasks, typically but not exclusively issued in blog posts by project leaders, trusted lieutenants and reputable contributors. To interpret and respond usefully to these posts and the discussion they generate, contributors will usually require a working knowledge of experimental processes and molecular structures in chemistry. This prior knowledge is apparent in the way that discussion of this work tends to develop according to standard conventions of scientific discourse. For example, when an update is posted inviting community input on the latest round of experimental work on potential drug compounds, participants generally recognize this as an opportunity to post interpretations of those results and recommendations for future work. In this way, the relationship between the proposed task and the activity it stimulates can be seen as following familiar conventions for reporting results and discussing their significance, such as those found in scientific research papers.

The aspects of the network's design that are open to change can also be explained in relation to pragmatic factors. These factors come into play within the cycle of problem solving that drives productive learning and knowledge construction in *The Synaptic Leap*. This cycle is essentially an ongoing dialogue between iteratively updated tasks and the activity that emerges among users who engage with those tasks. To understand how the cycle of problem-solving contributes to the evolution and development of the network's design, it is first useful to describe an early workflow in an open source drug discovery (OSDD) research project of the TSL malaria community.

Drawing on an important open access medical chemistry data set on NTDs (released into the public domain by GlaxoSmithKline in 2010), the malaria research community at *The Synaptic Leap* initiated a major new project in July 2011 to research promising chemical starting points for new medicines for malaria. Online activity began with blog posts at the hub site by the project leader. These outlined background and overall aims, identified the specific work needed and provided links to the network tools and resources that support this work (in particular, the information and knowledge repositories) and to a Twitter feed for receiving project updates. This initial call to action prompted asynchronous community participation at the hub (new blog posts and discussion of aims and needs), Electronic Lab Notebook (primarily data sharing and management) and wiki (updating project history). An ensuing process of community input and review served to further clarify project goals and tasks. Decisions were made about the lines of inquiry to pursue in the open data set and about designs for three rounds of experimental work in compound synthesis and evaluation.

Contributors completed this experimental work in their physical laboratory environments over a period of several weeks. As results became available, the data was uploaded to the Electronic Lab Notebook or forwarded to the project leader to be compiled into 'Results' posted at the hub site and shared through Twitter. Another cycle of community input and review followed to identify implications and plan for the second round of experimental work. The outcomes of this review process were fed back into the network through project and task updates. By November 2011, the results of the third round of experimental work were available and posted at the hub site. At this time the project leader also created a Google+ group for the project to supplement the Twitter feed as a means of rapidly sharing project updates, and also to extend the network through the addition of an alternative and more mainstream space for discussion. By March 2012, work had progressed far enough for participants to consider publishing the key findings of the research project in a peer-reviewed journal. Sharing results with the wider scientific community in this traditional way remains important to strengthen the credibility of open science methods, and thereby facilitate their growth. Collaborative writing began in a shared document using the project wiki, and the project leader created a dedicated Mendeley group to gather and share relevant research papers.

Activity at the Google+ group was initially minimal, with comments on the project leader's posts limited to brief statements of acknowledgement that rarely evolved into extended discussions. In May 2012, a Facebook group was added to provide convenient access for users of this larger social network. Over the next few months, these Google+ and Facebook groups gradually developed into distinct spaces of critical discussion where participants engaged in in-depth peer review and posed new problems – activity that was initially concentrated at the main blog site. Throughout this period, the project leader continued to monitor the network for consensus and to feed decisions back into the network. These were communicated via periodic task updates posted at the hub site, and also were shared or posted in all the social media environments. The cyclical workflow described here broadly follows the traditional phases of scientific research, moving through problem definition, experimental design and data collection, data processing and analysis, and discussion of results with respect to their significance for future research and dissemination. Applied in an online learning network designed for open science, however, each phase of the scientific process is potentially subject to ongoing peer review that can, moreover, inform activity in other phases (Figure 12.3). This approach contrasts with traditional, closed science in which peer review is usually limited to the initial grant application and to the end products of research, such as published research papers.

Running in parallel with and also feeding into this asynchronous work cycle were a series of synchronous online sessions, including both streamed face-to-face events and fully online interactions. These were reserved for contexts of social interaction that demanded more immediate and nuanced interpersonal exchange. For example, the project leader hosted weekly team meetings, a public conference and public consultation event at the University of Sydney to provide project updates, invite open discussion and, in the case of the public events, recruit new contributors and online participants. To allow real-time participation and discussion for those unable to physically attend, many of these events were streamed live through the Adobe Connect web conferencing platform. The project leader made monthly use of Skype for international one-

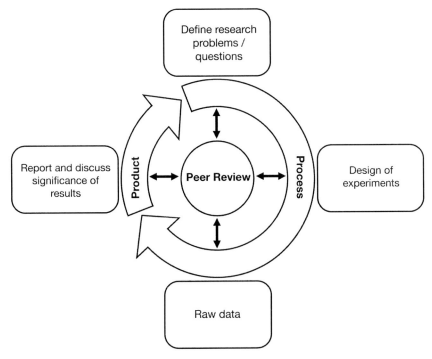

FIGURE 12.3 Open peer review on the cycle of knowledge construction

to-one coordination sessions with members of the Medicines for Malaria Venture, a key project partner. One-to-one or small group Skype conferences were also used in situations where delicate negotiation with remotely located experts was required – in order to build trust in the integrity and rigor of the network's open source processes, as a precursor to network participation. Finally, there was some experimentation during the project with using the Google+ web conferencing environment ('hangouts') as a more convenient and convivial alternative to Adobe Connect for small to medium sized collaborative meetings of up to 10 participants.

The ways this activity unfolded across the multiple digital environments and modes of one tropical disease research community illustrate how the network's design has evolved largely in response to emerging project needs. As the cycles of problem-solving activity proceed, new project needs emerge out of peer review, and constraints on efficient network participation become more apparent. These forces encouraged innovation in the set design of the network. There has been a progressive addition and collective configuration of secondary digital environments in response to needs arising from cycles of project work and, at the same time, the emerging online practices of participants. Moreover, many of the digital environments used by the network support different facets of the epistemic and social activity depending on how they are configured for use in different project scenarios. By virtue of this entanglement, the ongoing negotiation of online work practices has allowed the set, epistemic and social design of the network to slowly evolve through pragmatic processes of co-creation and co-configuration.

Abstracting and Synthesis

In this chapter we have observed how the set, epistemic and social design choices that constitute the evolving architecture of this network align with principles of open science. Since collaborative projects of this kind depend on widespread participation, the first priority for set design has been to establish and maintain a technology infrastructure that anyone can access and use to make productive contributions. Sustaining this kind of broad accessibility and participation in an open science community has required flexible and ongoing set design. The totality and configuration of set features has evolved to accommodate the emerging needs of the different open science projects hosted at *The Synaptic Leap*, and the emerging collaborative practices of the projects' participants. Another principle of open science is that all contributions remain transparent to current and future users, which allows the quality of epistemic activity in the network to be regulated through a meritocracy of open peer review. It is with respect to this principle of transparency that features of set design (open and accessible technology infrastructure, persistent communication) can be understood to intersect with important aspects of both epistemic design (quality of knowledge work through the meritocracy of open peer review) and social design (explicit guidelines for interaction that encourage a culture of trust) in the architecture of productive open science. The epistemic activity of open source collaborations centers on compelling projects of shared interest. The research projects currently coordinated through TSL adhere to this principle by focusing on the morally compelling problem of tropical diseases in developing countries. The network promotes itself online and through live events. It channels participants' desires to make a difference - and to develop their knowledge of research methods in medicinal chemistry - into open source drug discovery and synthesis projects, in a range of disease research communities. The epistemic design of the network is further realized at the hub site through a system of pre-set 'subject' genres for blog posts. Chief among these is the 'Request for Help', which serves as the basic task unit for triggering epistemic activity in the form of project contributions and associated discussion.

None of these design elements would operate reliably, however, without clear and consistent leadership and guidance. This is a significant design issue for networks that employ open science methods. The flexibility of multiple platforms and modes of collaboration enhances accessibility, increases traffic and boosts participation. However, the resulting complexity risks user confusion and fragmented activity. The role of trusted organizer – fulfilled in different ways by the founders and project leaders – is therefore an essential social design feature of this network. To harness the advantages and mitigate the disadvantages of collaborating across diverse and changing environments, members in this leadership role perform three important duties: actively monitoring the collaborative activity that occurs in the different parts of the network; posting regular summaries of project progress that serve to keep activity connected and on track; negotiating with the project community to select and configure digital environments and resources to minimize technical barriers to participation.

Despite these demands, the flexible and evolving design of *The Synaptic Leap* and its multiple secondary environments are proving to be productive for open science research. Indeed, the online collaborations have yielded peer-reviewed publications in chemistry, biotechnology and NTD research journals (Orti *et al.* 2009, Woelfle *et al.* 2011a, 2011b). The open source approach of TSL allows for adaptive workflows that have the potential to overcome many limitations of traditional approaches to research in science. In the latter, workflows are generally more rigid and often confined to siloed groups. Peer review is also restricted primarily to the preparation of grant proposals at the beginning of research projects, and then again at the end when papers are submitted for publication. By contrast, the open design and operation of TSL reduces the possibility of duplicated effort and enables peer review at every stage of the research process. It infuses traditional scientific methods with the kind of agility and efficiency associated with rapid prototyping in the engineering and design professions. As the example of *The Synaptic Leap* demonstrates, this model of collaborative research holds great potential for fast, high quality, cost-effective biomedical research and, indeed, research in other areas of science.

Note

1 Accessed at www.thesynapticleap.org. Please note that the network as described in this chapter may have evolved since the time of writing.

References

Coffin, J., 2006. Analysis of open source principles in diverse collaborative communities. *First Monday* [online], 11(6). Available from: http://firstmonday.org/htbin/cgiwrap/bin/ojs/index.php/fm/rt/printerFriendly/1342/1262 [Accessed 20 September 2012].

McConnell, S., 1999. Open-source methodology: ready for prime time? *IEEE Software*, July/August, 6–11.

Orti, L., Carbajo, R. J., Ursula, P., Eswar, N., Maurer, S. M., Rai, A. K., Taylor, G., Todd, M. H., Pineda-Lucena, A., Sali, A. and Marti-Renom, M.A., 2009. A kernel for the Tropical Disease Initiative. *Nature Biotechnology*, 27(4), 320–321.

Wenger, E., White, N. and Smith, J. D., 2009. *Digital habitats: stewarding technology for communities*. Portland, OR: CPSquare.

Woelfle, M., Olliaro, P. and Todd, M. H., 2011a. Open science is a research accelerator. *Nature Chemistry*, 3(10), 745–748.

Woelfle, M., Seerden, J -P., de Gooijer, J., Pouwer, K., Olliaro, P. and Todd, M. H., 2011b. Resolution of Praziquantel. *PloS: Neglected Tropical Diseases*, 5(9), e1260 [online]. Available from: www.plosntds.org/article/info%3Adoi%2F10.1371%2Fjournal.pntd. 0001260 [Accessed 5 February 2013].

World Health Organization (WHO), 2012. *Accelerating work to overcome the global impact of neglected tropical diseases: a roadmap for implementation – executive summary* [online]. Geneva: WHO Press. Available from: http://whqlibdoc.who.int/hq/2012/WHO_HTM_NTD_2012.1_eng.pdf [Accessed 23 January 2012].

13

VIRTUAL CHOIR

Sharing Experiences of Singing Together Apart

Lucila Carvalho and Peter Goodyear

Overview

The Virtual Choir[1] involves people collaborating at a distance from one another, singing alone to have a part in an online choir. There have been several Virtual Choir (VC) projects and they provide compelling examples of what can be achieved through committed collaborations within informal learning networks. An intriguing aspect in this case study is the intensity of the emotional experiences evoked by the artifacts created in VC, for those who have participated as choir members and on those who experience one of their productions. For this reason, before discussing the Virtual Choir's architecture in more detail, we would like to invite you to experience the Virtual Choir. The following link provides access to Virtual Choir 3.0: www.youtube.com/watch?v=V3rRaL-Czxw&feature=fvwrel.

Composer and conductor Eric Whitacre had the idea for the first Virtual Choir when he watched a YouTube video of a young fan singing one of his compositions in 2009 (Virtual Choir 2011). Whitacre then used social media to invite his fans and other potential participants to sing in a virtual choir. Since then, three projects have been completed: Virtual Choir 1.0 (VC1), VC 2.0 (VC2) and VC 3.0 (VC3). VC1 began in May 2009 and involved 185 singers from 12 countries. The final product was a video of the choir, which reportedly received one million hits in two months (Virtual Choir 2011). Virtual Choir 2.0 had 2,052 singers from 58 countries. Virtual Choir 3.0 involved 3,746 singers from 73 countries.

Each project involves individual video recordings made by people singing to the scores of a pre-defined composition, chosen by Whitacre. Potential participants find information about upcoming projects on Whitacre's personal webpage or via other social media sites. Resources made available to the participants include videos of Whitacre (e.g. virtually conducting or explaining the project), audio files (e.g. examples of a soprano, alto, tenor or bass performing the piece), sheet music and practical information, such as how to record and upload videos, how to contact a member of the Virtual Choir team, etc. Once individual videos are completed, would-be choir participants upload their files, to be edited and cut together by professionals in Whitacre's team. The creation at the end of each project consists of an edited video of a virtual choir, which merges the video of Whitacre virtually conducting with the individual videos of choir members, and other visual effects (Figure 13.1). In addition to examining the designed architectures for the successive Virtual Choirs, we also use this chapter to explain why it is we see this as an example of collaborative knowledge creation.

The architecture of the Virtual Choir reflects a decentralized approach to the deployment of the network, where there is not just one space exclusively dedicated to collaboration. Even though a dedicated space hosts information and resources related to the Virtual Choir projects at Whitacre's website, the exchange and sharing of impressions are also hosted within a variety of social media environments (e.g. Facebook, Twitter, discussion forums on YouTube, TED Talks). Whitacre takes advantage of social media to successfully promote, encourage and engage participants as they complete their tasks, and afterwards, once projects are completed, to promote the projects. Choir members interact within these different environments in order to ask for support and information, as well as to share personal accounts of their stories, experiences and feelings in relation to participating in the project.

Since the first Virtual Choir in 2009, an increasing number of participants and other stakeholders have joined the projects and, consequently, new challenges have emerged, along with increased levels of complexity in the projects themselves. The new challenges appear not only at a technical level but also at a musical knowledge level, where Whitacre, for example, takes on more challenging musical tasks (e.g. with greater variation in rhythms and more complex musical motifs). Recent projects have seen the adoption of more powerful technologies in order to support the production of the final artifact: the video of a virtual choir. VC3, for example, incorporates new streamlined technologies through a partnership with Google, which resulted in the creation of dedicated spaces for the 'virtual choir community', such as hangouts, master classes and online seminars (Whitacre 2010). VC3 also includes other co-producers sponsoring the project (seen in icons on the Virtual Choir's blog page). These increased levels of complexity are also reflected in the deployment of the final creation: artifacts produced for VC1 and VC2 were deployed via YouTube, but VC3, in addition to the YouTube video, also involved producing an audio video installation, which was launched in April 2012 at Lincoln Center in New York, and is being presented at venues across the world, including at the Olympics in London 2012. This installation involves High Definition video and surround sound 'to create an immersive and visceral audience experience' (Virtual Choir 2012).

FIGURE 13.1 Virtual Choir: production of VC3

Virtual Choir projects shape a musical experience that transcends the boundaries of immediate real space and time. Individual recordings can be produced at home (from any location on the globe) and during an extended period of time (e.g. six months). A single participant may also submit more than one part, that is, one may produce a video singing as a baritone and another as a bass. This was seen in VC3, where 3,746 videos were received from 2,945 people – a number of participants were singing more than one part. Therefore, the resulting artifact of a virtual choir is composed of video recordings of people who may be located at opposite ends of the world, who have sung the musical piece at different points in time, and who may fulfill more than one singing role within the same choir, to an audience that may be anywhere across the globe, listening at any time. That this is accomplished with a sense of communion is a remarkable achievement.

On a social level, the three projects seem to have had an impact not only on choir members, but also on audiences. Within the various discussion forums and dedicated spaces for interactions about the Virtual Choir projects there are several accounts of choir members describing life-changing learning experiences and profound feelings of connection, even amongst people who had never met in person (Arca 2012, Virtual Choir 2012). There are also accounts of non-members who felt moved by the projects, and their realization of human unity, of crossing boundaries and bringing people from all over the world together to deliver or to hear beautiful and touching creations (Virtual Choir 2012).

Set Design

Virtual Choir's set design requires that choir members are able to access a number of resources in both digital and material spaces. The material space plays an important role in the projects because participating members are expected to complete their individual tasks at home (or in some other location that offers the right degree of quiet, privacy and technology). The successful completion of the project requires that members produce individual videos, and to do so they need to have access to a set of resources including: a quiet room, a computer, a pair of headphones, a web camera and so on.

The use of a decentralized approach in the deployment of the network results in communication being realized via a number of digital spaces such as on blogs, YouTube, Twitter, Facebook and Myspace. Even though Whitacre's website contains a dedicated space that hosts information and resources related to the projects, the network also relies on freely available social media, in addition to other Internet resources and software applications. Digital resources include, for example, a web connection and a browser to access social media sites and software applications to support recording and watching videos, access and visualization of PDF files etc. An important characteristic of most of these resources is that they are either freely available or are commonly used software applications. Similarly, people are also likely to already have most of the essential material resources required to participate in the learning network: a computer, a camera, a quiet room, black clothes. As a result, virtual choir projects can be realized at a relative low cost for participants.

The digital space has two main functions: on one hand it is used as a repository for storing representations of the knowledge necessary to learn how to complete the task (see also Epistemic Design below). On the other hand, the digital space involves using a variety of platforms to nurture and provide a home for social interactions. Therefore, set design relies on social media spaces for maintaining ongoing interactions and keeping choir members engaged. There are regular updates to participants about what is being accomplished at various milestones of the project. Personal stories and experiences are also shared (see also Social Design). However, what is important to note, in terms of set design, is how the space supports those types of activities: sharing, engagement and interaction. In this sense, the adoption of software applications and material resources that choir members are likely to be familiar with seems to be of great importance. One of the effects of deploying these projects via social media is that participants do not need to learn about the design or layout of the environments. In fact, since participants are likely to already use these social spaces independently of the Virtual Choir projects, they will not need to join a new environment, or learn about what they have to do or how to navigate or to respond to others. Participants who are following the Virtual Choir via Twitter or Facebook, for example, receive updates and news within their already preferred (digital) social spaces, and in this way, they do not need to 'visit' a new site because the Virtual Choir reaches them in their own 'homes'. In addition, spaces for interaction are mostly realized through discussion forums (e.g. on Whitacre's blog, Facebook, TED Talks) and therefore use a well-known structure of posting and answering posts.

The layout of Whitacre's webpage is *busy*, hosting a lot of information about his professional life and interests. Nevertheless, a separate space exists for the tasks and activities related to Virtual Choir projects. In its current version, the Virtual Choir blog shows information related to VC3 covering topics such as: credits of those who participated in the project, sites of the installations, statistical information related to the countries where videos were produced, a map plotting the choir singers in their original locations, knowledge resources for completing the tasks, history showing information related to previous projects and also a Twitter feed. The page dedicated to knowledge resources still hosts information for the tasks related to VC3, which is stored for reference purposes. Help is provided via frequently asked questions (FAQ) pages. The information is well organized and its layout is easy to understand and to navigate through, enabling participants to find information about the different components of the project.

In summary, the set design for both the material and digital spaces within the Virtual Choir case study takes advantage of technology, software and/or resources that are of a familiar nature to choir participants – things that come readily to hand. Most of the material resources will be those in the immediate surround-ings of the participants' everyday life: a room in their house, the computer they already have, a camera, headphones, black clothes and so on. Similarly, digital resources are displayed using familiar structures and layouts, via common or freely available software applications and taking advantage of social spaces that are frequently used.

What is most important is that the set up of the material and digital spaces ultimately facilitates the stretching of real-life boundaries, realizing a virtual encounter of thousands of people. The project allows for individuals physically located in distant corners of the world to share a common experience; it allows for such a group to sing together, even when in reality none of the members sang at the same moment and location. Moreover, while the knowledge creations of the initial projects were mostly deployed solely in the online space, the latest Virtual Choir also brings the virtual into the physical. Embracing a combination of physicality and fantasy, VC3 is incorporated in installations and in perfor-mances with live audiences. As a result, in addition to being available online, VC3 has also been presented at different venues, such as Lincoln Center in New York, the Titanic Visitors Centre in Belfast, the Cirencester Festival (UK), on the Millennium Bridge in London during the Olympic and Paralympic Games, at the Ikon Gallery in Birmingham (UK) and the World Unity event in Mexico. Virtual Choir projects traverse real-life boundaries, crossing the material and digital spaces, in a fluid movement that brings the physical to the virtual and the virtual to the physical.

Epistemic Design

Overall, the knowledge involved in the Virtual Choir activities is of two kinds: (i) specialist knowledge related to music, choral singing and specifics about the musical piece to be learned, as well as (ii) practical and technical advice for producing, recording and uploading videos. The epistemic design therefore involves knowledge related to teaching and learning the procedures and skills necessary for the delivery of a Virtual Choir project. Tasks relate to the production of an individual video recording where the participant sings the selected piece of music and the delivery of this video to Whitacre's team. Knowledge resources are available at the dedicated space for the Virtual Choir projects in Whitacre's webpage and are accessible mostly via links to PDFs, videos and audio files. PDFs of individual parts are to be used in combination with Whitacre's videos of instruction, and together compose the essential resources choir members need to access in order to successfully complete the tasks. Other knowledge resources further support the tasks and these include examples of videos produced by other choir members, or help with common technical questions.

Procedures and musical information are unpacked through detailed explana-tions. For example, one of the knowledge resources for VC2 is a video of Whitacre reading through the sheet music of *Sleep*, page by page, commenting on specific parts and advising on his vision of the music (Virtual Choir 2012). The video shows Whitacre as he introduces choir members to abstract concepts related to choir performances in general, and what he expects in terms of the delivery of *Sleep* specifically. Whitacre introduces specialist knowledge related to choir performance (e.g. discussing the importance of 'diction' in music). He models the pronunciation of certain consonants and vowels, and highlights specific parts of the music showing how certain words should be sung. Detailed information includes explanations about the need for long sounds as one sings words like 'moon' and 'soon'. Specialist terms are also introduced, such as the use of 'legato' and 'crescendo' in music, with straightforward explanations: *legato* is about 'singing in long fluid unbroken lines' and 'not note to note'; *crescendo* when one 'is getting louder' (Virtual Choir 2012). Specific instructions include: the timing of pauses; when one should breathe; alerts for when specific parts (alto, tenor, bass or soprano) will be in more evidence; and letting choir members know at what beat to stop. The knowledge is organized around procedural needs and provides a very specific account of what is required and why. In combination, the knowledge resources tell choir members about the notes and rhythm they will need to sing, when to start singing, simple instructions about the gestures for following the conductor and other details such as how to position themselves in front of the camera, how to use light, the importance of headphones and why they should wear black clothes.

The epistemic design displays and organizes valuable information about the task at hand: how one is to prepare the video recording and how to upload the video file for the creation of the virtual choir. There are also interesting learning opportunities for those new to music, choir singing and performance. Abstract concepts seem to be well explained and easy for a novice to follow. Nevertheless, assumptions are made about the knowledge one needs to bring to participation in the Virtual Choir projects. For example, one needs some ability to read music and to interpret the signals from a conductor. One also needs to know whether one's voice is a soprano, bass, tenor or alto, so that one can choose the correct part to sing.

Social Design

Whitacre reports that the Virtual Choir projects started as an experiment in social media (Virtual Choir 2012). The 'experiment' consisted of an invitation to those who were already in Whitacre's immediate (virtual) social group to participate in the project, and those were people in his circle of fans. He then relied on a snowball effect, where his fans would invite their friends, and the friends their friends, and so on. What is special in terms of the social design of the Virtual Choir projects is that a great deal of attention is dedicated to the way the communication amongst choir members takes place. As a result, one of the central aspects in the Virtual Choir case study is the emphasis placed on promoting social interactions and keeping choir members engaged, which are realized through the various social networking spaces that host discussions amongst choir members and the audience, and Whitacre's team's strategies for keeping members engaged.

The use of different social media meant that the Virtual Choir projects, at least initially, could be announced within potential participants' existing social networks. That is, participants typically first heard about the projects from Whitacre directly (if they were a fan) or from a friend. Currently, a Facebook page hosts the interactions amongst choir participants, but other social spaces are also used, such as YouTube, Twitter, Whitacre's blog and others (see Set Design). The creation of these dedicated social spaces seems to reflect Whitacre's awareness that an important part of these projects relates to fostering a sense of community, of bringing people together and facilitating connections between them, even if in most cases, members are unlikely to meet face-to-face.

Knowledge and meanings seem to be mostly context dependent and bounded to the specific social learning context of the Virtual Choir projects. That is, choir participants involved in the network learn skills and procedures with a specific task in mind: the production of their video component that will be incorporated as part of the final virtual choir creation. Their involvement in the projects appears to also allow for personal learning experiences that are highly valued and, in most cases, would be very unlikely to occur otherwise. Several accounts of these experiences can be seen throughout the various social media sites associated with the Virtual Choir projects, and many of these mention a sense of connection to fellow human beings. The passage below, for example, illustrates a story told by Whitacre at a TED Talk (Virtual Choir 2012), where one choir participant describes the remoteness of her location, and how that makes choir singing a physically impossible task, which was nevertheless realized in the virtual space through her participation in the Virtual Choir:

> It is a dream come true to be part of this choir, as I have never been a part of one. When I placed a marker on the Google Earth Map, I had to go with the nearest city which is about 400 miles away from where I live. As I am in the Great Alaskan Bush, satellite is my connection to the world.
>
> *(Virtual Choir 2012)*

Similarly, there are several accounts reporting the emotions evoked as a result of the experience of participating in such a project, the intense feelings of connection and the grandeur of their achievement. The two passages below illustrate such experiences:

> It is events and creations like these that will bring the human race closer and closer and bring more hope for true peace on this planet. Eric, your vision

and creativity is an asset to the wellbeing of our species. I believe you deserve a Nobel Prize or Humanitarian award! Keep it up!!!

(Virtual Choir 2012)

Eric does not just write music, he writes the emotions that connect with everyone, to me he writes the unthinkable. I listen to his music and it inspires me to write something with hopes of it sounding as passionate as his music.

(Virtual Choir 2012)

The videos, both for the instructions but also the individual creations, convey an image that reflects intimacy, shaped through the setting and the way the cameras are positioned and used. The videos are shot as close-ups, most of the time using a computer camera (web-cam), and in the home or office settings (e.g. choir members' houses, Whitacre's office). The individual artifacts show a video-singer closer to the viewer and a background scenario where the viewer can have a glimpse of the environment the singer is in. As a result, these artifacts reflect private, personal places, which in turn reinforce a sense of connection between the singer and the viewer. Similarly, Whitacre's videos of instruction also reflect the same intimacy, being shot in his office and using close-ups in such a way that viewers can 'imagine' Whitacre is sitting in the room next to them as he goes through the detailed instructions for how to complete a task. The video-instruction for the recording of the musical piece has Whitacre's image on a close-up looking directly at the camera. The choir member watches Whitacre's video as he or she follows his conducting movements, and looks closely into Whitacre's eyes. Once again, the image evokes intimacy and a sense of connection as if one is singing while looking into Whitacre's eyes. The same feeling of proximity is reflected in the way Whitacre manages social media and interacts with choir participants. He keeps choir members informed as the milestones of the project are reached, updating others about personal matters related to choir members and reflecting a sense of intimacy in his remarks. For example, he regularly refers to choir participants as the 'gang'. All of these reflect an emphasis on the subject, on realizing the connection at a personal level. The passage below illustrates how this personal connection with Whitacre was felt by one of the choir participants:

I was very struck and amazed by how much of a connection I had. . . . Even though when I watched Virtual Choir 1, I was thinking, 'This isn't choral singing.' But when I sang my part and Eric conducted, the connection that I had with him – looking into his eyes and watching him conduct was every bit as real to me as if I were standing on a stage, and that surprised me.

(Arca 2012)

In summary, the Virtual Choir projects seem to reflect a successful architectural structure with an emphasis on the epistemic and social design. Whitacre and his team use a decentralized approach to reach potential choir members, but other subtle strategies are employed to keep those who join the project engaged and interested, to create a feeling of belonging and partnership within the project and to keep a sense of connection between choir members and with Whitacre, which ultimately is reflected in the artifacts created.

Set, Epistemic and Social Co-creation and Co-configuration Activities

As the Virtual Choir projects evolved, so did the set, epistemic and social co-creation and co-configuration activities. As new Virtual Choir projects came to life, more elaborate resources, strategies and roles came into play. Lessons learned through the realization of each project were incorporated in each new cycle, and therefore VC2 and VC3 were not merely another attempt at a virtual choir experience that more or less mirrored VC1, but each new project incorporated feedback, strategies and ideas learned as a result of the previous experience, which resulted in reshaping the learning resources, the setting and the technologies employed to support the project and the roles and involvement of various stakeholders. There are also different digital and physical boundaries traversed. Examples include reports of choir members who go on to meet in 'person' (Arca 2012) and of external choir groups who choose to join together with the Virtual Choir project.

> The fun part about this is that many of us have met. We've been able to come together at different concerts and events and meet Eric and each other, so it's been a very rewarding experience. I strongly urge you to participate in the next one in the fall!
>
> *(Virtual Choir 2012)*

As timelines and new cycles of Virtual Choir projects have evolved, greater interest has arisen, which in turn has brought in an increasing number of participants, coupled with the need for better infrastructure. This has been addressed with the establishment of new connections via sponsorships and partnerships with Google/YouTube. In terms of the technological infrastructure, while the VC1 and VC2 projects were delivered via YouTube, VC3 used Vimeo, an online platform for curating and sharing video collections. In addition, VC3 has a dedicated channel within YouTube. The use of new streamlined technologies meant that an application was specially developed to support components of VC3 (Virtual Choir 2012). This application allows videos to be extracted and placed on an instance of Google Earth in Whitacre's website, resulting in greater visibility of the physical distances these virtual choir participants are traversing in the digital space, and providing clues about the diversity of the group. See, for example, the plotting of participants on Google Earth (Figure 13.2).

The most recent version of the Virtual Choir continues to value the ability of choir members to share their experiences, and so VC3 incorporated new spaces to house the 'virtual choir community' with, for example, a dedicated space for participants to upload their own videos and a 'hangout' on Google+ (Virtual Choir 2012). These new social spaces also meant new affordances for ways of connecting, which go beyond the sharing of personal meanings related to participating in the experience. The dedicated Google+ hangout for VC3, for example, offered a space where virtual choir participants could 'meet and practice together' in the virtual world, so they could work and help each other as they learn about the task at hand (e.g. they could help each other with pitches, or have separate subgroups for practice e.g. sopranos, basses, tenors and so on). The improved and streamlined ways of capturing and storing videos also include lessons learned on how to tag videos so that they can be more easily found on YouTube.

In terms of knowledge and learning, an interesting aspect of the Virtual Choir projects' co-creation and co-configuration is that choir participants are also given opportunities to collaborate in the production of knowledge resources – a chance to actively contribute to the project (beyond singing a part) – by sharing Whitacre's responsibilities in producing the learning resources. If participants choose to do so, they become collaborators and co-creators of the knowledge resources that others will be accessing as they complete their own individual parts. An example can be seen in Whitacre's VC2 post: 'For the sheet music, can someone with Finale or Sibelius skills (or bow-staff skills) make four separate PDFs of the vocal parts of *Sleep*? One for soprano, one for alto, one for tenor, one for bass' (Virtual Choir 2011).

However, it is important to note that participation in such activities depends on having some specialist knowledge and skills (e.g. of Finale or Sibelius). So although there is an openness to offers of help, these explicit requests are not necessarily for the music novice. One needs to be able to combine one's own knowledge with that of others to help advance the creative process. Similarly, as part of the VC3 project, Whitacre invited participants to share their videos with other participants. Specifically, he asked participants to self-evaluate their videos and those who considered they had performed well in their individual creations would then submit their videos for consideration: 'Other people's videos are not publically available however, if you have a recording that you believe is good enough for others to use to learn from let us know and, if chosen, we'll feature it on the Resources page' (Virtual Choir 2011).

Thus, choir members have opportunities to re-signify their outputs, which would then become learning resources in addition to being their individual vocal creations – to be incorporated as part of the main Virtual Choir artifact. As a result, roles shift: participants who may otherwise have had a more narrow social role, focusing solely on the production of their individual sung piece, are given

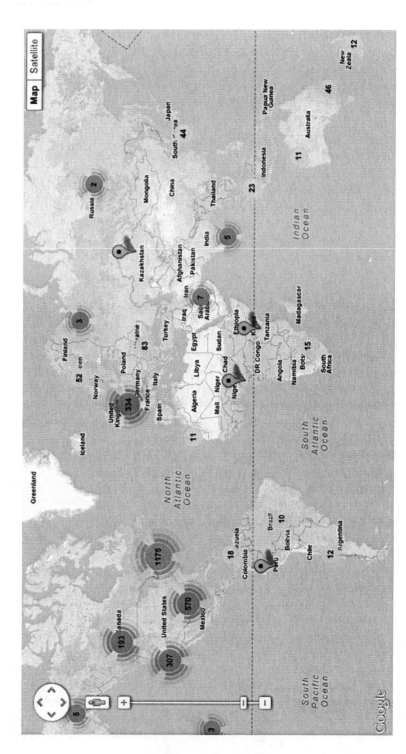

FIGURE 13.2 Virtual Choir: map showing the location of choir participants

the possibility of greater participation by sharing their knowledge through digital artifacts: singing demonstration pieces, creating PDFs of musical parts and so on.

The level of complexity of the learning tasks also changes over time within the new cycles of projects, in terms of the music structure that choir members are asked to learn and perform, which in turn affects the level of technical complexity required to complete each project. The pieces Whitacre chose for VC1 and VC2 (*Lux Aurumque* and *Sleep*) both have what is described as a homophonic musical structure: that is, these musical pieces require choir singers to work to the same rhythm at the same time, and they use soft and warm consonants (e.g. 'lux'). In technical terms (for the production of the final video), the homophonic approach allows more space for fudging the timing a little as the technician aligns the different audios and videos. VC3 involved more complex rhythms, since the musical piece (*Water Night*) takes polyrhythms into account. In effect, that presents a different type of challenge for choir members in terms of the output they are to create – singing to a musical piece that involves lyrics and musical motifs and different rhythms – which in turn also brings a different technical challenge in terms of synchronizing the audio recordings.

In spite of the complexity of its specialist knowledge, and the technical challenges for the production of its final creation, the most interesting aspect of the Virtual Choir projects is rooted in the experience it evokes. The projects foster a sense of a social identity, as those who participate develop a sense of belonging to the 'Virtual Choir social group'. Participants talk about the intensity of sharing a common language and are proud of identifying themselves as authors who contributed to a creation that is perceived as a beautiful and moving artifact. Choir participants not only report intense feelings of connection with the experience itself but they sometimes report a need to come back and review the product of their experience. One of the participants remarks: 'Just had to come here for my daily dose. One of the most beautiful, human experiences I've had the honor of being a part of' (Virtual Choir 2012). Another choir member sees their participation as a life-changing experience that defines 'who they are':

> The world carried on, life continued as it should, I didn't forget I was a part of this, but it took a back seat I guess. Today someone dropped a Facebook note about our *Sleep* getting close to 1M views, so I played that, and transported into that time for a moment. Then I came here, and was reminded of the hypnotizing effect this extraordinary piece has on us all. It has kind of become a time machine for me, a transcendent moment that defines who I am, and it will always affect my daily life.
>
> *(Virtual Choir 2012)*

Participants continue to co-configure activities once projects finish or once the final creation is completed, and new activities take place fostering an ongoing social connection amongst members, traversing the boundaries of the initial project itself (Arca 2012). As a consequence, choir members continue to attend the virtual social spaces even after the final creation has been completed. Such movement comes both ways, from the participants who continue to be connected to the spaces but also from Whitacre, who continues to nurture participation. Whitacre fosters interest by providing updates to members about the progress of the completed projects (e.g. launches at different venues, interviews conducted, how many viewers have seen the final videos and other news), as well as offering personal accounts for what has happened in some of the members' lives (e.g. someone underwent heart surgery and Whitacre invites choir members to send their best wishes). As a result, the community is active, and does not cease to exist once projects are completed. Moreover, Whitacre plans ahead: at the end of VC2 he was already referring to VC3, and a call for interest in VC4 is also already on display on Whitacre's blog.

Abstracting and Synthesis

The Virtual Choir case study illustrates the realization of a series of successful task-based projects, each of which involves significant amounts of informal learning. The main problem this case study illustrates is how design elements can be used to address the essential learning needs of participants, while at the same time nurturing a sense of belonging and inclusion. These elements combine to supplement participants' intrinsic motivation – so that they can engage in, and contribute to, the completion of a specific task, within what can be described as an informal learning environment.

Informal learning environments presuppose a learning context that is distinct from those in formal education. In this case, choir participants do not receive a qualification at the end of the project, and although some members may be professional singers in the music field, the virtual choir goals do not relate to professional development, career interests or ambitions. Such informal learning contexts are usually non-compulsory and therefore tend to rely heavily on learners' personal motivations, engagement with the tasks and/or the social context of the learning experience. Gee (2005) has proposed the notion of 'affinity spaces' to describe spaces that people with shared interest are drawn to, referring to these as 'semiotic social spaces'. The focus of Gee's notion of affinity spaces is the way in which people acquire and attribute meanings to signs. That is, the emphasis seems to be on the meanings attributed to the artifacts in the space where people with shared interests or goals meet. Lave and Wenger's (1991) notion of 'communities of practice' is also applicable to sets of people who share common interests in a particular domain as, for example, in a craft or a profession. However, Lave and Wenger emphasize people and their experiences, focusing on membership and learners' social identities, different levels of participation and the regular nurturing of engagement. In our case study we believe that both meanings (affinity and community) are relevant: the understandings evoked by the artifacts within the setting of the learning experience as well as the personal and social meanings fostered. Choir members have to have an interest in the task at hand – contributing to a group creation that they value – at the same time that they also value how their participation affects their personal and social identity. So here, the perceived complexity (a task that does not seem too difficult to accomplish, where enough learning material/support is organized and accessible, and a task that is perceived as contributing to a worthwhile creation) in addition to perceived social and personal values will dictate whether people allocate their time to engage in collaboration with others and ultimately contribute to the end product.

Virtual Choir houses a lot of learning resources but the way knowledge is communicated tends to be realized through an emphasis on the participants, specifically on how the experience affects and influences individual emotions, personal achievements (e.g. one is proud of being associated with the final artifact) and social identity (e.g. a shared sense of belonging). By perceiving Virtual Choir as a relevant group to be associated with, choir members are able to develop a sense of a shared goal, to feel that they have membership within this social context, which is then reflected in their contribution to the group's creation.

The architecture of the Virtual Choir exemplifies how design elements may be assembled together to support sharing of information related to a task-based project (through knowledge resources) as well as the fostering and nurturing of connections (through regular updates and the sharing of participants' personal experiences). There are three physical sites where stakeholders may be situated: the home space of a virtual choir member, the home space where Whitacre is located and the home space of members of Whitacre's technical team. These stakeholders 'meet' via social media in the digital space, that is, via the computer screen. Within the social media space, stakeholders exchange information about the task and share their personal impressions of their experiences (Figure 13.3).

The decentralized approach via various social media sites takes advantage of technology, software and resources that are familiar to choir participants. Most material elements are found in the immediate surroundings of the participants' everyday life: a room in their house, the computer they already have, a camera, headphones and so on. The digital elements also rely on a familiar structure and layout and the use of common or freely available software applications, and take advantage of social media sites that are likely to be commonly used by participants. Easy access to these resources seems to be a crucial component of the success of the network. In addition, the use of well-crafted instructions, learning resources and availability of technical information provide effective support to choir members in completing the task at hand. Other essential design elements are those that evoke emotions and intimacy (e.g. close-up videos, regular updates, remarks that stress a group creation or a shared goal), shaping and reflecting the personal and social characters of the informal learning experience. These design elements are tied together in the virtual space

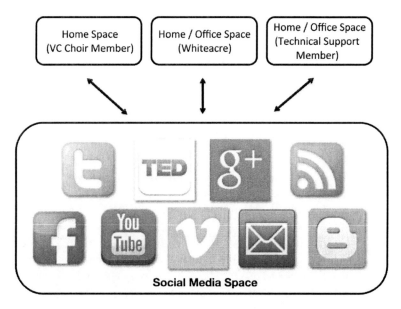

FIGURE 13.3 Virtual Choir: key structural elements

(Figure 13.3), facilitating the sharing of meaningful knowledge and experiences, and the realization of a shared creation.

Note

1 Accessed at http://ericwhitacre.com/the-virtual-choir. Please note that the network as described in this chapter may have evolved since the time of writing.

References

Arca, R., 2012. Making real connections through virtual choir [online]. *Suite 101.* Available from:http://suite101.com/article/making-real-connections-through-virtual-choir-a408299 [Accessed 8 July 2012].

Gee, J. P., 2005. Semiotic social spaces and affinity spaces: from the age of mythology to today's schools. In: D. Barton and K. Tusting, eds. *Beyond communities of practice: language, power and social context.* Cambridge: Cambridge University Press, 214–232.

Lave, J. and Wenger, E., 1991. *Situated learning: legitimate peripheral participation.* New York: Cambridge University Press.

Virtual Choir, 2011. *Singer instructional for Eric Whitacre's Virtual Choir 2011* [online]. Video. Available from: www.youtube.com/watch?v=dWCTKnbqE6s&feature=relmfuacre. com/the-virtual-choir> [Accessed 29 June 2012].

Virtual Choir, 2012. *Eric Whitacre's Virtual Choir 3: Water Night* [online]. Video. Available from: www.youtube.com/watch?v=V3rRaL-Czxw [Accessed 9 July 2012].

Whitacre, E., 2010. Interview. In: *The Strand.* TV, BBC World Service. April 30. Available from: www.bbc.co.uk/programmes/p00795yk [Accessed 30 May 2013].

14

ISPOT

Your Place to Share Nature

Ana Pinto, Kate Thompson, Chris Jones and Doug Clow

Overview

Learning happens anywhere, anytime, anyhow, and the iSpot network has been created to capitalize on these learning moments of everyday life. iSpot[1] is a British-based social network developed by the UK Open University (OU) as part of a larger project called Open Air Laboratories (OPAL). The iSpot website brings together those who enjoy the thrill of observing and identifying natural species, irrespective of their level of expertise or interest. Whether it is a child exploring the environment with parents, an adult interested in informally learning about new species, an enrolled student from the OU or an expert biologist, the iSpot learning network caters for everyone with an interest in the natural world.

The main aim of the iSpot network is to offer ordinary people opportunities to learn about natural sciences by sharing photos of their observations of reptiles, birds, fish, fungi, mammals, invertebrates and/or plants and to receive help identifying them. While observing nature is a simple task, identifying species can be a very difficult enterprise. Thus, once a member adds an observation to the website, another network participant responds by identifying the species. Identifications can be added by anyone, regardless of their level of expertise, and iSpot has a team of volunteer experts working to help with identifications. In this sense, the provision of support for identification through social networking constitutes one of the central purposes of the iSpot network.

There is no prerequisite for joining the network other than a willingness to enjoy and learn about the natural world. The basic resources needed are access to a computer with connection to the Internet and a digital camera, or a mobile device with those capabilities. People can sign in through their social media account, such as Facebook or Twitter, or by filling in a short online form.

The high level of activity within the site provides a compelling example of how a learning network can be formed through structured informal processes. In January 2013, there were well over 20,000 members registered and there have been over 150,000 observations uploaded to the site since the network was launched in June 2009.

Set Design

The layout of the iSpot website is clean and uncluttered. The central part of the main page hosts the latest images of species added by its members. General information is presented on the bottom half of the main page and additionally under the 'News' option on the main navigation menu. Under the 'Help' section on the menu bar, members can find specific information for using the site, including videos with basic instructions. The other sections on the menu bar are 'Surveys', 'Forums', 'Groups' and 'Keys'. Other than involvement in observations and identifications of species, all members can initiate or participate in forums, and take part in surveys. The 'Groups' section provides introductory guides for each of the eight taxonomic groups utilized to classify observations within the website: amphibians and reptiles, birds, fish, mammals, invertebrates, plants, fungi and lichens and other organisms. The 'Keys' section provides more resources for those willing to make identifications (Figure 14.1).

The iSpot network relies on members being able to access resources in both material and digital spaces, as members are expected to upload in the digital environment photos of observations they have made in the natural setting. An observation may consist of more than a single image, and entails filling in a simple form with some mandatory details (see Figure 14.2). These include the group to which the species belongs (Birds, Invertebrates, etc.), date of the

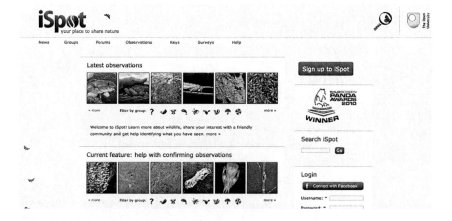

FIGURE 14.1 iSpot: home page

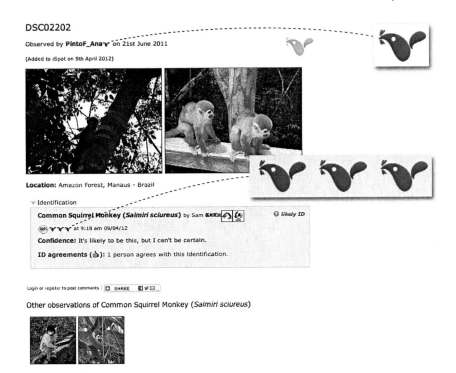

DSC02202

Observed by **PintoF_Ana** on 21st June 2011

(Added to iSpot on 9th April 2012)

Location: Amazon Forest, Manaus - Brazil

Identification

Common Squirrel Monkey (*Saimiri sciureus*) by Sam ●●●●●   *likely ID*

at 9:18 am 09/04/12

Confidence: It's likely to be this, but I can't be certain.

ID agreements ( ): 1 person agrees with this identification.

Login or register to post comments | SHARE

Other observations of Common Squirrel Monkey (*Saimiri sciureus*)

FIGURE 14.2 iSpot: an observation

observation and the location. A map function is available on the website, and is used to record the exact location of an observation.

Figure 14.2 illustrates the icon used to represent the group 'Mammals'. Each of the eight groups has its own icon. These design elements have multiple functions within the overall design (set, epistemic and social). The icons appear in a row in the main page below the images of the latest observation added to the website, as well as below the images of observations still requiring confirmation of identification. They provide a link to each of the groups, allowing members to create their own learnplace when customizing the main page according to their area of interest (Figure 14.1). This design feature may also be useful for people with low levels of literacy (whether young children or adults) who may use these visual cues to navigate through different taxonomic groups.

iSpot has the support of voluntary representatives from a range of scientific groups and schemes. These representatives are 'badged' with a logo that provides a link back to their schemes' or societies' websites (currently there are almost 100 listed). The links become resources for learning, along with other supporting materials available to facilitate the task of identification. These support tools are also key design elements within the network and will be discussed with respect to epistemic and social design later in this chapter.

The tasks involving the identification of species require effective engagement with the learning resources. The set design of iSpot provides support to members with different levels of expertise through a component designed to guide members to relevant and appropriate online educational resources: the identification keys. The keys are displayed via questions and/or statements to be answered by members as they go through the process of identifying a species observed. The design of the keys aims to encourage the user to accurately describe details of a species. The keys on iSpot use a novel Bayesian model, rather than the traditional 'dichotomous' approach; this means that users do not have to answer the identification questions in any set order. The identification keys that are available are classified according to experience – into those suitable for beginners and those for experts.

The keys for experts are more specific (such as a key to the species of female *Rhipicephalus* [*Boophilus*] ticks), requiring a higher degree of specialist knowledge. This is in contrast to those available for beginners (such as a *minibeasts* key, which is described as a basic key to major groups of invertebrates found in gardens and similar habitats). In an identification procedure, a series of questions are answered, each about a different feature of the species to be identified. Once the user selects a key, and before they begin the task of identification, they are taken to a setting up page. For example, in the case of the *minibeasts* key for beginners, the initial question relates to whether the user wants to give extra weight to common species or to treat all species equally. Once the users have selected their answer, new questions are generated. In this new page, a number of *characters* are listed and the user chooses answers to each character from a list of pre-defined options. For example, the user is asked to identify the number of legs on the *minibeast* (eight, twelve–fourteen, many, none, six). When an answer is selected, the identified character is moved to a new list, containing the defined characteristics of the species (for example, six legs, two wings, hard body), and displayed at the bottom of the page. As the list of characteristics is updated and refined, a third list of most likely species (located on the right of the page) is also shown. Other tabs available allow the user to view and compare species, or choose 'diagnostic characters'. The images displayed demonstrate the characteristics and species, and are sourced from existing iSpot identifications.

All digital resources within iSpot are displayed in a simple, well-structured layout. A 'my spot' section appears on the main page when a member logs in. Links to any content that a member has contributed to the website or has added to their favorites is shown in this section. The member is also notified when an identification, agreement or comment has been added to an observation they made.

In addition to iSpot's dedicated website, members' activities may occur within many other different digital or physical spaces. iSpot uses Twitter, as well as a direct link to face-to-face projects, the Bioblitzes. Bioblitz events involve ordinary people and experts engaging as a group in surveying and photographing wildlife at pre-determined sites during a specified period of time (usually for 24 hours). The iSpot set design offers a Bioblitz tag as an option under 'descriptive tags' so all observations are uploaded within the same section. iSpot members may then help with any unidentified species observed during group events.

iSpot designers have created a platform for learning that goes beyond the website and extends to the outside world. iSpot has been designed to build upon a system of activities that supports and encourages learning at scale. This system involves not only the users, experts, mentors and iSpot keys brought together in a process of formal learning, but also broadcasts (e.g. BBC TV through its nature programs). In this scenario, from the outset, iSpot's designers assumed that members' habits, identities and real-world probes would influence activity on the website. Still, they envisaged minimizing the resources required to participate in the network in order to facilitate access for all as far as possible. The minimum requirements in the material world are some form of access to nature (such as gardens and urban organisms) and a tool for capturing and uploading a digital photograph (which, of course, requires access to the Internet). A key strategy of the designers was to provide links to other existing sites that already offer excellent resources for supporting identification of wildlife (e.g. field guides). By avoiding duplication of resources already available online, designers were able to create a simple but efficient learning network. Not limiting the accessibility to the site unnecessarily was an important strategy, especially when considering that some people have limited opportunities for being exposed to taxonomic knowledge about specific entities of their surrounding environments.

iSpot's design elements reflect principles that coherently support the active participation of members. For instance, the request for notifying the location when uploading a form not only signals the importance of *place* for an effective identification of a species, but also relies upon active interaction with the natural world. An implicit assumption is that the user is aware of the location where they made the observation and can articulate this to the site through the 'Add an observation' process using the Google Maps solution developed for iSpot. In this scenario, a sketch of the architecture of place should account for the wide range of local resources members may come across during their diverse learning journeys, including the 'agency' of the natural world. A case in point is how seasonality interferes with patterns of human and non-human activity (e.g. some naturalists and animals become a lot less active during mid-winter across the UK). Both the natural world and the human-made material world (e.g. scientific tools, digital technologies, transport to access surveying sites, etc.) play significant roles in the success of activities using the iSpot website.

Epistemic Design

iSpot involves a complex architecture to account for members with varying levels of expertise and for learning processes that involve networked relationships.

The epistemic design emphasizes a social view of learning, though relationships are not strongly collaborative and links vary considerably in strength (Jones *et al.* 2008). Elements of the set design regulate participation through a structure that bridges a spectrum of learning: informal, structured and formal.

The exchanges between networked members tend to focus on specialist (scientific) knowledge related to the identification of species. In spite of the mostly informal nature of the iSpot learning network, scientific names are regularly added to all identifications within the site. This combination of learning specialist knowledge in an informal setting seems to sit well with iSpot members. In terms of knowledge and learning, it is interesting to note that iSpot's design philosophy situates members as active producers of knowledge; all members actively collaborate in the production of knowledge artifacts. Nurturing these types of participation results in an active community that continues to grow and, in some cases, even contributes to research.

As mentioned earlier, the most common form of participation involves members having observed and photographed natural elements in the physical environment. The learning task that follows requires members to upload the observation and fill in a pre-defined form. Every observation uploaded in turn becomes a learning resource for all members. Participation may also include more complex tasks such as identifying others' observations, or confirming existing identifications. One option when members 'add an identification' is to declare how confident they are, based on a pre-determined selection. These include: 'I am as sure as I can be', 'It's likely to be this, but I can't be certain', 'It might be this'. Knowledge building may be facilitated through designed elements such as this, enabling members to engage in structured 'discussions' about the species identified, and move towards the advancement of ideas in the network. Once an identification is proposed, new resources related to the species are added to the observation. These include links to the *Encyclopedia of Life*, the NBN map (a map from the UK's National Biodiversity Network showing the geographical distribution of official observations of that species) and other observations of the same species. These extra resources provide scaffolding for further learning. The aim is to facilitate complementary tasks related to confirmation of the identification, that is, to prompt members to verify the identification and choose 'I agree', or alternatively, 'add a revised identification'. In any case, members may also 'add comments'. An important effect of this fixed upload format is that participants quickly learn how to use the basic designed elements of the digital environment. In addition, the design mirrors the scientific practices of field biologists. By replicating the kinds of recording sheets that practicing scientists use, as well as the types of knowledge that they record, members are scaffolded in their learning of both domain specific knowledge (the species identified) as well as the scientific process.

Although members of the iSpot network contribute a significant variety of identifications, a dedicated team of experts is also present, and they can often identify the majority of observations fairly quickly. More than half of the observations uploaded without an identification receive an identification within an hour. By providing a number of keys (see Set Design), the epistemic design takes into account the varied levels of expertise and provides a space where everyone is able to learn and contribute to the construction of knowledge artifacts. However, while a wealth of digital resources is available to support members who choose to learn about different species, they may rely only on fellow members to identify their observations. Thus, one interesting aspect of iSpot relates to the way social networking provides an effective channel for verification of knowledge through the harnessing of collective intelligence. Conole (2013) calls attention to the potential of this kind of global scale 'open research', which is becoming increasingly attractive (see also *The Synaptic Leap*, Chapter 12 of this volume). In this context, iSpot has become a pioneer in using structured informal learning to feed into research, while also enabling members to take on more formal learning opportunities within the same platform. The OPAL surveys are an example of this. There are six links to different OPAL surveys on the iSpot site. These encourage members to participate in biological surveys that will contribute to scientific knowledge about the geographic spread of species (such as the 'bugs count survey' or 'biodiversity survey') as well as human impacts on biodiversity and environmental systems (such as the 'climate survey' or the 'water survey'). This approach connects Citizen Science, where volunteers participate actively in the scientific process (see Silvertown 2009), with a specific concern for learning by the volunteers.

The social and epistemic interactions between members, relating to the observations, can be quite loosely coupled. In a typical interaction, one member posts an observation, another member identifies it and a third member may add a comment. Other spaces in iSpot can be used for more collaborative practices, particularly within the forum, where stronger ties may be forged through dialogues and discussions. These more collaborative knowledge-building relationships tend to occur amongst experts who already belong to overlapping formal or informal communities of practice outside the iSpot environment. This sharing of experience may have an impact on the construction of their individual identities both within the iSpot community and within their boundary community of practice in their field of expertise/study. These experts, depending on their chosen degree of participation, may aspire to engage in learning themselves, at times making identifications outside of their specific fields. There are eight groups for classifying observations but experts from any domain may choose to participate in identifications and discussions outside their main fields. Their expert status is displayed only for the group to which it applies. An aspect worth noting is that novices can benefit from being able to model how to engage in identification based on their observations of the behaviors of more experienced members or experts.

Social Design

The iSpot learning network brings together members with a range of experience and expertise in the natural sciences. In this friendly and productive environment, people from diverse walks of life can actively engage in learning about both the local and global natural environment. While most observations are likely to occur in the immediate surroundings of participants' everyday life, interactions transcend the immediate space and time. Even with members who are distributed very widely in geographical space, a sense of community may be achieved once they share a common interest.

Thus, the iSpot network involves members with a wide range of interests and backgrounds. Roles and divisions of labor are democratically shared and well supported by the designed elements of the website. For instance, all members can suggest identifications, show agreement and add comments. However, iSpot uses some design features that identify expertise and roles (for a detailed analysis of this feature, see Thompson *et al.* 2013). The badges and icons next to a member's name are one example of this. Alongside each comment or observation entry one can see an author's ID and his/her badges or icons. As a result, for each entry in the site, the level of expertise of a member (e.g. an expert, a novice) and the domain of expertise (e.g. invertebrates) are immediately apparent. This element of the set design contributes to the enactment of both (i) a particular way of structuring knowledge (epistemic design) – as one can visualize the ways of communicating specialist knowledge in a certain subject area – and (ii) roles (social design) – as one can visualize the knowledge status of members – within the learning network.

In order to stimulate and develop members' expertise, and to help ensure the scientific accuracy of identifications, iSpot has in place a *reputation system*. The system rewards those who actively participate in the network by compiling each member's number of observations, agreements, identifications and posts on forums. The more members participate in the network the more social points (stars) they accumulate. Additionally, they may also acquire the icons representative of expertise in a particular group – these scores depend on how much expert opinion agrees with the identifications they have made. In Figure 14.2, for instance, while the member who originally posted the observation has one icon next to her name, the user who added the identification has three mammal icons. These icons appear not only beside the members' names but also within their profiles in the reputation column.

While icons are used to signal the level of expertise of the member involved in the identification, as well as to which group the observation belongs, the badge to the right of the member's name represents his or her affiliation to a specific professional group (Figure 14.3).

Therefore, how expertise is claimed within the website follows particular and interesting rules. While a badge represents a specific scheme, society or

tree

Observed by **PintoF_Ana** on 16th September 2012

(Added to iSpot on 18th September 2012)

Location: Kiama, NSW, Australia

▽ Identification

Canary Island Palm (*Phoenix canariensis*) by David  ⓘ *likely ID*

🌿🌿🌿🌿🌿 at 1:01 pm 18/09/12

Confidence: It's likely to be this, but I can't be certain.

Notes: Very widely planted in warm temperate regions including Australis

ID agreements (👍): 1 person agrees with this identification.

FIGURE 14.3 iSpot: badges indicate professional organizations

organization to which a member belongs, the icons represent the result of expertise enacted within the website. Expertise resulting from members' participation on iSpot depends upon the *merit system*. In this context, the experts play an important role not only regarding identifications but also in relation to the attribution of merit points within the merit system. The number of points attributed is based on the reputation of the member who agrees with the identification. This system seems to work well in bringing together experts and non-experts in a convivial learning environment. The system provides feedback on the scientific expertise of members, while allowing them to visualize the hierarchical position each member occupies in the hierarchy of knowing/ knowledge. The dynamic nature of the points attributed to each member may result in roles and divisions of labor shifting as members' expertise is increased. An analysis of the reputation system (Clow and Makriyannis 2011) shows clearly that experts' views make a much larger contribution to the number of points attributed than do non-experts' views.

Badges are assigned to organizations through application to the iSpot team, who verify their authenticity. In return, organizations represented by members have their events publicized on the iSpot website. The associations between iSpot and numerous schemes and societies represent an important aspect of its social design (and epistemic design, through the badges link). One well-established association is with the Bristol Natural History Consortium (BNHC) that hosts Bioblitz events (as described in the set design). The iSpot network offers a direct link to the BNHC website to encourage its members to take part in Bioblitz events. As mentioned earlier in this chapter, these face-to-face events aim to promote committed and long-term community involvement in monitoring and protecting the natural environment. Such activities involve more than informal observations and may forge continuing social engagements. Meanwhile, the BNHC's website promotes a number of further links. This organization uses popular social media sites such as Facebook, Twitter, Flickr, YouTube, etc. to promote various events. This use of social media not only facilitates engagement of event organizers, volunteers, naturalists and the general public, but also allows for promotion of new events and sharing of previous Bioblitz experiences. Therefore, while both iSpot and BNHC have a dedicated digital space for Bioblitz, the communication is realized within several different spaces.

iSpot's social design promotes a type of literacy that has been regaining currency lately, that is, *family literacy* (see Wasik 2012). Family literacy constitutes a powerful type of social learning in which all people, no matter how young or old, share experiences and jointly learn. These shared experiences are particularly visible during Bioblitz events. For instance, within the videos and photos that appear in the Bioblitz Facebook page, one can see young children surveying sites alongside adults. Such events bring the generations together, provide access to tools (both conventional and newer, hi-tech), facilitate diverse ways of learning, and encourage the continuation of traditional approaches to interactions with the natural environment. 'The actions, the deployments of artifacts . . . evoke the worlds to which they were relevant and position individuals with respect to those worlds' (Holland *et al.* 1998, p. 63).

In such settings, while young children may be using toy science instruments, older ones might use new technologies (e.g. digital cameras, iPads, etc.), and 'grandpa' can bring along an antique magnifying glass. Meanwhile, the experts can use low-tech plastic pots for collecting species or state of the art instruments (e.g. a mini microscope). In this way, tools, technologies, nature and people all become integral resources mediating learning; activities and knowledge creation are distributed across a heterogeneous network of elements.

An aspect of iSpot less visible on the site, but somewhat visible in the field, is the activity of a team of regionally based 'iSpot mentors'. The iSpot mentors take part in local nature events, presenting iSpot as part of a range of activities to develop the public's interest in nature. They have reached over 55,000 individuals through these face-to-face events. A key component of the iSpot social (and epistemic) design is the continuous encouragement of its members to take on increasingly active roles. Whether it happens on a more informal basis through participation in projects or volunteer work with the network of natural history societies and biodiversity recording and monitoring schemes, or formal enrolment in a tertiary course with the OU, iSpot seeks to extend and expand members' involvement in enjoying and protecting the natural environment.

Set, Epistemic and Social Co-creation and Co-configuration Activities

The iSpot environment supports members of the public, higher education students and experts, from any country, all learning and possibly collaborating within the same platform. As discussed throughout this chapter, the most common form of participation occurs when uploading a photo of an observation using a pre-defined form (Figure 14.2), a task that requires that members add information related to the species group (e.g. Mammals), and when and where the observation took place. These uploaded images, supported by features of the set, epistemic and social design, become themselves part of the structure of the website (the set), the tasks to be completed and the knowledge created (epistemic), and are the focus around which social interaction takes place. As new observations and identifications are added to the website, co-creation and co-configuration take place. The main page of iSpot is continually updated with the latest observations as well as any observations that still require confirmation of identification.

On examination of posted observations and subsequent identifications by network members, it appears that most postings include the minimum details required about an observation. However, in some cases, additional comments are added and 'conversations' emerge within the form structure. When suggestions, ideas, impressions and personal feelings are added within the basic form, network members tend to engage in extensive collaboration. Personal stories, which may include a sense of wonder and excitement about the events surrounding the original posting, as well as the stories that follow, seem to encourage further sharing of information within the community. In some cases, these observations have relatively high numbers of agreements. Perhaps when a story is associated with an observation, members are more likely to contribute to the identification as well as the comments. On other occasions, the type of observations that enable a story to accompany them may appeal to a broader section of the community. In any case, the unfolding of knowledge about the context of the observation seems to be as important in these cases as the identification itself.

Discussion forums are the other space in which activity occurs. In general, forums involve further discussion about one particular observation or relate to general topics involving wildlife. Unlike the sharing of observations that are regulated by pre-defined forms, postings in discussion forums allow for easier change of topics, and those discussions that continue over a long period of time can be challenging for members to follow and/or take part in. The composition of members participating in the discussion forums may also influence the content and direction of postings. The rating of expertise, discussed previously, which is important when establishing the identity of a specific observation, is also represented in the forums. In some cases, members rated as experts within the iSpot community engage in what is probably closer to a debate in the discussion forum, particularly when the topic is more general, such as personal positions about conservation. Issues may also arise when discussions involve ethics and research practices within different groups.

An important aspect of co-creation and co-configuration occurs when members participate in events, such as Bioblitz. A typical scenario involves a member following the link from iSpot to the BNHC, which serves as a portal with information on events taking place in many regions across the UK. A number of organizations have been running their own Bioblitz events, and the BNHC encourages more institutions to join the Bioblitz National Network. Members who take part in such events are guided by experts to ensure maximization of their productivity. Participants who are also members of iSpot are encouraged to upload their observations to the iSpot site, and a Bioblitz tag is created so that observations on iSpot belonging to that Bioblitz can be gathered together. The linking of iSpot and the Bioblitz network helps improve the scientific quality of the data collected, as iSpot demonstrates the scientific relevance of participation in the site. These events reconfigure and enact design elements from the set and epistemic design into a new social context, with face-to-face, community contact, rather than individual observations. Even with the different social context, the design is still productive. Members can make further contributions when they 'visit' other digital environments linked to these networks. For instance, on the dedicated Facebook page for Bioblitz, people can watch videos of previous group events in which they may have taken part, and can also add comments or start new discussions. Videos often present whole families working together to survey a site. Another interesting feature is the addition of works of art depicting observations made (paintings, illustrations, etc. of nature).

Abstracting and Synthesis

The main design problem this case study addresses is how design elements can bridge between diverse elements in a network, traversing across a range of strong and weak ties, bringing together people of all ages and with a wide range of goals, interests, abilities and knowledge in a productive learning network. The iSpot network accommodates over 20,000 members, and in order for such a large number of participants to feel that they are contributing to the network, and in order for roles to be realized, a complex process for acknowledging, acquiring and displaying expertise is used. The necessary elements of professional scientific practice are reproduced in this network, and it serves the purposes of situating members in the ways of knowing within the sciences, scaffolding their practice and managing the large numbers involved. The iSpot case study illustrates useful design elements for those informal learning networks committed to delivery of high quality open content while providing its members with rich informal learning opportunities and options to embrace formal studies.

The iSpot learning network has many functions and may fulfill diverse purposes: as a platform to engage in informal or formal learning about nature; as a repository for storing representations of knowledge necessary for identifications; for social networking; as a forum to discuss or seek orientation about practical problems involving interactions within the natural world; and as a database for research in the natural sciences. Despite its informal feel, iSpot aims to motivate members to move into a range of learning journeys. These include routes out to complementary activities (such as Bioblitzes), natural history societies and biodiversity schemes (such as badges links), as well as formal learning enrollment with the Open University (such as the *Neighbourhood Nature* course). By reaching as many people as possible and catering for their learning regardless of previous scientific knowledge, the network promotes a commitment towards a responsible interaction with the natural environment.

One of the main purposes of the designed elements reported in this chapter is to scaffold members' experience of the scientific process of recording data and identifying species. In this context, the reputation systems, as well as the identification keys, represent distinctive design elements. The reputation system appears to be extremely powerful in motivating members and promoting further participation within the iSpot ecosystem. Meanwhile, the keys constitute an interesting combination of set and epistemic features. The expertise required to use the keys is reliant on the ability of the user to answer questions with the level of specificity required. Observation skills, as well as scientific terms, need to be developed before expert keys can be used effectively. The provision of a range of keys, suited to beginners, users with some experience and experts, ensures that all members are supported within the environment. The key itself is an important, rigid part of scientific practice that the set and epistemic design effectively apply to scaffold users both in their initial selection of a key (according to expertise, and then to the entity to be identified), as well as through the identification process. The scientific framework remains rigid within the overall design.

The iSpot network creates links between a range of participants, using ties of varying strengths, and connecting the natural and digital environments. The digital environment connects members around the many areas of common interest within the natural world, and across a range of organizations that share similar goals. It encourages members to leave the digital space, and collect more information, to share with fellow members of the network, through programs such as Bioblitz and OPAL surveys, as well as the usual observation posts. The organized group events, alongside the maps that indicate the number of observations made in different locations, help members to feel connected in a vast natural and digital space. The associations with many different schemes and societies sit well with iSpot's intention of generating a positive impact on the world. While reproducing some aspects of the social context commonly associated with scientific practices, iSpot also manages to successfully integrate science and fun, and appeal to people with varying backgrounds.

Learning situated within these contexts helps to induct new people into distinctive communities of practices by forging social identities. In all cases, these people are appropriating knowledge, practices, values, norms, etc. of the social and scientific worlds. The 'surveying' activities constitute social practices that become integral to the life of these communities, promoting social learning experiences that have the potential to bring both affective and cognitive benefits. Perhaps most importantly, this type of active participation within these social groups can lead to conceptual understandings that can then be (re)applied, to the benefit of all in the community.

Note

1 Accessed at www.ispot.org.uk. Please note that the network as described in this chapter may have evolved since the time of writing.

References

Clow, D. and Makriyannis, E., 2011. iSpot analysed: participatory learning and reputation. *Proceedings of the 1st international conference on learning analytics and knowledge*, 27 February–1 March 2011, Banff, AB. New York: ACM, 34–43.

Conole, G., 2013. *Designing for learning in an open world*. New York: Springer.

Holland, D., Lachicotte, J. R., Skinner, D. and Cain, C., 1998. *Identity and agency in cultural worlds*. Cambridge, MA: Harvard University Press.

Jones, C. R., Ferreday, D. and Hodgson, V., 2008. Networked learning a relational approach: weak and strong ties. *Journal of Computer Assisted Learning*, 24(2), 90–102.

Silvertown, J., 2009. A new dawn for citizen science. *Trends in Ecology & Evolution*, 24(9), 467–471.

Thompson, K., Ashe, D., Carvalho, L., Goodyear, P., Kelly, N. and Parisio, M., 2013. Processing and visualizing data in complex learning environments. *American Behavioral Scientist*, 57, 1400–1419.

Wasik, B. H., ed., 2012. *Handbook of family literacy*. New York: Routledge.

15

UTILIZING INFORMAL TEACHER PROFESSIONAL DEVELOPMENT NETWORKS USING THE NETWORK AWARENESS TOOL

Maarten de Laat, Bieke Schreurs and Rory Sie

Overview

The Network Awareness Tool (NAT) is a Web 2.0-based tool that enables professionals to become aware of existing networked learning relationships (within or between organizations) that can help them with real, urgent, work-related problems that are part of their daily practice. In most cases, such problems arise unplanned, *ad hoc* and are usually dealt with informally. However, these problems serve as a kind of 'social hub' that brings together professionals in order to develop a solution that allows them to continue working (De Laat 2012). These everyday work-related problems provide not only an opportunity for professionals to seek each other's help, and build meaningful networks; they are also a catalyst for informal learning. Informal learning tends to deal with implicit knowledge, embedded in day-to-day practice, and is a result of spontaneous learning activities (Billett 2001, Davenport and Prusak 2000, Eraut 2000, Marsick 2001, Boud and Hager 2012, Hargreaves and Fullan 2012). While observable, explicit knowledge is relatively easy to obtain, through reading or training courses, informal learning in the workplace allows for the acquisition of deeper, tacit components of knowledge (Lane and Lubatkin 1998).

Networked learning is a perspective that aims to understand learning processes by focusing on how people develop and maintain a 'web' of social relations, used for their learning and professional development (De Laat 2012, Goodyear *et al.* 2004, Haythornthwaite and De Laat 2012, Steeples and Jones 2002). In the context of this chapter, we define networked learning as a form of informal learning situated in practice, where people rely strongly on their social contacts for assistance and development (De Laat and Coenders 2011). Networked learning can occur through the use of ICT, but networked learning activities can also happen face-to-face in the workplace. This explicitly assumes informal learning networks to be already present, in the form of everyday social relationships (De Laat 2012). This bottom-up approach is different from the top-down approach that, for instance, Sloep *et al.* (2012) employ. They view a learning network as a tool that supports the professional, for example by facilitating peer support in a virtual learning environment (e.g. Biebkracht: Sie *et al.* 2012, p. 6 and Chapter 9 of this volume). Contrary to this view, we see learning networks as existing social phenomena. From this perspective, learning cannot be designed: it can only be designed *for* – that is, it can be facilitated or frustrated (Wenger 1998, p. 229). This means that tools and spaces can be designed to facilitate learning and there is a need here for people with the ability to do so – to be architects for learning: 'Those who can understand the informal yet structured, experiential yet social, character of learning – and can translate their insights into designs to service learning – [as they] will be the architects of tomorrow' (Wenger 1998, p. 225).

In our (bottom-up) view, professionals and their managers ideally need to become the architects of their own professional learning spaces. For example, to design for learning the architect can make sure that 1) the desired artifacts are in place, like curricula, expert advice, procedures, tasks etc. and 2) the right people are at the right place, in the right kind of relation to enable learning to happen (Wenger 1998). The Network Awareness Tool (NAT, in Dutch 'Netwerk in Beeld' [NiB]), developed at the Scientific Centre for Teacher Research (LOOK) at the Open University in the Netherlands (De Laat and Schreurs 2011), focuses exactly on the latter. We believe that greater awareness of how professionals are connected, and how these connections are driven by their work-related problems, may help to raise awareness about the presence of learning spaces, populated by the networks/communities, in which professionals participate (De Laat 2012). This awareness facilitates learning between professionals as they can (independently, or with the help of a facilitator) jointly utilize the architecture of these professional development networks (Schreurs and De Laat 2012a). To do so, professionals first need to get insights into their own networked learning relationships and the networks that exist around them. NAT can be used to collect and map the informal reality of social learning networks (Schreurs and De Laat 2012b). As such, NAT facilitates the visualization of already existing social learning spaces.

In this chapter we will describe the architecture of NAT and how NAT is used to facilitate design for learning. We will describe how the design elements of NAT can contribute to the understanding of informal networked learning activities by the professionals. The chapter is based on data gathered at a gymnasium in the Netherlands (the ABC[1] Gymnasium) in which the Network Awareness Tool was used to understand the structure of these networks. The examples show how design elements of NAT support professionals to enhance the structure of their learning network. The ABC Gymnasium is a young gymnasium (a school that prepares students for university entrance) in the Netherlands. The study was conducted as part of a project that was set up to stimulate teachers' networked learning activities within the school, in order to form a topic-driven network or community of practice. To this end, 53 teachers were asked to indicate in NAT the people with whom they learn and what work-related problems they discuss while learning with each person. Additionally, the teachers were asked what they value in ABC Gymnasium about networked learning. We conducted individual interviews with 16 teachers and organized group discussions with four groups of five to six teachers to analyze the output of NAT. The NAT output (e.g. network visualizations) acted as input to further facilitate design for networked learning in the school.

This chapter discusses some of the key design elements of NAT, following the sections on set, epistemic and social design, hypothesizing how these elements influence the enhancement of the learning network structure within this school. The chapter also illustrates how these design elements can be abstracted to inform the design of online tools in other contexts.

Set Design

The design of NAT is based on the idea that learning relationships (in our context at least) are emergent. They exist in both realized and unrealized forms of networking. Some network relationships are active, in the form of explicit relationships. Others may be potential relationships or tacit, implicit relationships.

In general, NAT consists of three main design elements (detailed examples will be provided below). First, there is the network elicitation space. Here, users are asked to fill in their personal learning topics and indicate their learning ties around work-related topics. Peers' names that are already in NAT's database are automatically recognized to prevent duplicate entries. Second, there is the visualization space, in which the inserted information is processed and visualized. Work-related (learning) topics are presented in a tag cloud and ties between the professionals associated with these topics are visualized in the form of a learning network structure. Users can actively navigate in the visualization part and look at the visualization from three different perspectives. They can view their own personal learning network, the learning network around a certain topic, by selecting topics in the tag cloud, and they can see the overall learning network structure between professionals from the entire organization. Third, we integrated a personal profile page with name, email address, working location and the user's expertise.

NAT's set design incorporates elements to support professionals' awareness of three types of relations. First, NAT provides support for the visualization of active learner–learner relationships, but also learner–learning topic relationships (active ties). Second, NAT acts as a supporting instrument in the sense that it helps learners identify candidate contacts, from whom they can learn (potential ties). Third, NAT allows professionals to visualize relationships that exist, but those that professionals may not have mentioned yet (tacit ties). In the section below, we will explain how NAT's design supports professionals in becoming aware of these active, potential and tacit ties.

Active Learning Ties

An important purpose of NAT is to elicit existing active learning ties around relevant and actual topics like, for example, work-related problems. NAT includes a space for professionals to input the learning interactions they have in a physical setting. Professionals are asked to identify their learning interactions on a specific topic by employing a so-called *ego-centric* network data collection method (Scott 2000, p. 72, Sie *et al.* 2012). In detail, this is performed as follows: a professional is asked about the contacts that she has learnt from recently. She then specifies which topic they discussed and to what extent this contributed to her learning. In other words, a *value* or *weight* is assigned to each learning relationship, and *meaning* is given to the learning relationship by specifying what was learnt. The input feature, therefore, incorporates a weighting feature in the tool by means of a rating system. Users of NAT can rate the frequency of their contacts using stars (4 stars = daily, 3 stars = weekly, 2 stars = monthly, 1 star = less than monthly). Besides frequency, they can also rate the quality of this tie in terms of learning – that is, the value of this tie in relation to the topic at hand. This is done using stars as well (ranging from low quality = 1 star to high quality = 5 stars). In addition to information about each of the ties, the tool also collects data about the importance of the entire network on each topic. Ratings can be given for the impact this network has on one's own learning, on changing one's practice and the relevance the network has for the development of the organization. In Figure 15.1, an example of importing NAT's ego-centric network data is shown. 'My themes' (top left) provides an overview of the professional's topics (i.e. the work-related problems that initiate informal learning). The column in the middle 'My contacts in . . .' is used to import the contacts that contributed to learning on this topic. And 'Theme info' is used to provide information on what the subject is about, and to rate the extent that the network has contributed to the professional's learning experience.

When a professional imports all the learning topics and the associated contacts, an *ego-network* will emerge. In the visualization part of NAT, this ego-perspective is represented in the form of a network structure. In Figure 15.2, in the center of the screen, an ego-network of professional 'PG' is visualized by showing all the ties that are connected to this professional.

Potential Learning Ties

Besides supporting awareness of active ties, the imported information and the design elements in NAT can also be used to point out possible connections

FIGURE 15.1 Example of ego-centric network of a professional of the ABC Gymnasium

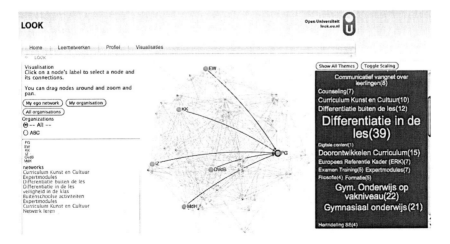

FIGURE 15.2 Ego-network visualization of teacher 'PG' of the ABC Gymnasium

between professionals. Haythornthwaite (2002) studied the nature of ties in online communication and noted that whereas some research had emphasized the use of Computer-Mediated Communication (CMC) for maintaining and reinforcing strong ties, in fact the real benefit may be in the realm of latent, or potential ties: ties for which a connection is possible, but that have not yet been activated by social interaction. Her finding is a source of very useful insights that can improve design for networked learning. In the field of recommender systems, a similar approach was adopted decades ago, when like-minded users were given recommendations about items based on the actions/preferences of other fellow users. A well-known example is the recommendation module at Amazon.com ('Customers who bought this item also bought . . .'). An important characteristic of a potential tie is that it is not yet established by individuals, simply because professionals may not be aware of a potential learning source they can connect with. Only by becoming aware of other people dealing with similar problems, or of people who have relevant expertise, can a potential learning tie be found. This is not limited to the case where such people exist in another organization; it can also be true within one organization, and even between colleagues who work closely together. Only by making this information explicit can latent ties be converted into active learning ties. NAT can be a plugin to the organization's CMC or work platform, and thus caters to communication within and between organizations.

NAT elicits potential ties by pushing implicit information from a so-called 'two-mode network' (learner–topic instead of learner–learner relationships) to the users. We are then able to visualize relations between professionals and topics relevant for their practice (who learns about what) and learning relations between people: who learns with whom. In the section below on epistemic design we will explain how users can discover potential learning ties. Here we will solely explain the design elements.

When users log in to NAT they do not merely see their ego-network, as is shown in Figure 15.2. They can also see all the other learning topics active within their organization (as indicated by the circle in Figure 15.3). Next to the list of existing learning topics, they can see for each topic all the professionals who are connected to it. For each topic, this list is divided into one's known contacts (active ties) but, more importantly, also the contacts one was not aware of (as indicated by the square in the middle column in Figure 15.3). If one clicks on these possible learning contacts, one is presented with information about that person: this includes name, email address and specific expertise of the target person. This information is extracted from the personal profile page.

The visualization part of NAT sheds another light on these potential learning ties. This is based on the idea of *structural balance*, a well-known theory in Social Network Theory that asserts that people form ties more easily with people

FIGURE 15.3 Potential learning topics and potential learning sources, with extra contact information

who are already related to other people they know (say a friend of a friend is my friend too). Especially when it comes to transferring tacit knowledge, people rely on colleagues whom they can trust and colleagues who are close to them or share the same practice (Borgatti and Cross 2003). Therefore, the visualization of the network structure (rather than listing them as in Figure 15.3) provides additional information about shared ties between professionals. In Figure 15.4, for example, 'PG' could be a good potential learning source for 'CV'. They are learning around the same topic and they have many ties in common ('KK';'IZ';'HL').

Tacit Learning Ties

To conclude the key elements in the design of NAT, we will now illustrate how we implemented design elements to provide users with information on tacit learning ties. The idea of the existence of tacit learning ties is based on the

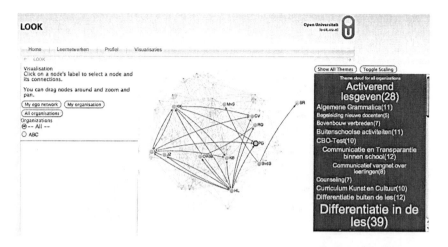

FIGURE 15.4 Network around the topic 'buitenschoolse activiteiten'

definition of tacit knowledge by Polanyi (1967), who first suggested that 'we know more then we can tell'. The knowledge of complex processes is often implicit. This kind of knowledge is mostly revealed through practice; it is often embedded in a particular context and usually transmitted through social networks (Schmidt and Hunter 1993). During their practice, professionals show other professionals how to deal with complex issues. But professionals are often not aware of these social learning activities. Of course we do not claim that we can grasp the whole complex process of the transfer of tacit knowledge within an organization, but we make an attempt to elicit tacit learning ties: ties by which professionals inspire other professionals without them knowing that they were a source of learning. To elicit tacit ties, we integrated the Web 2.0 idea of *signaling* in NAT. With NAT we signal users of potential ties. We push information that is loosely similar to the social network feature often seen in online social networks as 'people you may know'. In our system, the tool pushes information about informal networked learning activities that users are mentioned in, i.e. 'learning topics you are mentioned in by others'. In other words, rather than showing 'people you may know', the design of the tool facilitates awareness about 'people who know you'. This can stimulate the users to think of learning networks that they are engaged in but that they did not think of, or were not even aware of. This is essential for visualizing informal networks, which often deal with tacit and implicit knowledge. On the import side, tacit ties with topics are represented in a list under the heading 'Also mentioned in', shown in Figure 15.3. In the visualization part, professionals can see arrows pointing to them in a learning network. These ties are from people who mention the professional as being a valuable learning source.

NAT in Relation to Epistemic Design

Now what do professionals learn by using NAT? NAT is designed to be used as a reflection tool, to give professionals opportunities to gain insights into their own social learning activities and those of others in and beyond their organization. But it is more than just a learning analytics tool. NAT also holds the potential to stimulate new learning ties and give insights into the social learning content and social capital of an entire organization. NAT tries to elicit knowledge that is transferred or created between professionals. This implies the visualization of both codified knowledge and tacit knowledge. NAT does not aim to make a clear distinction between the two, but it does intend to elicit more than a professional's explicit expertise, or the transfer of codified knowledge.

In addition, NAT's design aims at assisting informal learning in the workplace at three distinct levels of the organization's network (cf. Sie *et al.* 2012, para. 2.2.2). First, on the individual level, it allows a professional to identify her ego-network. The visualization of the ego-network promotes professionals' *self-reflection* by making them aware of the people that they learn from (Social Design) and what knowledge they hold (Epistemic Design).

Second, on the group level, NAT can detect and visualize relationships that revolve around a specific topic or tag. To do so, it uses the topics (work-related problems) or 'themes' that NAT users specify when they label the learning relationship that they have with a fellow professional. In the case of professional informal learning, such a theme can be knowledge about a specific course subject, such as differentiation in the classroom.

Figure 15.5 shows an example of a network around the theme 'differentiation in the classroom' ('differentiatie in de les'), which comprises 39 professionals. These members share a common practice or interest in this topic. In this case, the members of the group have all indicated that they are learning around the theme of differentiation in the classroom, and the network ties show to what extent they are learning together on this subject. On the topic level, professionals can identify the density of a learning network around a certain topic and/or detect clusters or simply find out that there are multiple networks on the same subject that are not connected at all. The visualizations can also be used to identify key persons within a network based on the number of ties (incoming and outgoing). Using the scaling option will change the size of nodes in the network based on their connections. The following quote from the focus interview illustrates the ways teachers were looking at the specific learning network 'differentiation in the classroom':

> This [network structure] seems logical. The people represented in this network visualization do talk a lot about differentiation in the classroom. You can look at [this visualization] from different perspectives. For example it strikes me that our female colleagues are more centered in the middle.

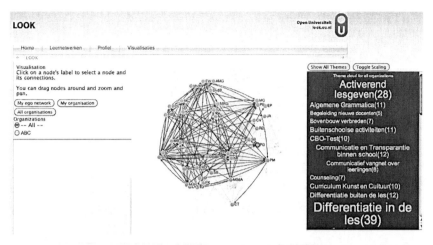

FIGURE 15.5 Network around the topic 'differentiatie in de les'

> Apparently differentiation in the classroom is more discussed amongst female colleagues.
>
> *(Teacher, Focus Group Interview)*

Third, at the organizational level, NAT makes it possible to visualize the networks of the entire organization. This design element allows users to get an impression of the overall connectedness within their organization. Typically, managers are interested in this type of visualization. If an organization is relatively unconnected, or has so-called low *network density*, knowledge may remain localized in small networks and therefore remains hidden from the rest of the organization. Conversely, if an organization is perfectly connected, it could mean that the interactions either contribute to a perfect knowledge exchange within the organization (which is unlikely) or, more intuitively, that knowledge exchange is suboptimal (something like 'everybody is talking with everybody all the time'). In other words, the intensity or quality of the learning relationships may be lower.

The overall representation of networks also allows one to see the clusters of individuals that emerge in an organization. Within these clusters, knowledge and meaning are shared but, between clusters, little or no knowledge is shared. This provides an opportunity to transfer knowledge from one cluster to another, in order to be more creative. Burt (2004) denotes such opportunities as *structural holes*. In the context of designing for learning and utilizing the potential of informal professional development networks, this is what NAT on this level aims to do. By visualizing the existing networks, NAT facilitates reflection on how knowledge sharing and participation in networks can be enhanced. Such insights may help managers in also becoming architects of the kind we described earlier: facilitating the development of an effective learning network within their organization by implementing strategies that facilitate communication across potential learning ties; or by organizing the management of urgent learning topics more efficiently, around a core group of professionals who are already dealing with these issues; or by connecting potential ties between professionals in different clusters, to stimulate the possibility of horizontal innovation.

Finally, NAT provides an overview of knowledge that is being created informally, by listing all the topics in the form of a *tag cloud*. This tag cloud shows the topics that professionals are working on in terms of their development, driven by everyday work-related problems (see the column on the right in Figure 15.5, listing all themes). As such, this tag cloud presents an overview of the informal learning agenda of the organization. Topics that are mentioned more frequently appear larger in the tag cloud, making it easier to identify popular themes.

This tag cloud could also represent the identity of an organization. What is happening in the workplace? What are the work-related problems that professionals in the organization are trying to solve by forming social learning networks? During the interviews with the teachers at ABC we asked them to reflect on the meaning of the tag cloud, and the following interesting quotes emerged in the focus group interviews:

> Do we recognize this? Yes, completely. This is not surprising. What I find powerful about this tag cloud is that these results are from all the individual teachers. It is not a result from one meeting, but from individual conversations between people. It shows what lives here. This is the reality. It is a confirmation of what we ascertain a couple of times, but now it comes from all the individuals, and that is beautiful.
>
> *(Teacher, Focus Group Interview)*

> The tag cloud says something about the identity of the ABC Gymnasium: We care about our students and the quality of our education. . . . What we are occupied with and what differentiates us from other Gymnasium schools.
>
> *(Teacher, Focus Group Interview)*

Also, the tag cloud can help teachers to build their own social learning network or help managers to evaluate what is going on in the school. The following quote illustrates how the school principal plans to use the tag cloud over time:

> Topics need to become larger and smaller. If this theme is the same size in two years, we are not performing well. Over the years we can make a

comparison. You can see with what we are occupied. This topic [for example] is very large. It shows what we are occupied with at this moment. If a theme is going well in the school, the size may be smaller, then it will be mentioned less in conversations.

(School Principal, Focus Group Interview)

Tonight I have a meeting with the parents. I also want to discuss this with them. What if there were tag clouds from different schools? Would we recognize the tag cloud of our own school? We think we do, but actually we do not know for sure. I would like to test this and compare this with other schools. I would like to see the differences.

(School Principal, Focus Group Interview)

The final quote represents what teachers want to do with the results represented in the tag cloud:

The tag cloud represents what topics exist here. The topics that are represented larger gain more attention. Can you relate this directly to yourself? The large topics receive public support. Can you act on this yourself? We have to do something with it. Otherwise we won't start talking about it. We have to talk about the topics we struggle with.

(Teacher, Focus Group Interview)

NAT in Relation to Social Design

NAT is inherently a social tool. It provides information for and about an individual professional, what connects them and how they are related. As was stated in the principal's quote: the end result of NAT is the collection of individual entries into the representation of the entire social learning architecture. However, NAT is not a tool that provides conventional communication functionality, like automatic emailing or chat functions, although we do provide a user's work email address, so that information can be used to establish contact. But, all in all, professionals can use their own means of communication to contact potential learning ties, or managers can organize meetings or events to stimulate social learning around specific topics that need a boost to stimulate innovation.

Users of NAT get information about the social learning networks within the entire organization. We do not predesign different roles within the system, but the roles of individuals within a social network emerge in the sum of all individual networks within the organization. Key players can be identified – central persons around a certain topic – and people can look for others with specific expertise. But also professionals in the periphery can be spotted. They can act as 'brokers' (Burt 2004) to external relations, for example, or may be motivated to get more in touch with their colleagues. In short, NAT is a learning analytics tool that reflects the informal learning networks that exist within an organization. It shows the social learning architecture as it happens in practice, but an architecture that, due to its informal nature, has no formal presence in the organization (De Laat 2012). By raising awareness about the presence of such networks, and the value they create (Wenger *et al.* 2011), NAT unveils a social architecture or a social space that can be further utilized and designed for.

Next to active learning ties, individuals also see the learning ties through which other colleagues are connected to them. Often, these ties and the knowledge they hold are tacit for the recipient. The nature of tacit ties is well illustrated in the following quotes, obtained from the focus group interviews we held with the teachers of the ABC Gymnasium, asking them what they see in the visualization of the learning networks within their school:

> I wonder if colleagues are aware that they are a sparring partner for someone else.
>
> *(Teacher, Focus Group Interview)*

> I liked filling in NAT because it triggers you to think about who you talk to concerning certain topics. Normally you don't think about this. And on the sly you wonder who thinks about you. You are triggered to think about this. It is funny; you always chat about topics with colleagues without regarding it *per se* as a work conversation.
>
> *(Teacher, Focus Group Interview)*

Set, Epistemic and Social Co-creation and Co-configuration Activities

The notion of social design for learning in our context is not passive but actively involves the users as constructive learning professionals. Our work is infused by the notion of co-creation and practice-based research. In our approach when developing NAT, we work closely in co-creation with professionals, school leaders and administrators, who are actively involved in understanding, developing and promoting informal networked social spaces. We believe that – especially at this pioneering stage of understanding social professional development networks – we need to embrace the complexity of everyday informal professional development and try to paint a more complete picture to stimulate theory–praxis conversations (De Laat and Lally 2003). In research practice this often involves a way of co-creation between a researcher and, in this case, professionals at a school (Martens *et al.* 2012). This means that our participants are active participants in these research and development projects. This is important because we often try to influence or create a practice for informal networked learning in our work, which needs to be owned by the participants if it is to have any chance of sustained impact after the lifetime of a project.

To help facilitate sustained impact, we set up a kind of research team within the school or organization we work with. This team acts as a sparring partner that helps to interpret our findings and develop plans for future steps. It consists of teachers, school leaders, administrators, etc. and should, in fact, reflect all relevant layers of the organization (Homan 2006). This group of professionals forms the heart of the project, where the research findings are reflected upon in relation to the learning culture of the organization. With the help of this research team, (small-scale) studies are developed that will be carried out by our researchers within the organization. The cycle of practice-driven research is determined by this research team, with the studies taking place in the actual real-world environment. The importance of this approach is to acknowledge the unique social setting, dynamics and desires of each group as it is situated in practice.

Growth, Development and Evolution

Based on the results of co-creation in building NAT, we plan to add some future functionality and plan to adapt the NAT visualizations. During the focus group interviews at the ABC Gymnasium, for example, we asked the teachers what they think about the design of NAT. The tag cloud was really appreciated by all, but with respect to the visualization of the total network structure we received the following responses, which need to be addressed:

> The network representation is chaotic ... We cannot say much about the position of an individual within this representation.
>
> *(Teacher, Focus Group Interview)*

> With the representation of the tag cloud I feel an emotion. I can identify myself with this, but with this (network representation of overall network) I cannot. Here you have more chaos. There are a lot of ties. You also look more at the individuals. Why is this person here?
>
> *(Teacher, Focus Group Interview)*

> I believe I have already been looking for myself for the last 10 minutes.
>
> *(Teacher, Focus Group Interview)*

When users navigate from the import page to the visualization page, currently the first thing they see is a representation of the overall network. This can be perceived as overwhelming and the network can be seen as chaotic. Users are also intuitively looking for their own name within the network that is presented. To resolve this issue we plan to first show the ego-network perspective as represented in Figure 15.2 (Ego-network representation). Users first see what they already 'know', namely their own social learning network, and can then navigate further and see representations of other (theme) networks or the overall network. So users can start from a simpler representation of their own active ego-network and gradually move on to more complicated representations of the overall network. This will simplify the users' search for themselves and allow them to become familiar with the design of these elements and the information they express, such that they can, subsequently, interpret the more complex representation of the overall network.

To see the effect of the use of NAT, we also plan to develop NAT further, making it possible to look back in time, in order to study network dynamics and evolution, similar to work by Lomi *et al.* (2011). By adding a timestamp functionality, we will be able to see the growth of the overall network and changes in the networked learning behavior of individual users. Does the use of NAT increase the likelihood of professionals finding more peers to learn from? And do they become aware of tacit learning ties by seeing who is learning from them, or what other topics are relevant for their own learning space? And by doing so, we can easily visualize if users do become architects of their own learning network by developing new or more efficient learning networks around work-related topics, after being made aware of their network (neighborhood). Thus, we aim to increase one's *network cognition*. We view network cognition as a way of social creativity (Bhattacharyya and Olsson 2010): the ability to distinguish between suitable and unsuitable peers in terms of searching for *just-in-time* knowledge, advice or expertise.

Informal learning in networks is important in helping professionals to create new knowledge and to work on innovative ideas for solutions to problems that are on the edge of their domain. To optimize the results of their informal learning network, it is important for professionals to understand how informal learning is taking place by making informal learning activities within an organization visible. We aim to make NAT available as standalone reflection tools, or as exercises that professionals and groups can use regardless of our involvement. Further, NAT can be used as a plugin for existing online learning environments or content management systems within organizations.

Abstracting and Synthesis

In this chapter, we laid out the architecture of the Network Awareness Tool (NAT) that is currently under development by the LOOK Scientific Centre for Teacher Research. Also, we pinpointed the affordances of using such a network awareness tool on three distinct levels of the network measurement:

- First, the *network* level, at which the intensity and effectiveness of communication flows in an organization may be measured.
- Second, the *group* level, at which conversation themes can be distinguished. Users are made aware of the themes that drive the organization and which peers are working on which themes. Also, they are 'forced' to make their

learning ties explicit, as they can be mentioned by their peers (Figure 15.3, left column).

• Third, the *individual* level, at which users are made aware of their peers, and get to self-reflect on their learning behavior. By their learning behavior, we mean the ability to connect to the right peers in terms of efficiency (e.g. short paths) and effectiveness (e.g. the learning 'quality' of the relationship).

User feedback points out that users value the idea of viewing what their personal learning behavior is, and how they could possibly improve it, though the network visualization, especially on the organizational network level, seems to be rather overloaded with information. To solve this, we plan to change the order in which users see their network: we first show them their ego-network, which they are familiar with, and then show the more complex networks per theme, and per organization. In this way, the user gradually experiences more complex representations of the networks, which hopefully allows her to adapt more fluently.

Note

1 The original name has been anonymized.

References

Bhattacharyya, S. and Ohlsson, S., 2010. Social creativity as a function of agent cognition and network properties: a computer model. *Social Networks*, *32*(4), 263–278.

Billett, S., 2001. Learning through work: workplace affordances and individual engagement. *Journal of Workplace Learning*, 13(5), 209–214.

Borgatti, S. P. and Cross, R., 2003. A relational view of information seeking and learning in social networks. *Management Science*, *49*(4), 432–445.

Boud, D. and Hager, P., 2012. Re-thinking continuing professional development through changing metaphors and location in professional practices. *Studies in Continuing Education*, 34(1), 17–30.

Burt, R. S., 2004. Structural holes and good ideas. *American Journal of Sociology*, 110(2), 349–399.

Davenport, T. H. and Pruzak, L., 2000. *Working knowledge: how organizations manage what they know.* 2nd ed. Watertown: Harvard Business Publishing.

De Laat, M., 2012. *Enabling professional development networks: how connected are you?* Heerlen: Open Universiteit Nederland.

De Laat, M. and Coenders, M., 2011. Communities of practice en netwerkleren. In: J. Kessels and R. Poell, eds. *Handboek human resource development: organiseren van het leren.* Houten, Netherlands: Bohn Stafleu van Loghum, 417–428.

De Laat, M. and Lally, V., 2003. Complexity, theory and praxis: researching collaborative learning and tutoring processes in a networked learning community. *Instructional Science*, 31(1–2), 7–39.

De Laat, M. and Schreurs, B., 2011. *Network awareness tool: social software for visualizing, analysing and managing social networks.* Heerlen: Ruud de Moor Centrum, Open Universiteit Nederland.

Eraut, M., 2000. Non-formal learning and tacit knowledge in professional work. *British Journal of Educational Psychology*, 70(1), 113–136.

Goodyear, P. M., Banks, S., Hodgson, V. and McConnell, D., eds., 2004. *Advances in research on networked learning.* Dordrecht: Kluwer Academic Publishers.

Hargreaves, A. and Fullan, M., 2012. *Professional capital: transforming teaching in every school.* New York: Teachers College Press.

Haythornthwaite, C., 2002. Strong, weak, and latent ties and the impact of new media. *The Information Society*, 18(5), 385–401.

Haythornthwaite, C. and De Laat, M., 2012. Social network informed design for learning with educational technology. In: A. D. Olofsson and J. O. Lindberg, eds. *Informed design of educational technologies in higher education: enhanced learning and teaching.* Hershey, PA: IGI Global, 352–374.

Homan, T. H., 2006. *Wolkenridders: over de binnenkant van organisatieverandering.* Heerlen: Open Universiteit Nederland.

Lane, P. J. and Lubatkin, M., 1998. Relative absorptive capacity and interorganizational learning. *Strategic Management Journal*, 19(5), 461–477.

Lomi, A., Snijders, T. A. B., Steglich, C. E. G. and Torló, V. J., 2011. Why are some more peer than others? Evidence from a longitudinal study of social networks and individual academic performance. *Social Science Research*, 40(6), 1506–1520.

Marsick, V. J., 2001. Informal strategic learning in the workplace. In: *Proceedings of the 2nd conference on HRD research and practice across Europe*, 26–27 January 2001. Enschede: University of Twente.

Martens, R., Kessels, J., Laat, M. De and Ros, A., 2012. *Praktijkgericht wetenschappelijk onderzoek: onderzoeksmanifest LOOK.* Heerlen: LOOK, Open Universiteit Nederland.

Polanyi, M., 1967. *The tacit dimension.* Chicago: The University of Chicago Press.

Schmidt, F. L. and Hunter, J. E., 1993. Tacit knowledge, practical intelligence, general mental ability, and job knowledge. *Current Directions in Psychological Science*, 2, 8–9.

Schreurs, B. and de Laat, M., 2012a. Network awareness tool – learning analytics in the workplace: detecting and analyzing informal workplace learning. In: S. Buckingham Shum, D. Gasevic and R. Ferguson, eds. *Proceedings of the 2nd international conference on learning analytics and knowledge,* 29 April–2 May 2012, Vancouver. New York: ACM, 59–64.

Schreurs, B. and de Laat, M., 2012b. Work-based networked learning: a bottom-up approach to stimulate the professional development of teachers. In: V. Hodgson *et al.*, eds. *Proceedings of the eighth international conference on networked learning*, 2–4 April 2012, Maastricht. Maastricht School of Management, 284–293.

Scott, J., 2000. *Social network analysis: a handbook.* 2nd ed. London: Sage.

Sie, R. L. L., Ullmann, T. D., Rajagopal, K., Cela, K., Marlies Bitter-Rijpkema and Sloep, P. B., 2012. Social network analysis for technology-enhanced learning: review and future directions. *International Journal of Technology Enhanced Learning*, 4(3), 172–190.

Sie, R. L. L., Berlanga, A. J., Sloep, P. B., Rajagopal, K., Drachsler, H. and Fazeli, S. 2012. Social tools for networked learning: current and future research directions. In: V. Hodgson *et al.*, eds. *Proceedings of the eighth international conference on networked learning*, 2–4 April 2012, Maastricht. Maastricht School of Management, 312–319.

Sloep, P. B., Berlanga, A. J., Greller, W., Stoyanov, S., Van der Klink, M., Retalis, S. and Hensgens, J. (2012). Educational innovation with learning networks: tools and developments. *Journal of Universal Computer Science*, 18(1), 44–61.

Steeples, C. and Jones, C., eds., 2002. *Networked learning: perspectives and issues*. London: Springer.

Wenger, E., 1998. *Communities of practice: learning, meaning, and identity*. Cambridge: Cambridge University Press.

Wenger, E., Trayner, B. and De Laat, M., 2011. *Promoting and assessing value creation in communities and networks: a conceptual framework*. Rapport 18. Heerlen: Ruud de Moor Centrum, Open Universiteit Nederland.

PART III
Synthesis

16

SYNTHESIS

Set Design, Epistemic Design and the Functioning of Learning Networks

Lucila Carvalho and Peter Goodyear

Introduction

This book documents an experiment in applying design-based constructs to the analysis of a wide variety of examples of learning networks. To shape this process, we provided the other authors with some guidelines – a first version of the analytic framework – as well as early versions of the Peep and Virtual Choir chapters. When we received their first drafts and their feedback on the issues that they confronted in their analyses, we revised and extended the framework to remove some ambiguities and we re-emphasized the point that it is when set, epistemic and social design elements come together to form distinctive structures that a clearer insight is gained into the relations between form and function. The analytic framework is certainly open to further refinement. In this chapter, we reflect on some lessons learned in the process of developing and testing it. To underline once more the importance of seeing connections between design elements, we take a slightly higher-level view of what the framework helps to expose. Because space is limited, we focus on just two groups of connections. One is between set design and activity. The other is between epistemic design, tasks and activity, though we also show how aspects of the epistemic permeate set and social design too. Relationships between set and activity bring us back to some of the discussion in Chapter 3 about *connecting ideas*, such as affordance and legibility. We expand on those in the next section of this chapter. In the section after that, we explain some concepts from Legitimation Code Theory, also first mentioned in Chapter 3. We show how these can provide additional tools for analyzing aspects of the epistemic design. The penultimate section presents a thematic treatment of some selected epistemic and set design issues, illustrated by drawing on case studies from Part II of the book. The chapter concludes with some thoughts about future research in this field.

Analyzing the Relations Between Set Design and Activity in Learning Networks

In Chapter 3 we mentioned the importance of being able to establish relationships between physical context and activity. The 'set' of a learning network is typically composed of interconnected entities, which, by and large, are object-like, place-like or text-like. These are not watertight categories, but one can say that most *texts* require certain kinds of interpretive work to be done by a person, if the text (and what it represents) is to have an effect on that person. Some very short texts, such as the word 'Exit' on a door, or 'Push' on a button, function rather like simple objects. The decoding work is relatively trivial. But understanding how more complex textual artifacts influence what people do, think, feel etc. is a more difficult matter and it is one to which we cannot do justice in this chapter. Readers interested in this area might look at some of the work on understanding multimedia communication and visual social semiotics (e.g. Kress and van Leeuwen 2001, 2006; Harrison 2003) including ideas about 'how people use signs to construct the life of a community' (Lemke 1990, p. 183). Finding meaning in complex ecologies of artifacts is also central to the 'semantic turn' in design (Krippendorff 2006).

Understanding how *object-like* and *place-like* entities affect activity is core to understanding set design. This is where connecting ideas such as *affordance, legibility* and *interpretation* are needed. The affordances of an object suggest to the perceiver what use it might be to them and how it might be used. Legibility is a quality of a place that allows people to 'read' and 'orientate' themselves in it. When someone 'reads' a place, this may include (quickly) perceiving some of its affordances, as well as more slowly interpreting its other qualities. Places that are experienced as requiring too much interpretive (decoding) work may be said to feel 'illegible' to those visiting them. Objects with confusing affordances can similarly impose unwelcome mental load and invoke frustration.

Cognition plays an important role in such 'readings', but it is not the only system in action. An affective system also influences the ways we judge the environment, for example by activating neurochemical signals in our brains (Norman 2004). These two systems are interconnected, and so certain affective states may be shaped by cognition and, likewise, cognition may also be shaped by affect. Affect influences our 'readings', our perceptions, the ways we decide about or react to something, regulating our thoughts, and adjusting our cognitive responses. Among the implications of this for learning are that affect and emotion may regulate whether one will be in a state that privileges focus and avoidance of distraction, or in a state of creativity, conducive to thinking outside-of-the-box, but more easily distracted.

In working out how material and digital objects and spaces can be said to have effects upon people's activities, educational technology has drawn some of its main ideas from work on Human–Computer Interaction (HCI) and interface design. Don Norman's writing has been particularly influential (e.g. Norman 1990, Norman and Draper 1986, Norman 2004). Looking across the analyses of learning networks in Part II, we cannot help but note two big issues that require further attention, and that have implications for both HCI and educational technology R&D. The first of these questions the purposes of design and the second questions the privileging of 'ease of use'. We address them in turn.

On the first of these, we note that educational technology and HCI share what might be called an *instrumentalist* ethic: good design is seen as that which helps people ('users') *achieve their goals* effectively, efficiently and enjoyably. This kind of design ethic seems so pervasive and self-evidently virtuous that it is almost unconscious, almost ideological. An important kind of imaginative act for designers in this paradigm is to think of the user, participant or learner looking at a screen (or tool or artifact) and asking themselves, 'How do I use what is here to achieve my goal?'. For Norman, and many others, a good design is one in which it is abundantly clear to the user what it is they need to do to complete their task.

The analyses in Part II leave us feeling uncomfortable about this instrumentalist, means–ends ethic. It is not that it is wrong. But it is incomplete. To make the point, we suggest imagining a person looking at a screen, or tool, or artifact and asking themselves, 'What can I do here?' Or imagine a person coming into a large building, and asking themselves, 'What is there here?', 'What might I find to interest or inspire me?' This more open, questioning, exploratory mode is also an important aspect of the relations between people and their environments, including the objects they use. It too can inform design. It warrants a place in analysis of existing designs, and in theory-building.

Designing 'sets' that are congenial for certain kinds of activity cannot, therefore, be reduced to means–ends analysis. It cannot always be the case that the users' pre-existing goals are the key to solving design problems. Sometimes, design will create sets that suggest new unpremeditated activities and that evoke unexpected feelings.

The second big issue refers to 'ease of use'. Reflecting on the chapters in Part II has led us to question a famous slogan, captured in the title of Steve Krug's web design handbook: 'Don't make me think!' (2006). In short, we suggest that designers need to take a more versatile approach to set design, such that design elements map appropriately on to 'fast' and 'slow' modes of thinking (Kahneman 2011 and see Chapter 3).

For both instrumental and evocative design, the ideas of legibility, affordance and interpretation remain useful. When someone looks at a screen on which is displayed a home page for a learning network, they should be able to get a reasonable answer to the conscious or unconscious question, 'How do I get this job done?' or 'What can I do here?' As mentioned above, three kinds of set design elements can help – texts, objects and places. That is to say, there can be (a) written instructions or (b) icons, buttons, tools etc. or (c) more complex, navigable, spatial layouts. While written instructions are often useful to some degree, there is a common feeling among designers that the necessity for reading instructions is a symptom of bad design. As Don Norman puts it, 'well-designed objects are easy to interpret and understand. They contain visual clues to their operation' (1990, p. 2). Norman's often-used example is that the shape and placement of a door handle should tell you whether to pull or push; it should *afford* pushing or pulling. Any door that needs written instructions is a design failure.

In set design for learning networks, non-textual design clues are often used to catch attention and guide activity. They can be simple (e.g. a button to click), or they can be quite complex assemblages of different kinds of entity (e.g. hierarchical menus with lots of options). Often, successful design will lead quickly and almost automatically to selection of an appropriate action. However, the quick response we associate with affordance (or high legibility) is not the only kind of *good* link between set design and activity. Sometimes it is right to cause the user to think, puzzle and wonder. Forcing some hard mental effort, problem-solving or serious reflection – engaging Kahneman's 'slow thinking' – is sometimes exactly the right thing to do. Since making sense of complex text imposes significant cognitive load – it demands 'slow thinking' – text is sometimes the best way of using set design to offer demanding tasks to people. But it is best scaffolded with other set design elements that are less cognitively demanding – such as subtle guides to navigation and attention, which rely on affordance. We might modify Steve Krug's slogan to say: 'Make me think! (But only about what I'll learn from.)'

So, up to a point, well-designed objects and places 'tell' people what to do, or what is expected from people when they interact with them. Objects should gently teach people how to use them (Miller 2010). Krippendorff (2006) refers to objects of design as having evolved to become more 'language-like'. People do not always focus on the physical qualities of things. Instead, they see what these objects, forms or shapes mean to them – and this 'conversation' is about the objects' affordances, what it is possible to do with them and how interacting or using these objects might affect them. On this view, the designer and other stakeholders involved in the design of a product can be seen as the 'source of a message' and the designed object or the product itself is 'the transmitter' (Crilly *et al.* 2004).

In design for learning, we argue, similar principles also apply. It is possible to investigate the 'legibility' of groups of elements that come together to compose the design of these networks, and within this context, we search for the 'messages' in the elements that appear to be key in expressing something to learners.

As our interest is in learning networks, the messages we pay special attention to are those related to knowledge and knowing. These may include, for example, figuring out how designers may combine certain set elements with the intention of enacting a particular pacing or sequencing of the way knowledge is expressed.

Each choice made, for each particular element – its position, size, appearance, connection with other elements, etc. – embodies the visions of the designers for what the problem at hand is, what they predict the learners will do, whether at this point a learner is supposed to, for example, pause and reflect or intensely interact with others and so on. But we are also interested in the activities that these design elements provoke, how they influence the behavior of learners and how learners reconfigure and reshape these elements as they interact within the network.

To make some of these insights more concrete, we have provided some thematic analyses of set design elements later in the chapter. Under the heading of 'Theme 5', we examine the affordances and legibility of set designs by identifying the intended effects of certain visual clues on participants' activity. Although some of these visual elements are almost imperceptible to people, they nevertheless stimulate particular types of response: they 'tell' people something they need to know about the space concerned. The other thematic treatment of set design (see 'Theme 4', below) is concerned with the entanglement of digital and material spaces in a number of the learning networks. It discusses the ways in which boundaries between the digital and material worlds need a degree of permeability. Before we can move to these thematic treatments, we need to introduce some further ideas relevant to *epistemic* design.

Analyzing Epistemic Design in Learning Networks: Insights from the Sociology of Knowledge

In Chapter 3, we said that an important aspect of our architectural analysis of these networks lies in exploring social connections: exploring issues related to social values, to what brings people together in terms of knowledge and knowing, the knowledge practices they engage in and the implications of these for design. In Chapter 3 we also talked about knowledge-building as an emblematic activity in networked learning. Indeed, one interpretation of networked learning is that it is when participants collaborate in knowledge creation. Scardamalia and Bereiter (2003) define knowledge-building as 'the production and continual improvement of ideas of value to a community, through means that increase the likelihood that what the community accomplishes will be greater than the sum of individual contributions and part of broader cultural efforts' (p. 1370). Bereiter and Scardamalia's extensive writings about knowledge-building help identify its key characteristics and also highlight the importance of situating knowledge-building in its broader social and economic context (see especially Bereiter 2002). In this section, we discuss ways of exploring connections between knowledge and social practices, looking at how sociological principles may both influence, and be enacted through, the design of certain elements within a networked environment. We do this, in part, by exploring some further examples from the case studies in Part II. In Chapter 3 we mentioned the analytic utility of ideas from Legitimation Code Theory (LCT; Maton 2014, Maton *et al.* 2014). We offer a brief introduction to some selected aspects of LCT here.

Legitimation Code Theory (LCT) is an approach in the sociology of knowledge that builds on and extends Basil Bernstein's code theory and Pierre Bourdieu's field theory (Maton 2014, Maton *et al.* 2014). The approach provides useful tools to analyze knowledge practices in a given knowledge community, and it may support those interested in examining the relationships between design elements and the structuring of tasks proposed. In order to engage in such analysis, we are assuming that learning networks can be seen as providing educational contexts where certain pedagogical interactions take place, and where people are exchanging views and experiences related to knowledge and knowing. Another assumption is that the nature of knowledge may be different in these learning networks. In fact each network is likely to be differently shaped by underlying principles structuring the knowledge practices of the participants: what counts as relevant knowledge and practices may differ from one network to another. Each network is likely to reflect these differences in their epistemic and social design assemblages, in the activities of participants more broadly and in the particular ways network participants co-configure the space.

The LCT lens allows us to explore what the measure of achievement is to be in a given network. It helps unveil what the 'rules of the game' are in a learning network – the implicit norms and agreements for that particular social group. We see two LCT dimensions as especially important to our research: Specialization and Semantics. Specialization is concerned with 'what makes actors, discourses and practices special or legitimate' in a given context (Maton 2007, p. 98). This dimension is based on the premise that every knowledge claim involves two distinct parts: it is about 'something' (what is claimed) and it is made by 'someone' (who articulates a claim). Specialization therefore offers analytical tools for exploring different measures of legitimacy, considering that practices may emphasize epistemic relations to the object (ER) (what and how people know) and/or the social relations to the author (SR) (who is considered a legitimate knower). When applying these analytical tools, specific specialization codes are attributed, depending on whether the emphasis on these relations is stronger or weaker (ER+/− and/or SR+/−). As a result, there are four possible combinations of codes: knowledge codes (ER+, SR−); knower codes (ER−, SR+); elite codes (ER+, SR+); and relativist codes (ER−, SR−). Importantly, specialization codes reflect both the epistemic and social relations, considering that these two relations are always present, there is always 'something' (object) and 'someone' (subject) in every knowledge claim, even though these two may be differently emphasized. This dimension helps us in seeing whether legitimate practices tend to stress knowers and/or knowledge structures, as we search for the underlying principles structuring knowledge within the network context, and the types of design elements that reflect such structuring. In the next two sub-sections below, we suggest how Specialization may be applied in the analysis of some design elements in these networks. See 'Theme 1' for a discussion about ways that design elements may reflect the nature of knowledge and 'Theme 2' for an exploration of matters related to legitimacy of knowers, such as learning from a valuable adviser.

Whereas Specialization is concerned with the bases for claims to legitimacy of knowledge practices, Semantics helps us unveil issues related to the processes of knowledge-building. It focuses on examining the structuring of knowledge through its relation to context dependency and condensation of meaning (Maton 2011). It allows us, for example, to investigate connections between the design of learning tasks (e.g. sequencing, pacing, selection of knowledge that is expressed) and the activities of networked participants. Semantics proposes two analytical codes of 'semantic gravity' and 'semantic density'. 'Semantic gravity' conceives knowledge in relation to degrees of context dependency. The stronger the semantic gravity (SG+), the more that meaning is dependent on its context in order to make sense to people; the weaker the semantic gravity, the less dependent meaning is on its context in order to make sense (Maton 2009, 2013). As we saw in the case studies in Part II, in some networks knowledge is more likely to be very context dependent; that is, knowledge practices are more likely to make sense to people within a specific social group. For example, cumulative knowledge-building in The Synaptic Leap (Chapter 12) involves abstract scientific concepts being applied in a specific context, which only make sense for those who are working in a specific area of biomedical sciences and chemistry.

'Semantic density' is about the degree of 'condensation of meaning', and this may refer, for example, to symbols, terms, concepts, phrases, etc. (Maton 2013). The stronger the semantic density (SD+), the more meaning is condensed; the weaker the semantic density (SD−), the less meaning is condensed. As discussed earlier in this chapter, this connects to ideas of affordance, legibility and interpretation, and underlies the analysis of how epistemic design elements reflect meaning. An example of an epistemic element in our networks that shows a higher level of condensation of meaning would be the icons in iSpot (Chapter 14). We discuss these more explicitly under the 'Theme 5' heading below.

Semantic gravity and semantic density have been used in the analysis of classroom activities, for example in biology and history classes at a secondary school (Maton 2013), allowing researchers to trace trajectories of knowledge practices related to context dependency and condensation of meaning over time, within a classroom context. Maton (2013) shows different semantic profiles (through 'semantic waves'), identifying some of these as associated with enabling knowledge-building. For example, semantic profiles identified as enabling cumulative learning were more likely to show a specific pattern that grows bigger over time, from concrete to greater levels of generalization and abstraction.

In applying these concepts to our analysis of the epistemic design of the networks, we search for elements that suggest a weakening or strengthening of semantic density through, for example, the analysis of the sequencing of tasks proposed. We search for designs that appear to encourage 'semantic profiles' that would favor knowledge-building processes in our networks; that is, 'design profiles' that suggest a sequence of tasks where students are exposed to increasingly progressive levels of generalization and abstraction. For example, in Peep (Chapter 4), we use these concepts to support the analysis of the tutorials and assignments, looking at the sequencing, pacing, selection of knowledge and how their structuring changes over time, as Peep students go through their lessons. Such analysis reveals a 'design profile', which is composed of learning tasks that reflect a progressive strengthening of semantic meaning. For instance, early tutorials introduce students to basic elements of programing, using everyday examples – such as comparing the use of a programing language to the English language. These early tutorials are followed by other, more complex tutorials, such as using programing to draw with code, increasingly adding to the complexity in meaning. Moreover, the 'code editor' – a key design element in Peep – allows students to navigate between the effects of using highly condensed terms (the programing language they are learning to design with) and the effects of their designs (the image produced).

Video resources made available to network participants, such as those in the Virtual Choir case study, can also be analyzed for movement between weakening and strengthening of semantic meaning. We are able to differentiate between knowledge that is relatively decontextualized to more context dependent and simplified meanings, for example when analyzing passages where Whitacre unpacks specialized technical terms and their use in choral singing, in a way that is accessible to novice choristers.

In terms of our architectural framework, Semantics offers support for the analysis of how certain design elements may encourage knowledge-building practices in a learning network. Specifically, our interest is on investigating how epistemic elements may sustain, influence and encourage certain practices in a given network. Such key design elements are likely to be perceived as expressing specific meanings and so are not just elements on the stage, but instead they reflect a particular structuring of knowledge that, in turn, may influence the activities of learners. LCT helps us unveil how design features of an environment may address issues related to legitimate knowers and knowledge. We illustrate ways of applying these concepts in the next three sections ('Theme 1', 'Theme 2' and 'Theme 3') with examples from case studies in Part II.

Theme 1: Design that Reflects the Nature of Knowledge Practices in a Field

The analysis of Peep (Chapter 4) suggests that one of the functions of the network is to introduce students to what is considered interesting and special within this specific area of design. Elements in the design of Peep are carefully brought together to reflect some of the practices of the field, at the same time also supporting students in forming a sense of a community. For example, the design of learning tasks encourages students to explore the work of specific professionals (experts in the field) as part of their assignments, a process that could be seen as introducing students to ways of recognizing legitimate knowers in the field. Not surprisingly, we can also identify design elements that show an emphasis on knowledge as an object, on developing certain skills and procedures, therefore exposing students to ways that design is practiced within the field. For example, the environment includes a space for students to externalize, represent and write about the thread of the development of their conceptual ideas. They are also encouraged to offer their views about each other's designs by saying what they like or dislike in the work of their peers. In this sense, students are acculturated into ways of practicing design that reflect some of the practices in the 'real world'. At the same time, they are learning about what is possible in terms of design knowledge and how others may interpret the same design briefs.

Similar analysis can also be applied to some elements discussed in the case study of iSpot (Chapter 14), which appear to have been designed to reflect some of the scientific practices of field biologists. iSpot incorporates epistemic elements that mirror artifacts used by practicing scientists, such as recording sheets. They also include scaffolds that gradually introduce the keys system for identifying new specimens. In short, iSpot offers opportunities to learn about fauna and flora in ways that are grounded in some of the scientific practices of biology. In terms of our analysis using Specialization, this would be an example of a design element that enacts an emphasis on the epistemic relations – the procedures and skills people in that field need to learn.

Theme 2: Design that Involves Learning from a Valued Adviser

Issues concerned with 'legitimate knowers' are apparent in a number of the case studies in Part II. In terms of enactment through design, an interesting feature of the Flagship Program is the fact that it allows for customization by a facilitator; that is, by an adviser who will provide guidance to subsets of participants in the program. Here, participants have the ability to choose their (digital representation of an) advisor according to their beliefs about who would be the best facilitator. So the environment promotes a type of 'master and apprentice' (virtual) relationship while taking into account the social values of learners. It offers design elements that enable learners to be guided by someone whom they perceive as a legitimate knower. (They are given the option of an elder, an expert professional or a peer.) In terms of our analysis using Specialization, this is an example of a design element that enacts an emphasis on social relations.

The analyses of several other case studies such as iSpot (Chapter 14), Qstream (Chapter 10) and ISQua Knowledge (Chapter 11) reveal other ways in which issues related to being a 'knower' are reflected within the particular social networked context. iSpot (Chapter 14) presents an interesting discussion of the 'social rules' underlying claims for legitimacy within the site. The authors of Chapter 14 point out that, while the use of a 'badge' next to a member's ID denotes that member's affiliation to a scheme, society or organization, the use of icons represents their level of expertise, gained through interactions within the website, as a result of a *merit system*. These visual representations link the 'knower' to the 'type' of knowledge they hold. The merit system seems to regulate some of the relationships between participants and, as a result, within the social context of the environment, experts' roles involve both (a) responsibilities related to learning tasks (the identifications of observations), and also (b) recognizing other members' efforts (through the attribution of merit points when the expert agrees that an observation made by a novice member is correct). Such an agreement by a 'knowledgeable' member of iSpot increases the status of the novice. What this reveals is that the reputation of a member is of critical importance: activities of the network are structured around hierarchical positions participants take within the network, related to knowing/knowledge, the visibility of one's status as a knower and who makes a 'legitimate' knower within the network.

In the design of Qstream, the idea of seeing how one sits amongst the social group of learners is also enacted through visualizations, where a particular design feature in the network enables participants to see their individual performance in relation to the performance of others (see Chapter 10). These features enable learners to monitor how their own answers compare with the cohort on the particular course they are taking. Interactions with the broader community of learners are also enacted through elements that allow participants to choose whether they would like to incorporate their own views on a specific theme, leaving a trace for other future course participants, and engaging in discussions with other network members. Such features illustrate ways in which design elements may facilitate social connections between network members.

The ability to reach those professionals perceived as 'valuable knowers' in the field is one important function in the design of ISQua Knowledge (Chapter 11). The network incorporates several features to enable 'experts' and 'novices' distributed across the world to come close together to discuss issues related to quality and safety in health care. Some of these features include, for example, *Expert-led discussions*, *ISQua talks*, *Debates* and so on.

Theme 3: When Design Enables and Addresses Social Change

Several of the networks examined in Part II have design thinking at their core – in the sense that the core network activities involve design processes. Peep is an obvious example, but researchers involved in The Synaptic Leap (Chapter 12) also work to a design-based model to frame the research problems they investigate within the network. Their activities revolve around a cycle of process improvement, initiated with the public posting of a research problem and sharing data within the community. Network participants are then asked to investigate, identify and reveal flaws in the current approach. They make suggestions for how the approach may be improved and those in charge of the project act on these suggestions. New problems are then identified and the cycle begins again. This type of open science process involves the network participants themselves in design. Their 'design problem', nevertheless, relates to biomedical matters: for example, finding the compounds to successfully combat a certain disease. Researchers engaged in these practices are enacting a different way of practicing academic research, challenging traditional models where scholars only make research data available for the community once conclusions have been published, and where a specific scholar, or small group of scholars, is recognized as the author(s) associated with that particular knowledge (Farrell and Hooker 2013). Knowledge practices such as these seem to be underwritten by implicit agreements between participants that within this particular network 'what' is known is much more important than 'who' knows. That is, in terms of Legitimation Code Theory, legitimate practices within this network place an emphasis on knowledge as an object, rather than on authors as the knowers.

The Biebkracht network (Chapter 9) consciously uses a participatory design process for the ongoing development of the network, through a customized version of an agile software development method. Their methodology involves a rapid prototyping approach, using a framework where initial ideas are made available via small design results, and these are then open for testing and evaluation, and potential improvements. These results then inform the next steps in an iterative design process. The Biebkracht project takes an organic conceptual approach, where some of the essential qualities include openness, flexibility, finding effective ways of capturing participants' expertise and experiences, and enabling these to rapidly inform the next phase of design work. The intention of following this design process was to create a learning network firmly grounded in participants' views, so that it 'would fit like a custom made suit' (Chapter 9). Importantly, this participatory approach acknowledges broader cultural changes that are strongly associated with technological innovations, and which are challenging the traditional functions of librarians and libraries in the community. As books are made easily accessible through online means, and as information is made readily available through the Internet, librarians' usual practices and their status as knowers are both being challenged by the changes in the broader knowledge practices of the community. They require that librarians rethink and reshape well-established practices. The Biebkracht project brings these professionals together to discuss these issues, which may help them to reposition themselves in the field. In other words, a core purpose of this network is to find ways of addressing major transformations in the library sector.

Similarly, Diseña el Cambio (Chapter 8) also revolves around the idea of exposing network participants – teachers, students and their families – to a simplified version of a design process. Participants experience design thinking and ways of designing solutions to local problems, a process that empowers children with the tools and procedures to identify and address important issues in their own communities. The network offers much more than participation in a competition or a 'challenge'. Its broader underlying function is to teach 'everyday people' a systematic way of addressing problems in the community. As a result, those who participate in the network may shift from a passive to an active social role as they engage in bringing about social changes, and in sharing 'design for change' methods more broadly. In so doing, the model adopted in Diseña el Cambio is shaped as a process that systematically emphasizes skills and procedures, tools and knowledge that are relevant to problems of interest to the children. In other words, organizing principles underlying knowledge practices within the network place an emphasis on the epistemic relations: on knowledge as an object. By learning about and applying such skills and procedures, anyone can gain the capacity to achieve great things within their community.

We now shift back to looking at some design issues emerging from the Part II cases that illuminate some of the connections between set design and activity.

Theme 4: Design Traversing and Connecting Digital and Material Spaces

Many of the case studies described in Part II involve networks where participants interact wholly or largely through the Internet. In some cases, such as Peep, the Aalborg class and Diseña el Cambio, a good deal of participant interaction also takes place face-to-face. Moreover, much of the activity that matters most to people is firmly situated in the material world. There is life beyond what is readily visible in the shared digital platforms used by these networks. We do not want to get caught up in a philosophical discussion here about where a network begins and ends, or about whether the digital and material can really be separated. The point we want to pursue in this section is that design for learning networks will normally be improved if attention is paid to the little things that allow participants' activity to shift smoothly between the digital and the material. We will use three case studies to develop the argument: the Virtual Choir (Chapter 13), the Flagship Program (Chapter 6) and NAT (Chapter 15).

Two aspects of the Virtual Choir bring the relationship between the digital and material worlds into particularly sharp focus: (i) performance events in the material world; (ii) individual creation of sung pieces. When a Virtual Choir production is complete, it becomes available on the website and can be played by anyone with a good Internet connection and the means of hearing the performance. In turn, this requires either headphones or a quiet room. When the Virtual Choir performs (on demand), implicit requirements are placed on the performance space. But the Virtual Choir does not only perform in private spaces. Some performances take the form of live events and ongoing installations. For example, there has been a Virtual Choir performance at Lincoln Center in New York, and the Virtual Choir was also part of an installation during the 2012

London Olympics. Many design elements have to be configured to realize an event: the choir 'singing together apart'. This does not happen at a single point in time or space. Rather, the event is materialized through the production and running of a multimedia artifact. This artifact is slowly brought into being through the activities of thousands of individual singers, carrying out their tasks at different times in a variety of locations.

In this sense, elements of the set design shape individual and social processes, ultimately enabling the realization of the Virtual Choir production. These elements are intimately woven together, to express and realize a sense of togetherness at many different layers of the production. At the same time, however, the provision of tools alone would not guarantee the realization of any of the Virtual Choir projects, or what is achieved through them. Broader social processes also play a crucial role: they shape the technology, stimulating the evolution and guiding the selection of tools and methods for using them. In this sense, activities outside and inside the network reorganize the material elements and how these come together to form the set for the Virtual Choir. As discussed in Chapter 13, the effects in people's lives are powerful; expressed in the feelings of togetherness–alone, in the sense of realizing something impossible, in bringing together all sorts of people, with all sorts of experiences, from all sorts of backgrounds and ages, to make beautiful music.

We also see entanglements between the digital and the material in the Flagship Program (Chapter 6). For example, the *proximal* function of this network is to provide professional development for teachers leading curriculum innovation, equipping them with tools and skills that are useful for agents of local change. The much more socially valued *distal* function of the network is to embed the national curriculum and improve children's learning. That is, beneficial effects must be felt by people who are not direct participants in the network.

As shown in Chapter 6, the online program was originally created to provide guidance to participants about ways of setting up local project teams, mainly consisting of other teachers in their school. Network participants were given opportunities to interact with other would-be school and curriculum leaders across Australia to discuss curriculum initiatives. A pre-condition for joining the network was that one had explicitly been given a leadership role within a school in Australia. Otherwise one would not be able to join, contribute, share or interact with the program content and other participants. As a result, material elements that enable participants' activities as school leaders therefore also constitute an essential requirement for joining and participating. Once participants bring their experiences to share with others in the digital realm, these experiences are also likely to be influenced by discussions with other network participants. In this sense, the local community is also likely to be reshaped and reconfigured and, eventually, the whole process is expected to result in substantial positive changes in the material, social and epistemic framings for activities in the local schools.

Another way of looking at this would be to say that the original network expands. The program acts as a catalyst, extending the network by *indirectly* reaching a broader number of teaching professionals and having beneficial effects on their practices. This web of connections also links the physical to the digital and the digital back into the physical. As participants bring (reifications of) the experiences that they have within their local schools into the digital realm, to share with other network participants, these experiences become resources that underlie discussions. And as participants learn new skills and knowledge in curriculum innovation within the digital realm, they then bring these experiences, as resources, back to the physical and into the future (compare with the SHARP learning cycle in Chapter 2). So the network is continuously evolving and expanding beyond the digital into the physical, here represented by the involvement of others in the local schools.

For this to work effectively, the boundaries between the digital and physical realms need to be permeable to certain kinds of object – so that experiences in the physical world can be shared efficiently in the digital, and so that digital resources can be deployed in the physical.

For example, some elements of the set design (e.g. PDFs) were crafted to make it easier for participants to use them to shift ideas between the digital and physical worlds. Connections were made between the digital learning resources and the online project workspace, for instance through the presence of web links that take participants to key resources in each section. This helps participants produce printable versions of key resources, so that they can work in the online workspace, while referring to a material version of some of these resources that they hold in their hands. It also makes it easier to take material resources into their schools. In a similar way, the design of the Virtual Choir site also makes it easy to print the sheet music needed for singing. (In passing, we might observe that the field of learning technology R&D seems ideologically hostile to paper. Recent work by Pierre Dillenbourg and colleagues is successfully reclaiming the special virtues of paper as an interface – see e.g. Bonnard *et al.* 2012.)

Finally, the case study of the Network Awareness Tool in Chapter 15 involves a different kind of tangling between the digital and physical. NAT can be used to enhance the visibility of existing relationships in a physically situated learning network by constructing digital visualizations of them. The digital foregrounds significant interactions happening within the physical. The digital tool is, therefore, woven into the material world, enabling people within the school to discover and build on existing relationships. Conversely, relations in the physical world become embedded in the digital, as mapped by NAT.

Theme 5: Visual Clues and their Influence on Learner Activities

We illustrate how designers may add visual elements that afford particular messages through two examples from Part II, exploring the ways visual clues in these environments may affect learners' behaviors. Our first example is found in the iSpot case study (Chapter 14). One of the interesting discussions in the iSpot chapter revolves around a small design feature, represented through the icons that appear besides the users' IDs. Occupying a fairly small surface area of the screen page, in terms of Semantics these images can nevertheless be seen as condensing a number of meanings. Their 'message' relays the status of knowers, telling those in the environment about the 'topic under discussion' and the 'level of expertise' of its users. This particular element has the potential to fulfill different functions: relaying a message about who makes for a legitimate knower, at the same time acting as an agent to stimulate participation, and as a representation for a publicly awarded recognition of the valid contributions made by network participants. These small images are there for a big reason. They have a message to convey and they affect learners' behaviors. A posted entry from someone who has three butterfly icons next to their ID may inspire more trust than a post from someone with only one butterfly icon. They also stimulate participation – a member with only one icon beside their ID may be inclined to increase his/her participation in order to get more.

Our second example is found in the Flagship network (Chapter 6), where an unexpected effect on learners' behaviors is identified, and explained by the authors of the chapter as related to the design of the 'dashboard'. The dashboard includes a tab under which a list of modules is displayed. The designers' intentions were that users would be able to quickly access any of the listed modules and follow their progress status in each module. However, after analyzing the patterns of usage for the environment, the authors conclude that participants were more likely to go through the modules in the order they were displayed on the screen (in 9 out of 10 cases). This is in contrast to choosing a module of interest from the catalogue list and using these resources in a customized way according to their learning interests. The 'message' that those elements evoked was that they were to be used in a fixed sequence, even though designers had imagined they could be used in any order – people could choose. In sum, the 'message' was not fully conveyed: there were problems related to the legibility of those elements. They did not actually afford choice to 9 out of 10 users.

It is important to note that when we talk about 'legibility', we are not necessarily referring to only one isolated element. Sometimes this may relate to a combination of elements on the screen, or to the ways these elements are brought together to compose the set – some of which lies deep beneath the screen. In this sense, even the lack of a rich array of elements in the setting may still signal a message: a clean layout may be used to fulfill the design intention of focusing attention on a specific feature. In the Peep case study (Chapter 4) we saw an example of how an uncluttered visual interface is intentionally used as a design solution to focus learners' attention on specific programing issues.

Theme 6: When Design Makes the Invisible Visible

This idea that through design we are able to highlight something that may otherwise be difficult to see is found in a number of the case studies in Part II. As mentioned earlier in this chapter, the Network Awareness Tool (NAT) (Chapter 15) reveals significant relationships within a learning network that exists in the physical world. The purpose of the tool is to help people recognize relevant and useful connections, in terms of both social and epistemic dimensions, within their existing network. In epistemic terms, and at a micro level, NAT's visualizations would help users in identifying where to find the type of knowledge needed to address a specific issue they may be facing at work. These representations, when considered at a macro level, also reveal a certain epistemic architecture in the school's network. Or, from a social perspective, NAT provides users with visualizations to help them figure out who would be the person to contact when facing a specific problem. Who in that space would hold knowledge related to the problem? Who would be a 'legitimate knower'? In so doing, NAT reveals a certain social architecture in the learning network.

The use of the code editors in Peep (Chapter 4) seems to fulfill a similar function. However, instead of revealing connections between knowledge and people, the code editors act as a translator device between the meanings associated with the use of programing language. Here, what is revealed are the 'behaviors', in diverse representative modes, of a set of programing phrases and sentences, in terms of their design effects. Students are able to see what happens when they put code A and code B together. These code editors were a key feature throughout the environment, bringing the programing language to the front. They allow learners to navigate easily between visual and linguistic modes of representing programing, and enable them to engage in conversations about their learning of the programing language in a discussion forum.

Visual elements may also be used as a way to make social connections more evident, for example by revealing others in a network. Both Desiña el Cambio (Chapter 8) and Virtual Choir (Chapter 13) use Google Maps to plot each singer's location (Virtual Choir) and each project group's location (Desiña el Cambio). The resulting images show the number of participants worldwide, and in doing so, they offer a visual representation that shows that no one is alone; everyone is part of a larger community. Such a design element enacts part–whole relationships, helping participants visualize themselves in relation to their networked community.

There is much more that could be said about set design, epistemic design and the functioning of learning networks. In some ways, we are just scratching the surface. And there is also much more to be done in linking epistemic, set and social design into a coherent whole. So in the final section of this chapter, we share some ideas from our ongoing research program, and thereby offer an invitation for others to join the enterprise.

Future Research Directions

The work we have reported in this book is one part of a larger five-year program of research being conducted at the Centre for Research on Computer Supported Learning and Cognition (CoCo) at the University of Sydney. One of the other main strands of research involves empirical studies of designers who are engaged in design for learning, including design for learning networks. This empirical research is informing the development of better design tools and methods. Some of the design abstractions emerging from our analyses of existing learning networks will be used in providing conceptual building blocks for future design work – embedded in design tools and methods, for example.

The next phase of our analytic work on learning networks will switch focus from networks that are mostly online (where we have to trace activities out into physical spaces) to networks that form around physical spaces (where we will trace the digital extensions of the physical spaces). Candidate study sites include museums and galleries that are making innovative use of mobile devices (like the MONA example mentioned in Chapter 2) and new generation learning spaces in universities and colleges (see e.g. Boys 2011).

In addition to providing what we believe are richer insights into learning networks, and creating some better building blocks for future designs, we share the hope that this line of inquiry will also strengthen theoretical work in the field of learning network research, and in educational technology more generally. There are still some very hazy connections between ways of knowing, forms of knowledge, material and digital tools and spaces, social relations and the activities through which people actually come to understand and improve the world.

References

Bereiter, C., 2002. *Education and mind in the knowledge age.* Mahwah, NJ: Lawrence Erlbaum Associates.

Bonnard, Q., Verma, H., Kaplan, F. and Dillenbourg, P., 2012. Paper interfaces for learning geometry. *21st century learning for 21st century skills.* London: Springer.

Boys, J., 2011. *Towards creative learning spaces: re-thinking the architecture of post-compulsory education.* New York: Routledge.

Crilly, N., Moultrie, J. and Clarkson, J., 2004. Seeing things: consumer response to the visual domain in product design. *Design Studies*, 25(6), 547–577.

Farrell, R. and Hooker, C., 2013. Design, science and wicked problems. *Design Studies*, 34, 681–705.

Harrison, C., 2003. Visual social semiotics: understanding how still images make meaning. *Technical Communication*, 50(1), 46–60.

Kahneman, D., 2011. *Thinking, fast and slow.* New York: Farrar, Straus and Giroux.

Kress, G. and van Leeuwen, T., 2001. *Multimodal discourse: the modes and media of contemporary communication.* London: Arnold.

Kress, G. and van Leeuwen, T., 2006. *Reading images: the grammar of visual design.* London: Routledge.

Krippendorff, K., 2006. *The semantic turn: a new foundation for design*. Boca Raton, FL: CRC Press.

Krug, S., 2006. *Don't make me think: a common sense approach to web usability*. 2nd ed. Berkeley, CA: New Riders Publishing.

Lemke, J., 1990. *Talking science: language, learning and values*. Norwood, NJ: Ablex Publishing.

Maton, K., 2007. Knowledge-knower structures in intellectual and educational fields. In: F. Christie and J. R. Martin, eds. *Language, knowledge and pedagogy: functional linguistic and sociological perspectives*. London: Continuum.

Maton, K., 2009. Cumulative and segmented learning: exploring the role of curriculum structures in knowledge-building. *British Journal of Sociology of Education*, 30(1), 43–57.

Maton, K., 2011. Theories and things: the semantics of disciplinarity. In: F. Christie and K. Maton, eds. *Disciplinarity: functional linguistic and sociological perspectives*. London: Continuum.

Maton, K., 2013. Making semantic waves: a key to cumulative knowledge-building. *Linguistics and Education*, 24(1), 8–22.

Maton, K., 2014. *Knowledge and knowers: towards a realist sociology of education*. London: Routledge.

Maton, K., Hood, S. and Shay, S., eds., 2014. *Knowledge-building: educational studies in Legitimation Code Theory*. London: Routledge.

Miller, D., 2010. *Stuff*. Cambridge: Polity Press.

Norman, D., 1990. *The design of everyday things*. Garden City, NJ: Doubleday.

Norman, D., 2004. *Emotional design*. New York: Basic Books.

Norman, D. and Draper, S., eds., 1986. *User centered system design*. Hillsdale, NJ: Lawrence Erlbaum Associates.

Scardamalia, M. and Bereiter, C., 2003. Knowledge building. In: J. W. Guthrie, ed. *Encyclopedia of education*. 2nd ed. New York: Macmillan Reference USA.

CONTRIBUTORS

David Ashe is a Postgraduate Fellow and PhD candidate at the Centre for Research on Computer Supported Learning and Cognition (CoCo) at the University of Sydney, Australia, and is a member of Peter Goodyear's ARC Laureate Project team (Learning, technology and design: architectures for productive networked learning). David holds a degree in Agricultural Engineering, is a qualified mathematics and science teacher, and has spent many years in the IT industry. His PhD explores school students' thinking when faced with 'sustainability' issues, and investigates the interface between schools students' everyday and scientific reasoning. David is currently working as part of a team examining learning by design, as a learning strategy, within multidisciplinary teams.

Marlies Bitter-Rijpkema is Assistant Professor at the Centre for Learning Sciences and Technologies (CELSTEC), Open University of the Netherlands. Her research focuses on creative problem-solving and knowledge-building in virtual networks, knowledge support for distributed collaborative creativity and self-organized learning in innovation networks, as well as learning design and business modeling for open education and innovation. She currently directs a pedagogical design team developing learning and innovation networks for librarians.

Lucila Carvalho is a Postdoctoral Research Associate in the Centre for Research on Computer Supported Learning and Cognition (CoCo) at the University of Sydney, Australia. She is a member of Peter Goodyear's ARC Laureate Project team, within which she leads the research on analyzing learning networks. Her PhD research investigated the sociology of learning in/about design and ways of practically implementing principles from the sociology of knowledge in e-learning design. She has studied and carried out research in Australia, New Zealand, the

UK and Brazil. She has presented her work at various international conferences in the fields of education, sociology, systemic functional linguistics, design and software engineering.

Doug Clow is a Lecturer in Interactive Media Development at the Institute of Educational Technology at the UK Open University (OU). His work includes the Knowledge Network (a controlled-access publishing system for sharing expertise within the OU), and OLnet (a project funded by the Hewlett Foundation to increase the quantity and quality of research on Open Educational Resources). Doug's main interests revolve around teaching and learning using new technology. Specifically, his interests include online learning; open educational resources (OER); the boundary between informal and HE learning; mobile devices, mobile learners and mobile learning; virtual learning environments (VLE/CMS); learning technology standards; metadata; e-learning systems; educational multimedia; knowledge management and sharing; accessibility; usability; and student learning. He is an Editor of the *Journal of Interactive Media in Education*, which has pioneered the public, open review of journal articles since 1996.

Maarten de Laat is full Professor at the Open University of the Netherlands. He is Director of the Social and Networked Learning research programme, which concentrates on exploring social learning strategies and networked learning relationships that facilitate professional development in the workplace. His research is focused on informal learning in the workplace, lifelong learning, professional development and knowledge creation through (online) social networks and communities and the impact technology, learning analytics and social design has on the way these networks and communities work, learn and create value. He has published and presented his work extensively in research journals, books and conferences. He is co-chair of the international Networked Learning Conference and of the minitrack Learning Analytics & Networked Learning at the HICSS conference, as well as being a member of the steering committee of SoLAR (Society for Learning Analytics Research).

Wim Didderen MSc is Project Manager and Valorization Coordinator at the Centre for Learning Sciences and Technologies (CELSTEC), Open University of the Netherlands. He has acted in several positions in education in the role of initiator and/or instigator of innovative learning environments, with special emphasis on effective implementation of ICT in schools and online communication for learning. His academic background in Biology (Ecology) contributes to his view on facilitating effective learning in K–12 and higher education, as well as in networked learning for professionals.

Peter Goodyear is Professor of Education and Australian Laureate Fellow at the University of Sydney in Australia. He is the founding co-director of the Centre for Research on Computer Supported Learning and Cognition (CoCo) and convenes the University's Sciences and Technologies of Learning research network. His most recent books are the *Handbook of design in educational technology* (Routledge, co-edited with Rose Luckin and colleagues), *Technology-enhanced learning: design patterns and pattern languages* (Sense, co-edited with Simeon Retalis) and *Students' experiences of e-learning in higher education: the ecology of sustainable innovation* (Routledge, with Rob Ellis).

Chris Jones is a Professor of Research in Educational Technology at Liverpool John Moores University (LJMU) in the UK. Previously, Chris was a Reader in the Institute of Educational Technology at the UK Open University and before that a research lecturer in the Department of Educational Research at Lancaster University. Chris's teaching has been largely at postgraduate level and most of it has been conducted online and at a distance. His research focuses on the application of the metaphor of networks to the understanding of learning in higher education. Chris was the principal investigator for a UK Research Council funded project 'The Net Generation encountering e-learning at university' and he has published over 70 journal articles, book chapters and refereed conference papers. He is the joint editor of two books in the area of advanced learning technology – *Networked learning: perspectives and issues* published by Springer in 2002 and *Analysing networked learning practices in higher education and continuing professional development*, Sense Publishers in 2009.

Jaime Metcher is the Technology Strategist in the Centre for Innovation in Professional Learning at the University of Queensland in Australia. His role is to bring a technology perspective to the Centre's initiatives, seasoned with business and pedagogical considerations. In addition, he is responsible for identifying and recommending technologies that have a high enabling potential in the field of professional learning. These two streams come together in the creation of learning architectures for specific high impact professional learning interventions. Before joining the University of Queensland in 2009, Jaime was Senior IT Architect and Technical Manager at Med-E-Serv, the leading provider of online education for the healthcare sector in Australia. Jaime's role at Med-E-Serv from 1999–2009 produced a number of 'world first' applications of web technologies in the health-care and education sectors. His work involves responding to technical requirements and designing solutions that reflect best practice in educational design and technical architectures, as well as taking into account student and other user experiences of the services provided.

Crighton Nichols is the Director of Technology Projects at EducarUno, an education foundation based in Monterrey, Mexico, and a PhD candidate at the University of Sydney, Australia. He previously founded the Education & Research and Community Engagement & Localisation programs at One Laptop per Child, Australia. At the intersection of his work and research is the desire for a better understanding of the capabilities required to facilitate cross-cultural design and promote responsible technological innovation, especially pertaining to education.

Martin Parisio is a Postgraduate Fellow and PhD candidate at the Centre for Research on Computer Supported Learning and Cognition (CoCo) at the University of Sydney, Australia. He is a member of Peter Goodyear's ARC Laureate Project team (Learning, technology and design: architectures for productive networked learning). Martin's PhD research is an exploration of university built environments and designed spaces, examining designers' intentions, beliefs and attitudes towards effective architectural and spatial design for learning. His research interests include design for learning, educational technology, language education, systems thinking and pedagogy. He is an Australian Postgraduate Award (APA) scholarship recipient. Martin has taught educational technology on K–12 professional development courses and in teacher education courses in higher education.

Paul Parker is a PhD candidate at the Centre for Research on Computer Supported Learning and Cognition (CoCo) at the University of Sydney, Australia. He is the recipient of a scholarship awarded through Professor Peter Goodyear's ARC Laureate Project (Learning, technology and design: architectures for productive learning networks). Paul obtained an MA in Language and Literacy from the University of Technology, Sydney and has worked for over 12 years in a range of learning and teaching development roles in higher education. His professional experience in this context includes student academic language and literacy teaching, curriculum and assessment renewal, university teacher professional development and educational technology integration and evaluation. Paul's doctoral research explores the design and development of open networks for learning innovation.

Ana Pinto is a PhD candidate at the Centre for Research on Computer Supported Learning and Cognition (CoCo) at the University of Sydney, Australia. Her research focuses on analysis and design of productive learning networks in the field of Adult Basic Education. She is the recipient of a scholarship awarded through Professor Peter Goodyear's ARC Laureate Project 'Learning, technology and design: architectures for productive networked learning'. Ana's research interests include design for learning, educational technology, new literacies, adult basic education, lifelong learning, digital inclusion and social justice. Ana's academic background encompasses pedagogy, educational psychology, literacy education and information technology. She received her Master's in Information Technology in Education from the University of Sydney in 2001.

Tracy Richardson is Education Manager for One Laptop per Child, Australia. Tracy oversees the Educational Support initiatives of the organization – to empower teachers, school leaders and community members to implement the program locally. Tracy manages the online and face-to-face professional development offerings of the organization; the development of classroom resources and student programs; and partnerships with departments of education, universities, content providers and schools to deliver the best learning outcomes for students who use the laptops. Tracy taught in primary schools in Australia and the UK before moving into training and consultant work in classroom technologies.

Lynn Robinson is Professor, Deputy Director and co-founder in 2009 of the Centre for Innovation in Professional Learning at the University of Queensland in Australia. For over 15 years she has been engaged in the development of innovative, large-scale online professional development programs in both the private sector and the university. Using rigorous design and evaluation methodologies over repeated cycles of innovation, with her team she has codified professional learning analysis, design, pedagogical and implementation patterns. She has been a leader in numerous national initiatives for professional workforce capacity development in health, financial services and education. Starting with her early career as a general practitioner and medical educator, her involvement in the design and delivery of professional learning spans three decades. Before joining the University of Queensland in 2005, Lynn was a founding principal of Med-E-Serv, which was the leading provider of online professional development programs in the Australian health-care sector.

Thomas Ryberg is Professor (mso) (MA, PhD) in the Department of Communication and Psychology at Aalborg University (AAU), Denmark. He is part of the research centre: 'E-learning lab – Center for User Driven Innovation, Learning and Design' (www.ell.aau.dk). His primary research interests are within the fields of networked learning, Problem Based Learning (PBL), Computer Supported Collaborative Learning (CSCL) and Technology Enhanced Learning (TEL). He is co-chair of the International Networked Learning Conference (http://networkedlearningconference.org.uk/) and member of the Aalborg PBL Academy Management Board (www.pbl.aau.dk). He has participated in European and international research projects and networks (EQUEL, Kaleidoscope, COMBLE, PlaceMe, EATrain2), and in development projects in South East Asia and Latin America (VISCA, VO@NET, ELAC). In particular, he is interested in Problem Based Learning, and how new media and technologies transform our ways of thinking about and designing for Networked and Hybrid Learning.

Rob Saunders is Senior Lecturer in Design Computing in the Faculty of Architecture, Design and Planning at the University of Sydney, Australia. Rob's research centers around creative application of computing and the computational modeling of creativity. Using techniques from machine learning, robotics and surveillance he has explored the role of curiosity in creative processes and developed models of creative systems at individual, social and cultural levels. His models of curious design agents have demonstrated useful abilities for autonomous design systems, including problem-finding and open-ended exploration. His models of social creativity exhibit emergent dynamics, including clique formation and fashion cycles. Rob works with artists and designers across a range of disciplines to support and engage in the creative application of computing and has applied his research in the development of learning environments, design customization systems, smart environments, interactive installations and robotic artworks.

Bieke Schreurs is promovenda at the Open University of the Netherlands, and project coordinator of international research projects. Her research concentrates on how people build up networks to solve work-related problems and the impact social networks have on the way people create knowledge in the workplace. In her PhD she tries to stimulate practice-based research wherein research and practice are interrelated and instruments are designed to be used by both researchers and practitioners. Due to her former work as project coordinator of international research projects on ICT innovations in education at the KU Leuven, she has a special interest in media and learning, with a focus on learning analytics and digital learning materials. She has published and presented her work in research journals, books and conferences and she has written several successful international project proposals.

Beat Schwendimann is a postdoctoral researcher in the Centre for Research on Computer Supported Learning and Cognition (CoCo), University of Sydney, Australia. He is a learning scientist and science educator interested in how different forms of knowledge representations can help people learn. He conducted his PhD research as a Fulbright scholar at the University of California, Berkeley, exploring how collaborative concept mapping activities, embedded in a technology-enhanced science learning environment, can foster a more coherent understanding of biology. His research interests include: science education, teacher education, cognitive science, educational technology, knowledge visualizations, collaborative learning, epistemology and philosophy of science. He is a member of Peter Goodyear's ARC Laureate Project team, where he is studying how different forms of technology and knowledge visualizations can support inter-disciplinary groups of educational designers to collaboratively create learning environments that apply current scientific understandings of learning processes.

Tim Shaw is Director of the Workforce Education and Development Group in the Faculty of Medicine at the University of Sydney, Australia. He chairs the Implementation Science Working Party in the Sydney Catalyst Transitional Cancer Research Centre (TCRC) and works closely with the Sydney West TCRC on the development of educational programs. He has managed a number of substantial health workforce educational research and development projects in Australia, including: the development of the Australian National Patient Safety Education Framework; Basic Surgical Training online for the Royal Australasian College of Surgeons; the development of the Cancer Learning Knowledge portal for the Commonwealth Government; the development of the ISQua Knowledge Portal for the International Society for Quality in Health Care; and the use of new technologies to improve event reporting amongst junior doctors at Brigham and Mass General Hospitals in Boston. He was a contributor to the WHO Patient Safety Curriculum Framework for Medical Schools and the Patient Safety Education Project (PSEP) in the United States. His research focuses on implementation, knowledge dissemination and transfer and flexible learning.

Rory L. L. Sie is an Assistant Professor at the Open University of the Netherlands (OUNL). His main focus is on how we can use social network analysis and game theoretic solution concepts to foster successful cooperation in networks of learners, teachers and innovators. In a more general sense, he is interested in applying artificial intelligence techniques (e.g. recommender systems, agent-based simulation, semantic web) to support education and learning. He is former chair of the PhD councils of the OUNL and SIKS national research school. He has worked in several European-funded research projects and is currently work package leader on the Dutch government-funded Wikiwijs project on open educational resources. In addition to his academic employment, he coordinates IM-People's R&D work on intelligent matching techniques for recruitment.

Peter Sloep is full Professor in Technology Enhanced Learning at the Centre for Learning Sciences and Technologies (CELSTEC) at the Open University of the Netherlands, where he directs a research program on Networked Learning. His research encompasses such topics as networked learning (specifically but not exclusively for professionals), learning design, learning objects, standards for learning technologies and open educational resources, as well as knowledge sharing and creative collaboration in communities and networks.

Rangan Srikhanta is Chief Executive Officer of One Laptop per Child, Australia. A social entrepreneur, with a vision for large-scale change, Rangan decided to pursue his dream of making One Laptop per Child (OLPC) a reality in Australia. In 2009 he quit his job at international accounting firm Deloitte, and OLPC Australia was born, with the aim to assist around 1 million disadvantaged Australian children. Rangan was first inspired by the OLPC story while still a student at the University of Technology Sydney (UTS), where he earned a double degree in Business and Computing. Driven to deliver a comprehensive approach to social and educational change, Rangan and the OLPC Australia team have already delivered thousands of XO laptops to children around the country. Following three years of development, OLPC Australia recently launched the new One Education initiative: a practical and sustainable educational program that supports the XO. In 2013, Rangan continues to work towards OLPC Australia's long-term goal of bringing quality, accessible learning to all Australian children and taking the One Education initiative global. The distribution of 50,000 XOs to disadvantaged schools across Australia is an important next step in the exciting and important OLPC Australia journey.

Kate Thompson is a Postdoctoral Research Associate at the Centre for Research on Computer Supported Learning and Cognition (CoCo) at the University of Sydney, Australia. Her PhD examined the intersection of learning sciences theory (multiple external representations, computer supported learning and cognition) with simulation model use about a socio-environmental system. This sparked an interest in user-specific scaffolds and strategies for the interrogation of simulation models. Her background in environmental science has led her to a systems perspective and research on environmental education programs has involved mobile learning as well as virtual worlds, and more recently learning by design and education for socio-environmental synthesis. She has presented her work at various international conferences in the fields of the learning sciences, education and system dynamics modeling. Currently, her research as part of Peter Goodyear's ARC Laureate Project team focuses on developing methods for visualizing and analyzing collaborative processes using complex datasets, learning by design, as well as design for learning more generally.

Matthew Todd was born in Manchester, UK. He obtained his PhD in organic chemistry from Cambridge University in 1999, was a Wellcome Trust postdoc at the University of California, Berkeley, a college fellow back at Cambridge University, a lecturer at Queen Mary, University of London and, since 2005, has been at the School of Chemistry, the University of Sydney, Australia. His research interests include the development of new ways to make molecules, particularly how to make chiral molecules with new catalysts. He is also interested in making metal complexes that do unusual things when they meet biological molecules or metal ions. His lab motto is 'To make the right molecule in the right place at the right time', and his students are currently trying to work out what this means. He has a significant interest in open science, and how it may be used to accelerate research, with particular emphasis on open source discovery of drugs and catalysts. He is Chair of *The Synaptic Leap*, a non-profit organization dedicated to open biomedical research, and currently manages the Open Source Malaria project. In 2011 he was awarded a NSW Scientist of the Year award in the Emerging Research category for his work in open science. He is on the Editorial Boards of *PLoS One*, *Chemistry Central Journal* and *ChemistryOpen*.

Steven Verjans is Assistant Professor at LOOK (Scientific Centre for Teacher Research), at the Open University of the Netherlands. He specialized in e-learning and academic learning support in Learning.2.0 settings. His research interests include knowledge, professional learning, lifelong learning, technology, social media, personal learning environments and organizational learning environments.

Dewa Wardak is a PhD candidate at the Centre for Research on Computer Supported Learning and Cognition (CoCo), University of Sydney, Australia. As an undergraduate, Dewa's interests included web design, Internet communications and publishing, Internet power and politics, and Internet communities and social networks. After completing the Master of Learning Sciences and Technologies (MLS&T) at the University of Sydney, she was selected as one of the recipients of a postgraduate scholarship offered by Peter Goodyear's ARC Laureate Project (Learning, technology and design: architectures for productive networked learning). Dewa's current project focuses on understanding the role of visual representations, in particular free-hand sketching, and their use by educational designers in design team settings. Her research interests include design for learning, design of online learning environments, learning by design, collaborative learning, online learning communities and knowledge visualization.

Hanne Westh Nicolajsen holds a position as Associate Professor at the Department of Communication and Psychology, Aalborg University in Copenhagen, Denmark. Her main research interest is organizational use of ICT, focusing on the use of ICT in support of changed practices with regard to learning and innovation. In recent years her research has been divided between two domains. One domain is user- and employee-driven innovation with a focus on idea competitions and crowdsourcing within knowledge intensive organizations. Another domain – mainly driven by empirical experiments – is strengthening PBL (problem-based learning) and social learning processes within higher education, with a particular interest in the use of ICT and Networked Learning.

Pippa Yeoman is a PhD candidate at the Centre for Research on Computer Supported Learning and Cognition (CoCo), at the University of Sydney, Australia. She is the recipient of one of the scholarships offered by Peter Goodyear's ARC Laureate Project (Learning, technology and design: architectures for productive networked learning). After completing an MPhil in International Relations at the University of Cambridge she worked in commercial management consulting in health care in Africa and the Middle East. Her return to formal education was driven by a desire to understand something she had seen – an unusual learning ecology in full flight. Her PhD is an ethnographic study of this environment and it is informed by theories of materiality, human geography, social practice and non-representational theory. Within the scope of the Laureate Project, Pippa also participates in multimodal investigations of learning by design tasks in complex learning ecologies.

AUTHOR INDEX

SUBJECT INDEX